W9-DAF-651

Circles around the Sun

Circles around the Sun

In search of a Lost Brother

MOLLY McCLOSKEY

THE OVERLOOK PRESS
NEW YORK, NY

This edition first published in hardcover in the United States in 2012 by

The Overlook Press, Peter Mayer Publishers, Inc.
141 Wooster Street
New York, NY 10012
www.overlookpress.com
For bulk and special sales, please contact sales@overlookny.com

Cataloging-in-Publication Data is available from the Library of Congress

Manufactured in the United States of America
ISBN 978-1-4683-0025-3
10 9 8 7 6 5 4 3 2 1

For Mike, and for our mother

There had been an underlying sweetness to Mike, I would say that was the essence of him. He had been gorgeous, athletic, bright, deeply good.

He was very confident about his mind.

He was so introverted in high school that I tried to compensate by being extroverted.

What struck me was his eyes. I couldn't see the bottom, where they ended. They just kept going.

Mike was superb in the clutch. He probably won at least four games for us on the last shot.

He loved the Band, Dylan, Country Joe & the Fish, the Dead.

He was not a warm and fuzzy person. I was a little intimidated by him.

It was hard for him to be just one of the group.

He was an inner cosmonaut. But he wasn't the slightest bit off. He was one of the cool guys.

Mike was a sweet, vulnerable guy who was trying to find his place. There was an untethered quality. He was lost, good-hearted.

If I had to choose the five sanest people I knew at Duke, Mike would've been one.

Mike loved to go exploring, to just pick a canyon and follow it to the end.

He was interested in truth, in the way the human mind worked.

Mike liked being outrageous. That was part of his charm.

He is the last person I would've expected to develop schizophrenia.

I wouldn't agree that he'd be the last person to develop schizophrenia.

Mike is the most lonesome person I have ever known.

One

It was just after dusk when we pulled into the parking lot of the observatory, fifteen of us in three cars. My brother Tim had just gotten married and we'd rented a house in eastern Oregon for a family holiday after the wedding. The resort was all sage and pine, blue skies that seemed faded by the blank, unambiguous sunlight. The streets had names like Big Sky, Ponderosa and Bobcat. There were waist-high wooden signs to point the way and cheerful yellow arrows painted on the paths, and I had the feeling that when we packed up and drove away it would all evaporate behind us.

The observatory was part of the resort, but it was different from everything else on offer. A small poster on the wall inside the gift shop read:

> Looking into space is equivalent to looking back in time because the further away objects are, the longer it takes for their light to reach Earth. Light from objects further away than about 12 billion light years has not had time to reach Earth yet, since the universe has not existed for long enough. The edge of the observable universe is defined by the travel time of light rather than any physical boundary.

There were two people missing from what once would have been our family. My father, for the usual post-divorce reasons, does not attend gatherings presided over by my mother. My brother Mike does not attend family gatherings of any kind, ever.

I had seen Mike only a few days before. My mother and her husband Howard and I had taken him for lunch at a place called Shari's in an outlying strip-mall suburb of Portland, not far from where he lives in supervised housing. Shari's, the only restaurant where he was welcome, was bright and clean. The plastic menus were free of the residue of meals past, though their depictions of the 'special platters' were a little too luridly rendered to be appetizing. Shari's is the kind of eatery that sits off exit ramps and dots four-lane thoroughfares across America. Scenes from edgy, violent films are shot in places that look just like this.

Nobody said much. Conversation with Mike is not easy. His world is small – consisting of his visits to Shari's and his interactions with his case worker and with other members of the household. My mother asked how his tomato plants were doing, the ones he had on the deck of the house, and he told us he'd decided to quit growing them. The others were complaining because his watering sessions coincided with their sitting outside, below the deck.

'They got all wet,' he said.

My mother asked the obvious. 'Couldn't you just water the plants at a different time?'

He dismissed the suggestion. 'No. They don't understand. They're not smart enough to understand.'

'That's a shame,' Howard said vaguely, and we let the subject drop.

Mike didn't ask what the three of us were doing in Oregon, and we didn't tell him. He didn't know his brother was getting married that weekend. It had been more than twenty years since Mike had attended a family wedding. In the photos from that day, he looks – aside from his slightly outdated suit and the odd stiffness already visible in his fingers – rather well. He is slim, rakish, almost handsome. His hair and beard are neatly trimmed. He is, one might guess, a young man in possession of a flighty charm. Sometimes he appears oddly rigid, apart from us, even as he stands beside us. But to the untrained eye, there is nothing that suggests psychosis. These photos are among the last a stranger could look at and not know immediately that something had gone seriously wrong.

As we waited for lunch, fingering sugar packets, constructing Venn diagrams out of the rings of condensation on the table, I spied my mother in a rare moment of unguarded sadness. Her lips were pursed, and she was slowly pushing the straw around her glass of iced tea.

Back in the late seventies, after our parents' divorce, Mike lived

with us in Oregon for months at a stretch. My mother would come home from work and find him sitting in the living room on one of the high-backed black 'fur' chairs we'd hauled with us from house to house – one long leg slung over the other, one foot wagging incessantly, stroking his beard and having a conversation with himself.

'Hi, Mike!' she'd say, in exactly the same tone in which she greeted the rest of us, as though she were perfectly happy to find him there, just as he was, doing just what he was doing.

Maybe it was different when she went to see him on Sundays at Dammasch, the mental hospital in Wilsonville. When she saw him sitting in the corner of a lock-up, surely then some shadow crossed her face. Or maybe coming home afterwards, with a jittery dog in the back seat. (She used to take our dog along to visit him – Mike loved her so much – and the three of them would go for walks around the hospital grounds.) Maybe the day the dog threw up all over the car on the way home. Insult added to injury. Maybe then she cried.

Of course it must have happened countless times over the years, the waves of sadness, the tears, but my eyes were averted. As a teenager, my abiding wish was that my brother would quietly, miraculously, and without causing pain to anyone, as though he were simply ascending into heaven, disappear. Recognizing the impossibility of this, I had managed instead to create a blind spot where he existed – where, in a way, my mother did, too. For as improbable as it seems, I had no recollection of my mother ever having appeared anything like sad in his company – until that day in 2005 when we sat in Shari's waiting for our lunch, and she pursed her lips and stared into her iced tea and said nothing in a very particular way.

I looked away from her and over at him. It isn't easy to look at him, not so much because his face is a distortion of his youthful features, but because looking at him seems to call an impolite attention to that fact. To the fact that his face is puffed and grey where it was once lean and fresh and pretty. To the fact that his eyes – once animated by a youthful, reckless glee or narrowed into something cool, detached, superior – are now flat and expressionless.

So I try not to look too often or too closely. On the other hand, to look away seems the greater affront, so I bumble along in the middle. We all do it, the whole family regard him with a clumsy, furtive scrutiny. Every moment of seeing him is suffused with the awareness of what happened to his life – who he was and all the things he might have become and who, instead, he is now.

He ate a thick steak, quickly – his intake of protein is enormous – and said he was going for a cigarette. His speech was slightly slurred and his cadence monotone, the effects of the antipsychotic drug loxapine and the mood-stabilizer lithium. Loxapine eliminates or helps to reduce the severity of hallucinations and delusions – the so-called positive symptoms – but it can also cause sedation, indifference, agitation, slowed speech and tremors, as well as a Parkinson-like syndrome called tardive dyskinesia, which manifests in repetitive, involuntary movements of the tongue, lips, legs or arms. Lithium contributes to the slurred speech, and to his impaired concentration, attention span and memory. The other two medications he is on, lisinopril and benztropine, are given to alleviate the side-effects of loxapine and lithium, though they too have their side-effects. Lisinopril, which he takes for high blood pressure, can cause headaches and tiredness, while benztropine, taken to counteract tremors and rigidity, may cause drowsiness and nausea. Then, of course, there is the illness. Negative symptoms: *Poverty of thought. Passivity. Flat affect. Robotic fixidity and petrification of attitude and reactions. A small choice of modes of behaviour. A narrowed and restricted interest in present and past. Capable of enjoyment but unable to express it. Erosion of emotion and will. Impairment of empathy. Apathy. Slowness of movement. Underactivity. Lack of drive. Poverty of speech.*

By the time Mike came back to our large corner booth – far too large for just four, I suddenly noticed – the rest of us had finished our lunches. We paid the bill (my mother, as always at Shari's, tipped the waitress excessively) and edged ourselves out of the booth. Mike was staying on – for another coffee, another cigarette – so we would say our goodbyes at the door.

Embracing him is not something I have ever savoured. I still associate with him the smell of sickness, which hung heavy in his room in our old house. It was the smell of a body too long in bed, too long without a shower, and of the woollen skull cap he wore day and night and the layers of clothes he didn't change often enough. Although he no longer smelled like this, I felt the old reflexive recoil. And so I was surprised when I put my arms around him and didn't want to let go and didn't feel him wanting to either. We held each other for long enough that thoughts had time to form and pass away again, and one of my thoughts was of the unexpected duration of our embrace. I felt clearly that whatever it was – this unprecedented exchange of affection, this mutuality – was utterly sincere and strangely unembarrassed. I was also aware that at a certain point we would have to disengage. I wondered if I would be able to intuit the moment correctly, thus minimizing, for both our sakes, the awkwardness that would accompany our parting, an awkwardness that arises, always, from the sense of unearned intimacy we share.

As we let go, and as we all then moved towards the glass doors, I had to bow my head because I didn't want him to see that I was trying not to cry, and I knew that if I looked at him, I would certainly begin to cry. Crying just then would've been okay, if not ideal, in the dramaturgy of my family. We are not weepers but neither are we insistently repressed. But I wasn't sure how it would make him feel, knowing that seeing him had left me in tears.

At the ticket counter in the observatory we were each issued, in lieu of a ticket stub, a luminous lavender ring, which we were told to wear on an ankle or wrist or to hook around a belt loop or purse strap. We followed a path to a small enclosure, open to the sky, where six huge telescopes were poised. We went from telescope to telescope, queuing for glimpses of the sky. The moon – because of, rather than in spite of, its familiarity – moved us the most. That and the fact that our view of it was more dramatic than our view of the other items on offer, which tended to be diffuse and fibrous: the Andromeda galaxy; the cloud of gas and dust that was the Ring Nebula in Lyra; globular star clusters.

'The star clusters are dense groups of old yellow stars in the outer regions of the galaxy,' the guide told us. 'They formed early in the galaxy's history and they can contain thousands of millions of stars. They can range from a hundred to three hundred light years across.'

We murmured obligingly. What could we do with figures like that? Astonishing facts, but nothing that allowed the threads and clusters to compare with the single startling entity that was the moon. One half of it was lost in shadow; on the other half, we could see craters and welts. There it was, the moon, ours in a way Andromeda or Venus isn't, its surface less strange to us than the landscapes of the sub-Sahara.

On the far side of the enclosure, two more telescopes were pointed like cannons at the horizon. Through one, we could see Venus, briefly, before it sank from view. Through the other was Jupiter, which appeared to waver in a field of shimmering colour. We took our turns and in between stood in the dark like guests at a cocktail party, the clusters of my family dispersing and regrouping, the planets functioning as some recent piece of news to which the conversation kept returning. My mother mentioned a visit she'd made to Roswell, New Mexico.

'I always thought UFOs were nonsense,' she said, 'but some of those stories . . .' She raised her eyebrows and tilted her head, the look on her face only half sceptical.

I could picture her in Roswell. I could picture her feet, in plain white tennis shoes and at a slightly pigeon-toed angle, shuffling along through some UFO exhibit with a crowd of other would-be believers.

'When were you in Roswell?' I asked.

'When Howard and I took our cross-country trip in '92. We rented a camper van and drove.' She groaned. 'And drove . . . and drove . . .'

I didn't remember that they'd done that, and I was bothered by my forgetfulness. They would never be able to do that again: they were in their eighties. There were mysterious scrapes and dents on their car, acquired on trips to the corner store.

We fell silent and then, at the same moment, as though we'd heard a sound from the heavens, looked up again. The stars seemed to have changed, subtly, into something both stranger and more familiar, the way a word does when repeated over and over. As I gazed upwards – focusing on the star that I now knew to be Betelgeuse – I could feel my mother beside me.

The edge of the observable universe is defined by the travel time of light rather than any physical boundary.

She will die, I thought, and in the absence of the living source that begot it, a light will linger for many years – an invisible pulsation of influence. Her strict moral code and boundless generosity. A certain middle-class aesthetic of Super Bowl parties and *Phantom of the Opera* and coach tours to Europe. Her blithe way of being both absolutely present and capable of letting go, so that our various forms of deep unhappiness have never caused her to become deeply unhappy.

While we'd been discussing the plausibility of aliens, the views through the telescopes had changed. We could see binary stars now, and the spillage of the Milky Way had become clearer. We exchanged pieces of information we'd picked up from the guide.

Jupiter rotates so fast that a Jovian day lasts only ten hours.

A nebula is the after-effect of an exploding star.

A star explodes because . . .

Finally, the cold started to get to us and we began to trickle out of the enclosure and towards the parking lot. As those of us on the outside stood waiting for those still inside, we kept seeing, out of the corners of our eyes, darts of light – meteors from the Perseids. I caught myself feeling momentarily surprised, as though because we'd left the enclosure, the spectacle should have ceased. Eventually, shivering and impatient, a few of us drifted back in to find the others.

There were quite a few people still inside and I couldn't tell which of them belonged to me. What I could see were the luminous lavender rings given to us when we arrived, moving, as though by their own volition, through space. I had assumed they were just nifty admission tickets, pieces of glow-in-the-dark junk, but as the darkness had thickened and it had become more difficult to see one another, I'd realized the rings had a practical purpose, too: to keep us from bumping into each other. Now, a third possibility occurred to me – that maybe they were meant to make us think of ourselves as celestial bodies, wandering through the velvety blackness. In any case, the rings were about all we could see now, and as we shuffled between telescopes, careful not to thump our foreheads, the members of my family called out to one another, our voices low and tentative, hushed by the dark.

Two

I had spent the two weeks prior to that lunch at Shari's at my mother's house in Ocean City, New Jersey, a house she and Howard had just sold and were preparing to leave. She had given me several binders full of letters written over four decades, letters I had long known existed, had even randomly dipped into, but had not, until then, read through in their entirety.

Because I had no clear memory of Mike's pre-illness self – he was the eldest of six and I the youngest – and because this figure whose life the letters portrayed in such detail bore so little resemblance to the person I knew, I felt with far greater force, as I read them, the sensation that I had long felt vaguely: that there had been another son in the family, and that he had died around the age of twenty-three, when I was nine. Not long after that (so my story went), this other man had joined us, appearing suddenly, like a son my parents had given up for adoption at birth and who had finally tracked them down.

Over the next several years, something remarkable unfolded in front of me: psychosis. And yet, for all its strangeness and its certain emotional impact (the very factors that tend to encourage the formation of memories), the recollections I have of Mike from those years could be counted on one hand.

There was the evening of Tim's seventeenth birthday, when we came home from the pizzeria and Mike grew suddenly agitated, then manic, running in circles around the yard. There was the time Mike told my friend Becky, in that abstruse, guru-like tone of his, 'You're the tallest girl in the world,' causing us to collapse into fits of giggles as we repeated the phrase ad nauseam. There was the day I stood whimpering in the bathroom and he yelled at me to hold still as he removed a tick from my scalp. And there were the times during our first summer in Oregon when he took me with him to a mock-Tudor house on the lake shore, where he worked as a gardener.

I remember sitting in the living room and watching him emerge from his bedroom, in a woollen cap and a nubby blue sweater, to make his slouching way towards the bathroom. I remember that the air in the house felt different when he was in it, even if he was hidden in his room. And I remember one visit to a mental hospital. All the image amounts to is a strange, unlikely still of a group of us in a white hallway, seen from behind, at a moment of hesitation. We, the four visiting family members (Tim, my parents and me), are like people in a film who are being chased and deciding whether to flee to the right or the left. Our postures are odd, as though someone off camera had just yelled, *Freeze!* I don't remember seeing Mike, the room we went to, or anything that transpired. From his multiple hospitalizations, I have only this tilted and inane tableau.

That's about it, then. Nothing of the gin rummy games or the Chinese chequers the two of us used to play, nothing of the family day trips to the coast, the dinners in the house on Fourth Street or the games of H-O-R-S-E in the driveway, all of which I read about in his letters but cannot recall. Only those few snapshots, and a fleeting image of having once spotted him in our little downtown and turning a corner to avoid meeting him. But that image could just as easily be pure invention – an over-literal attempt to parcel up years of guilt into a single moment.

In 1982, when I was seventeen, I left Oregon and spent the next four years 3,000 miles away, at college in Philadelphia. When I returned to Oregon in 1986, I lived only a twenty-minute bus ride from Mike, who by then was settled in a supervised group home. My mother, in the meantime, had moved to Philadelphia herself. She came to Oregon a couple of times a year, and I sometimes went along when she was having lunch with Mike. But never once did I try to meet with him alone. I don't think the idea even occurred to me. And then, in 1989, I left the country and didn't come back. Two or three years could pass between my visits to Oregon, two or three years during which I would not see Mike or speak to him. Sometimes I actually forgot about him, and had to remind myself that we were six.

Throughout that time, all those years leading up to the summer of 2005, to our strange, prolonged embrace in the doorway of Shari's, a disconcerting image sometimes arose: I thought of him as a chunk of matter – earth or ice – that had cracked off from a larger mass and was drifting quietly, sadly away. As he drifted, he grew smaller, and I had the sense that he would drift and shrink until he was no longer there. It was a certain egotism on my part that gave rise to this image, for I seemed to have assumed that because he was disappearing from my life, he was disappearing altogether.

What struck me that afternoon in Shari's was not only the contrast between the person who sat across the table from me and the person described in the letters I had just read, but also the fact that Mike, aged fifty-five, was still so very, very present. I looked at him and felt ashamed and humbled and fascinated.

I have a friend, now in her mid forties, who suffers from a rare inherited neurodegenerative disease known as pallido-ponto-nigral degeneration, or PPND. The disease results from a mutation in the tau gene of chromosome 17. Its symptoms, including progressive Parkinsonism and dementia, appear by the fifth decade. After an average of eight to nine years, the sufferer dies, usually of aspiration pneumonia – an infection that results from breathing food, liquids, vomit or saliva into the lungs as a result of an impaired swallow mechanism.

Brigid was diagnosed in 2005. She wasn't shocked. She had watched her father die of PPND when he was about fifty, and she knew she had a 50 per cent chance of inheriting the disease. I knew that it had marked her, watching him deteriorate, losing him like that; but because she had always referred to his illness as 'Parkinson's', I'd had no idea that she had lived her life under this sword of Damocles.

I first met Brigid in 2001. Though she was from the Irish midlands, she'd been living in Paris for years, selling art, curating exhibitions between France and Ireland, sometimes teaching English for extra cash. I could see immediately that she was somehow different from my other friends, though I would not link her idiosyncrasies to the illness until later. Her bad memory I put down to her general air of abstraction and waftiness. She was unusually soft and forgiving – it would not have occurred to her to be critical of weakness in another person – and yet she carried herself like a grande dame, gliding down the street with what appeared to be the dignified bearing of an ageing aristocrat, but was more likely the beginnings of physical stiffening. She did everything with care – a tentativeness I attributed to some excessively genteel femininity. We would meet for coffee or a drink when we were both in Dublin, and I felt physically brash beside her, lumbering and inelegant and hasty. Sometimes I rang her in Paris. One night she said to me in a small, quiet voice, 'Molly, my hair is falling out.'

She stayed in Paris for as long as she could after the diagnosis, but when it became clear she was no longer able to look after herself, she left her beloved city and moved back in with her mother and step-father in the midlands. She has her own small wing in the house, and a chair that can be adjusted with buttons. She is surrounded all day, every day, by people who love her and treat her with absolute respect. Friends visit from Paris and from around Ireland. But paralysis has overtaken her. She cannot walk or eat without help, and is incapable of any facial expression. Only her eyes move. She is alarmingly thin, and has great difficulty swallowing. She can no longer really speak. When she does manage a few words, usually after body spasms which for some reason enable whispered bursts of speech, the first line delivered to a visitor is invariably 'I'm so sorry.'

Once, as her mother was showing me out, I said, 'Brigid's lucky to have you.' And her mother said, without the slightest trace of falsity, 'Oh, we're lucky to have Brigid.' Her mother had already nursed Brigid's father through the same illness. Another day, she bit her lip and said, 'This is worse. She's my blood.' I watch them and that is what I see: blood looking after its own, with dignity and generosity and no seeming awareness that any other response is possible.

But Brigid had a world. I saw her in it. I remember her when she was regal. Sitting, with that odd stillness, in a café off rue Jaucourt and ordering for us in her quietest, surest French. Or gliding up Baggot Street to meet me at the Shelbourne for a drink, greeting me always, 'Molly, *mo ghrá.*' Her thick black hair. The carefully applied lipstick. The parties and the openings. The romantic dalliances. The future. To have witnessed what the illness took from her makes a difference to what I see when I look at her now.

By early 2006, about six months after Tim's wedding, I had decided I wanted to know what had happened to Mike. This was not the first time I had set out to write about his illness. In the late eighties, *Oregon Magazine* had bought a piece I'd done on schizophrenia, but went out of business the month before it was to appear. A few years later the *Evening Press* in Dublin accepted a similarly themed article, then collapsed before its scheduled publication, suggesting a certain jinx was at work. By then, it had become a piece about pyramidal cells and maternal flu in the second trimester as a possible contributing factor to the development of schizophrenia.

But the letters had made me want to understand who he had been before he became ill, as well as who he was now. And I wanted to understand how what had happened to him had affected the other members of my family, how it might relate to our own stories and fears and psychological fault lines. I wanted to bring the two distinct halves of his life into a single story, one that would enable the vague sense of bereavement that had hummed through my life to find its object. My mother saw it as a form of tribute. She wrote to me, *I guess I was happy that Mike was to be commemorated in some way. It seems like a wasted life, but it should be celebrated . . .*

The first time I mentioned to Mike that I intended to write this book I was speaking to him by phone from my mother's house in Florida in the spring of 2006. I was planning to be in Oregon a few months later and to see him while I was there. I told him I was writing a book concerning our family, and that I was interviewing our parents and our siblings and would like to interview him. That his illness would lie at the heart of the book was something I intended to discuss with him in person.

'Would you be willing to do that,' I asked, 'to let me interview you?'

'Yeah,' he said, 'that would be fine.'

By the time I made it to Oregon, it was the following spring. The two of us went for lunch. It was soon clear to me that an 'interview', in the normal sense of the word, was not an option. His conversation, though peppered with seemingly penetrating insights, was disorganized and often self-contradictory. I also realized that it was highly unlikely my brother was going to address in a conversation with me the issue of his illness. Up to that point, and to this day, he has never acknowledged in my presence that he suffers from schizophrenia. I have never heard him say the word. Only once have I heard him refer, obliquely, to being ill, when he asked me, apropos of nothing we'd been speaking of, 'Did you visit me in Cedar Hills?'

The name didn't ring any bells. 'Was Cedar Hills an apartment building?' I said.

He smiled, barely, and looked at me with something like affectionate forbearance. 'It was a hospital,' he said.

Another time I asked him if he'd ever like to leave Oregon and live back east again. He told me he would, but that he couldn't leave Oregon because of his 'job' for Clackamas County Mental Health. There were too many people depending on him, he said. Clackamas County Mental Health is, of course, part of his support network. It is not his employer. No one there is depending on him.

It is impossible for me to gauge what his level of awareness is – and perhaps it varies with the day – though it is true that, even decades into the illness, a lack of insight into oneself, one's delusions, one's illness, remains a hallmark of schizophrenia. What I knew was that if he had never said the word *schizophrenia* to me, I could not bring myself to say it to him. What I said instead was something closer to what I'd said to him on the phone a few months back.

'Do you mind being in this book I'm writing about the family?'

He looked at me and said, 'I would expect to be.' And then, 'I don't murder anyone, do I? Do you write murder mysteries?'

'No,' I said, 'you don't murder anyone.'

About six months later, I was back in Oregon and I asked him again if he minded that I was writing about him in a book.

'No, I don't mind,' he said. Then he asked, 'Do you sell very many books?'

'Well,' I said, 'not *that* many.'

'Then why do you keep writing them?'

I knew, from the inconsistency of his remarks on a variety of subjects (one day he acknowledges our mother for what she is, the next day blandly insists we were all stolen at birth), that his answer to a question on any given day might contradict his answer on a different day. But I had decided from the start that were he ever to say, *No, don't write about me,* or, *No, I don't want to be in your book* – and he is capable of saying 'no' to things he doesn't want: seeing certain people, recommended medical care – I would shelve the project. While I was glad that he responded positively on three occasions to the question of being in a book I was writing, and consented to talk to me about his life, I also knew that a 'yes' constituted a cloudier kind of consent than it would in the case of someone who was not suffering from a mental illness.

My brother does not read books or newspapers. His illness and, to a lesser extent, his medication have severely limited his mental energy and concentration. It is highly unlikely he will ever experience a degree of remission that would enable him to read this book. Mike was diagnosed in 1973, almost forty years ago; remissions, though not unheard of, are extremely rare at this stage of the illness. But the hypothetical possibility exists, and so one of the questions I faced was how to write about his life in a way that he would find acceptable should he ever read the book.

I had long felt sadness over the loss of him. I had tried many times to imagine what it had been like for my parents to lose him. But I had never had much sense of what he himself had lost, or what he had suffered in the process. To understand and to depict this would be to portray him in his totality, both as a bright, shining boy of talent and promise, and as a troubled adult, stricken by a terrible illness that prevented him from realizing his potential as a human being and living the life he'd once seemed destined for.

Around the time I came into possession of the letters, and for much of the period I spent working on this book, I was often away from my own home in Dublin. My boyfriend at the time was working in

Kosovo, and I lived with him part-time there, then took work in Kenya for eighteen months. After that, I spent a spring in Paris. But the letters went with me everywhere. They served as aides-memoire and the raw material of Mike's story, but they also became something more. When I read them, I could see the kitchen tables at which they were typed. I knew the line of dogwood trees that the windows overlooked, the slope of the front yard, how there was so much shade out the back that the grass would never quite grow. I knew the rhythms of those days. I knew the love stories to which the letters referred, what was happening behind the scenes and what information was withheld. I knew the characters, however brief their cameos, and I recognized the significances embedded in what was ordinary: a certain road, a room in a house, the game of tennis. And when Mike's letters spiralled into incoherence, a grab bag of sentence fragments, mangled proverbs and random images both quotidian and hellfire, I understood, I like to believe, some of what he was trying to allude to.

What the letters had become was home. I wasn't sure which had the greater part in constituting home, time or space, because the letters blended and confused the two dimensions. They felt like forty years of time I could place on the table in front of me and enter as though it were a house.

Three

Long before I read those letters, before I talked to family members and Mike's old friends about what he was like as a young man, I had an abiding sense that his life had once exemplified everything promising and fine about my parents' early years together. He was the post-war dream and then the loss of that dream, and the period of his fracturing was the same period when certainty seemed to drain from us as a family.

What I know of my parents' lives before they were married, before my mother moved out of her own parents' home and began to record her life in thrice-weekly dispatches to her own mother, I know from their recollections, shared stories recounted to me from their now very separate worlds. I know that my father first saw my mother in a photograph. It was 1946 and he was just back from the Pacific. He had come down from upstate Pennsylvania to the Jersey shore to pick up his aunt, who happened to be at a neighbour's house when he arrived. The neighbour was my grandmother, and on her piano she had a photograph of a carefully coiffed blonde. In the softened focus, my mother's skin looked flawlessly smooth; her eyes shone. My father stared. Later, on the way home, his aunt asked him if he'd like to meet Anita, the girl in the picture.

Yes, he said, he would.

Three months passed, though, before it happened, months during which my mother had no idea how her future hung in the balance – how a man she'd never met carried a picture of her in his head, a picture he might easily forget, because not long after that day he left for baseball training camp in Martinsville, Virginia. He had signed a $300-a-month contract to pitch for the Philadelphia Athletics. My mother spent that summer working at a fish and chip place on the boardwalk in Ocean City, biding her time till she started grad school in September – she was going for a master's in education at the University of Pennsylvania. She loved working on the board-walk. She was young, and every day was an adventure and other people an endless source of fascination. It was just as she was finishing one of her shifts – a sticky, humid night at the tail end of August, her hair a stringy mess under its paper crown, the smell of fry oil rising off her – that he walked in the door.

He hadn't forgotten her. He was, however, a little surprised when he saw her. Her hair was chopped to a bob, and in her white uniform and flat shoes she looked tired and unglamorous, nothing like what he remembered from the photo. But he'd come this far, and he wasn't about to turn around and walk out. They made a date for Saturday night.

Neither of them drank then, but they went dancing. My father had a thing about the polka. *The polka!* My mother thought to herself, *What a rube.* She found him interesting enough, handsome, masculine, eager and exuberant in that just-back-from-the-war way, all innocence and experience tangled up together, but when she went home that night she wasn't exactly lovestruck. She had a lot on her mind; school was starting on Monday. (He would be at Penn, too, finishing his undergrad degree on the GI Bill.) And she was, according to her yearbook at Immaculata College, 'the practically perfect woman'. He was one of a zillion suitors she'd had.

That might've been that, then, were it not for the fact that the following Monday morning as she sat on a bench in a damp raincoat (there are details she will retain for ever) waiting to sign up for her courses, who – out of twenty thousand students – should step out of a classroom but Jack. (It was the coincidence they needed, because it wasn't likely they were going to wait around for one another. She'd have had many more suitors. As for him, he might have been a rube from upstate, but he was gregarious and impatient and wouldn't have stayed a bachelor for long.) Neither of them had any classes that afternoon so they decided to spend the day together. They went across the street to a luncheonette for a sandwich and then to one of the nearby department stores to look at a mock-up of something called 'The Village of Tomorrow'. Funny, my mother thought, they hardly knew each other and already they were looking at model homes.

After that, it was football games and dances and the Ivy Ball. By January they were pinned; by Valentine's Day formally engaged. He splurged on a diamond ring, and that afternoon took her riding for the first time in his new car – a beige Ford coupé they nicknamed 'Little Car'. Sometimes they met in the stacks of the Penn library and sneaked a quick kiss. By then, she had long since forgiven him his attachment to the polka.

My father's people were from Jackson's Patch in eastern Pennsylvania. The Patch wasn't a proper town but a dirt road with houses either side, owned – like all the patches surrounding Mahanoy City – by one of the mining companies. The men my father grew up around were drinkers, fighters, storytellers. They gambled at penny poker. They were also God-fearing Catholics, Irish nationalists and staunch union men. Coal defined their lives. In 1917, production in the region peaked at a hundred million tons. By 1925, the year my father was born, there was still a seemingly endless supply and no shortage of men willing to spend (and sometimes lose) their lives extracting it. Eddie, his father, worked underground, with dynamite, at the Mahanoy City Colliery – a dangerous place, full of rancid air and lethal gases, with the weight of so much earth above. When Jack was a teenager, Eddie took him down to the mines to show him the conditions. The object of the exercise: to scare his son into another life. It worked. My father was abstemious and law-abiding, avoided the toughs loitering on the corner – though he was far from timid. He could see that being a rebel rarely got you anywhere – there was a passing thrill, but then you're left with a hangover and shit for a life – and my father wanted to go places. He looked around and felt bigger than this town. He knew there was a difference between himself and his father, more than just a generation separating them. My father's childhood, in fact, had been pure bliss compared to Eddie's. By the time Eddie was twelve he had left school for good and was working ten-hour days as a slate picker, pissing on his own hands to disinfect the cuts made by the razor-sharp slate. Years later, my father would learn the term *white trash* and think that that was what they were; but by then he was rich – a Lexus, elegant suits and an impressive handicap – and could afford to love where he came from, to respect the way his father had suffered with good humour the indignities that came with poverty and toil. All his life, my father would judge people not by their origins but by the strength of their desire to rise above them. And he would never lose his awareness of how differently things might have turned out for him.

He finished high school at sixteen and in September of 1942 entered the University of Pittsburgh on a football scholarship. But by then the country was at war and my father, like everyone he knew, wanted to serve. After a year at Pitt, he went to the Naval Officer Training Program at Cornell to earn his officer's commission. With his commission, he had a choice: go to Annapolis for four years (by which time the war would probably be over and he'd have escaped with nothing worse than a few nasty tackles on the football field), or go overseas.

He was eighteen when he left for the Pacific theatre. He picked up his ship in the Philippines – an amphibious assault vessel – and continued on to Okinawa. The ship was used to ferry tanks, munitions and equipment between the big supply ships and forces stationed onshore. He was there for a year and a half. When the bombs were dropped on Hiroshima and Nagasaki, my father's crew got down on their knees and gave thanks. They'd been scheduled to invade mainland Japan, probably go into Tokyo Bay. The war was going to go on and on, and suddenly it was over.

Though they came from different worlds, my parents were shaped by the same era, its deprivations and its triumphs, its unambiguous values. Anita's father, Tony Morales, was born in Puerto Rico. His people were bankers, doctors and idle aristocrats. In 1917, Tony boarded a ship bound for America, and enrolled to study business at the University of Pennsylvania. He met his future wife, Fanny Sweeney, at one of the Sunday night ice-cream socials she and her sisters hosted in their parents' row house on 49th and Walnut, close to the Penn campus. Fanny's people were humbler. She was a first-generation Irish immigrant, the product of an arranged marriage – one of those dull, honourable unions sustained by the unquestioned

assumption that their business was not their own happiness but the betterment of future generations. Her father was a nightwatchman at a department store and her mother took in boarders for a few extra dollars. Fanny and Tony married in 1920 and six years later produced their only child.

Nita, as her parents called her, was three when the family lost everything in the stock-market crash. The engineering firm at which Tony had been working as an accountant went out of business; the money he'd invested in the market was wiped out. He got a job selling insurance door-to-door, a pursuit at which – with his air of polite reserve and his aristocratic bearing – he did not excel. And who could afford insurance? The family limped along for a couple of years, the monthly bills growing more difficult to meet. When the oil man came to collect, Nita sat quietly with her mother on the cellar steps, where they couldn't be seen. The day before Thanksgiving, the electric company disconnected them and they ate by candlelight. When the neighbour Mrs Levy mentioned their eating in the dark, Fanny pulled the word *ambience* out of nowhere and told Mrs Levy that she too should try candlelight for the holidays. Then she phoned City Hall and said they had a serious illness in the house, and City Hall got the electric company to reconnect them. When Tony finally defaulted on the mortgage, they lost the house and moved in with Fanny's parents.

Salvation came in the form of Roosevelt. Tony got work as an accountant with a Works Progress Administration programme. By 1937, he was back in the private sector and the family had moved to a home of their own in the suburb of Upper Darby. They paid $5,900 for a house that had previously sold for three times that much. Now, they were the beneficiaries of someone else's foreclosure.

Nita was a happy child, cheerful by nature. She roller-skated on weekends and went to the movie house on 52nd Street for eleven cents, played hide-and-seek and run-sheepie-run with the neighbourhood kids. She was a good girl, too, studious and devout. Confession, spiritual bouquets, Three Hours' Agony. After a slightly pudgy period, she had, by her final year in high school, grown into her looks. She had a prominent, slightly hooked nose that managed to add to rather than detract from her beauty – a single imperfection that kept her from appearing icy.

She won a scholarship to Immaculata, a women's college in Philadelphia. She had always been good with words, and majored in English, writing a social column called 'Of Spice and Men' for the student newspaper.

She conducted interviews, too. There she is, pictured with Monsignor Fulton Sheen – 'the burning-eyed one', who had just delivered a 'startling' lecture about Communism's grip on the world. In another issue she is seen beside John Powers, head of the famous Powers' Modeling Agency. Her prose is laced with the slightest hint of irony:

What appeared to be a few hundred 'love-sick maidens' lined the rotunda balconies and kept their eyes firmly fixed upon the doorway. What was the occasion? For whom were these girls waiting so expectantly? Mr John Robert Powers, of course.

Mr Powers gave the girls some advice, which seemed in perfect harmony with my mother's natural tendencies – the kind of words that would follow her through life, echoed by countless friends, acquaintances and colleagues:

> Always be the natural girl and everyone will love you. If you wish to be truly charming, spend yourself for others, forget yourself, and the glow of charm will brighten your face.

*

She married Jack in Philadelphia in August 1948. The match had gotten mixed reviews from Fanny and Tony. Tony liked Jack, but Fanny didn't approve. He didn't have money, for one thing. And he wasn't *from* anywhere. She thought her daughter should have held out for a doctor.

Nita didn't care that he had no money. He was a doer, they'd be okay. You can see from the photos of him what it was she fell for. Her favourite – at the bottom of which she scribbled, *Jack on the 1326* – was shot at a thirty-degree angle and from below. Sepia, inadvertently arty. He's looking down at the camera, standing in the V of a corner railing of the ship, the strength of his forearms apparent. The lips, the nose, could sometimes appear a little unformed (he was still a teenager), but in that light, at that angle, they are perfect. He has binoculars around his neck and wears a dark T-shirt, khakis and a cap. There is something Hollywood about the pose, like those shots of movie stars who'd served – even in uniform, especially in uniform, they still looked like movie stars. He's got this brazenly self-aware sensuality that seems a little risqué for the times, not to mention the situation: he was at war in the Pacific. He was nineteen

and in charge of a ship. Not the time, you'd think, to be looking that good.

My parents' first year of marriage was a busy one. My father was studying for his degree, coaching freshman basketball at Penn and playing pro basketball himself in the Eastern League for the Sunbury Mercuries. Thirty-five games a year, fifty dollars a game. (His baseball career had come to an abrupt, permanent end when niggling pains up the arm became full-scale adhesions and a doctor shot him up with novocaine and told him to throw real hard to work the soreness out.) My mother, meanwhile, was still in grad school but teaching five classes a day at a nearby high school for thirty-five dollars a week. After the Mercuries' games, she sat outside the locker room, correcting papers, waiting for her husband.

Their energy was fuelled partly by youth and partly by ignorance. They were ignorant of their own limits, of how complicated the future would become, how fragmented and compromised in comparison to the clean stark lines in which the present defined itself. The war was over, the men were home and they were heroes, and all anybody wanted to do was start a family and have a normal life and not be lonely or in danger any more. Sometimes my mother wondered how it could all feel so good after so many horrors, all the death – she didn't like to think about the things Jack had seen, and he didn't talk much about the war, not about the horrors, anyway. Everything he had seen and she hadn't meant there was a gulf between them. But that was how it was with men and women.

They rented a ground-floor apartment in Mount Airy, a quiet section of Philadelphia, home to young couples just like themselves. My father landed a job at Germantown Academy, a private boys' school, coaching football, basketball and baseball for three thousand dollars a year. At home, in the evenings, my mother made devilled tuna casserole and cauliflower salad and his favourite dessert – peanut brittle ice-cream ring. They listened to Fred Allen on the radio and watched Milton Berle on television. The whole country was falling in love with Milton Berle, this manic, vulgar comedian who wore wigs and dresses, checked pants and polka-dot

shirts, and who let people throw pies in his face. He was the opposite of Fred Allen. Allen was clever but his humour was dark, caustic,
and people had had enough of that. They wanted to put the bad
times behind them.

And yet, hovering around the fringes of this new world were
things that were not as simple or as frank as Uncle Miltie's humour.
Already, so soon after the clarity that the end of the war had brought,
there had arisen something edgy and confusing. Anxiety was in
the air – Communism and atomic bombs. It was hard to know
how scared to be. Nita had never been an alarmist, but the Alger Hiss
business was still going on and it was said that the government was
infested with Communists. She hoped that Hiss was innocent. It was
in her nature to favour a handsome, well-mannered intellectual like
Hiss over a slob like Chambers, the guy testifying against him.

In July, Hiss got off on a hung jury. Many people said you couldn't
let Communists slip through the net like that. The Red Army was
winning in China, and almost three hundred people working for the
State Department had recently failed security reviews. And, then,
on 29 August, the day Nita turned twenty-three, the Soviets conducted their first atomic test and the American monopoly on
nuclear weapons came to an end. That joke going around – that the
Russians could never bring a nuclear bomb to the US in a suitcase
because the Russians had yet to perfect the suitcase – wasn't funny
any more. No, better to watch Uncle Miltie and think about her
baby. Because Nita was pregnant.

Michael Edward McCloskey is born at 2.35 a.m. on 4 May 1950, in
Hahnemann Hospital on Broad Street in Philadelphia. A birth chart
done fifty-odd years later by an ex-girlfriend who has never forgotten him will show the following: a very strong sun and a very weak
moon. His ego, his outer personality, is robust, but the inner psyche
is weak. His mother knows nothing of strong suns and weak moons
or inner and outer psyches; she knows only that he is beautiful.
When they bring him home he is so small and delicate that she is
nearly afraid to touch him. In a letter to her mother that July, following a visit to the shore, she writes:

Dear Mommy,

*We certainly had a lovely stay, and it did Mikey a world of good. We took
him to Hoon tonite for his check-up. He weighs 12-6 and is 24½ inches
long. He is doing beautifully and starts cereal in two weeks. He's had
quite a social life this week. Tuesday we took him to the drive-in movies.
He behaved beautifully and we all had a good time.*

*I guess you were glad to see the 4th weekend pass. We may not be down
for a couple weeks. Next Sunday – the 16th – the people in the apartment
are planning a sort of weenie roast out here on the lawn. Some fun!*

Love, Jackie, Neetsie & Mikey

In the autumn of 1951, the family moves to the worst rathole my
mother has ever set foot in: a basement apartment in Bala Cynwyd,
next to the railroad tracks. All day long the Paoli local rattles the
windows and the figurines on the dinette set – a duo of indetermi-
nate ethnicity, with little sombreros or coolie hats, purchased at a
highway gift stand one leisurely Sunday afternoon. Money is tight,
as my father has entered grad school and my mother is at home
with the baby. But they are happy. In the evenings, they snuggle on
the sofa watching Edward R. Murrow's *See It Now* and *I Love Lucy*.
(My mother loves Ricky Ricardo. He reminds her of her father, the
way he says *pih-yamas* instead of pyjamas and *ham* when he means
jam.) It is late on one of those winter evenings, with the Paoli local
thundering past and the TV set still warm, that Steve is conceived.

Their stay in Bala Cynwyd is brief. When my father gets a job at
a high school in New Jersey, they move from the dark basement
apartment to the grand-sounding Barrington Manor where, for
seventy-eight dollars a month, they get a four-room, second-floor
walk-up in a sprawling housing development. Their front windows
look out at a mirror image of their own building, and the back
windows overlook the clothes lines, on which washing is forever
flapping. The clothes lines criss-cross a small common play area.
Beyond that, raw, flat New Jersey countryside.

By the time my mother has given birth to Steve, she and my
father have purchased a Cape Cod-style house in Haddonfield, New

Jersey. They have moved six times in five years of marriage and now, finally, they have joined the ranks of home owners. In the afternoons the sun falls on the back garden, and when the boys are napping my mother sometimes steals a few minutes with the paper and a glass of iced tea. On 20 June 1953, she reads that the previous night at 8 p.m. Julius and Ethel Rosenberg, convicted of espionage, were executed in Sing Sing Prison. The first fifty-seven-second jolt of electricity didn't kill Ethel. She had to be restrapped to the chair and given two more jolts before they pronounced her dead. My mother had seen pictures in the paper of Ethel Rosenberg's two sons carrying signs that said, DON'T KILL MY MOMMY AND DADDY. Honestly, she wasn't sure what to think. But she's sure that a mother should not be executed. Before Mike was born she had never held a baby in her arms. But this is what she does now, it is who she is. She loves the smell of a baby's skin and sometimes just presses her face against her boys' flesh, lost for a moment in the bliss of it.

For the summer, my parents take an apartment at the shore. My mother is sad to leave the new house for that long but she has been going to Ocean City for as long as she can remember, swimming at 13th Street, eating ice cream on the benches at the music pier. It's where she and Jack met, and going back there as his wife fills her with a deep satisfaction. Their apartment is a second-floor walk-up on St James Place. When they get a new washing machine, my father carries it up the stairs on his back, while my mother looks on, terrified and not a little impressed.

My father has raided their savings to buy a lot in nearby Somers Point and two pitching machines. He will charge twenty-five cents to guys who want to practise their batting. He levels the ground, rigs up heavy wire backstops, and installs the floodlights himself after one day's instruction from an electrician. Helping him to prepare the Stop 'n' Swat (she paints), my mother is scared to death of that electricity stuff – really, he hasn't a clue – but somehow it passes the examination of the state inspector. She half wonders if the inspector is just indulging Jack. People do that. My father's confidence and his willingness to give anything a go are infectious; something about him makes people want to climb aboard.

They are emblematic, a wholesome, post-war ideal: homemaker and breadwinner, mother and father, husband and wife. So much so that in September 1953 they appear in the *Ladies Home Journal* cover story, part of a series called 'How Young America Lives'. Titled 'Meet Mrs $10,000 Executive in the Home', the piece – a fourteen-page spread with dozens of photos – focuses on 'the earning power of a homemaker'. Household expenditures are tallied, along with the amount of money saved on skilled labour by having my mother do everything gratis. She cleans, cooks, tends sick children, washes, irons, cuts hair, grocery-shops, acts as her own beautician and as the family plumber ('toys in toilets, jelly beans down drain'); she shines shoes, refinishes furniture, washes windows, caters, sews the family clothes; she is secretary, bookkeeper, purchasing agent and all-around troubleshooter: '7 a.m. to 11 p.m. – no sky-high tycoon or strong laborer works harder than a Size 10 blonde with two children.'

The article highlights the couple's devotion to one another, particularly hers to him – 'Nita and Jack McCloskey, of Haddonfield, New Jersey, rediscover in 1953 terms what Proverbs summed up long ago: "Whoso findeth a wife findeth a good thing"' – and their shared dedication to the task of child-rearing. My father tells the magazine that before he got married, he knew he wanted 'not just love from a wife, but absolute devotion'. He has gotten it. Jack the Giant Killer, as he is now known by small-town sports writers for slaying teams greater than his own, is, like his teammates on the Sunbury Mercuries, a young man with a family, moonlighting to bring in a few extra dollars. My mother attends as many Mercuries games as she can, but some are 350 miles away, and on those nights she falls asleep saying the rosary, praying that the team makes it home safely. The minute Jack opens the front door, she is up, even if it's 4 or 5 a.m. If he wants, she will make him a proper breakfast and sit at the kitchen table while he details the highs and lows of the game. If he is not in a talkative mood, or simply exhausted, he eats a dish of ice cream and they go to sleep.

My mother doesn't get sentimental about many things, but says, 'I know how I really feel about the guy when I see his pyjamas hanging in the closet and realize he's not coming home that night. He's a kind of Horatio Alger hero or maybe Howard Ruark in *The Fountainhead* – he's fitted in so much of everything.'

They are a frugal couple and proud of their ability to stretch a dollar. Decor is strictly DIY. They paint a 'carpet' on the kitchen floor – crimson and black with tassels around the perimeter – and four of Jack's paintings hang on the living-room wall. (The art teacher at the high school encouraged him to take up painting to relieve tension.) On another wall is a twisted tree root my father found last summer, now painted white and mounted on red and brown board. They love entertaining – there is Jack playing the baby-blue piano for a small group of smiling friends, their heads tilted at an admiring angle – but are 'experts at parties on a

shoestring'. My mother lays out an inexpensive but filling buffet on the dinette, and guests are delighted.

The photos tell the story of their lives. There they are, dancing at a black-tie ball, elegant beyond their means. Sprawled companionably on the living-room sofa, typing teaching reports on the Remington. Together in the front yard – he with a gardening trowel, she handing him a seedling to put down. There is Nita trimming Mike's hair. Changing little Steve's diaper. Applying cold cream in front of the mirror, a framed painting of Jesus on the bureau beneath her. Hanging out laundry, stylish even in a tweed skirt and cardigan.

Two photos of Mike stand out. In one, Jack is slouched in an easy chair and Mike is sitting on his shoulders, his legs straddling his father's neck. He has one hand cupped under Jack's chin; Jack's face is turned towards him. The two of them are looking into each other's eyes, their smiles wide with wonder, mutually astonished by the mere fact of the other's existence.

The other photo is of Mike with Nita. They are lying on the floor in front of the piano, she on her back, he on top of her, also on his back. She is still, while he appears to be squirming. He is laughing,

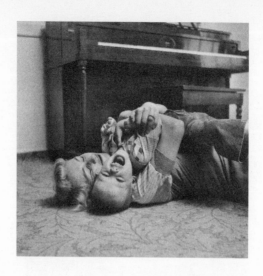

as though she were tickling him, which she is not; her arms are merely wrapped around him in an embrace. Just being held, it seems, is enough to awaken in him this irrepressible joy. As for Nita, her eyes are closed and there is the slightest hint of a smile on her face. Her expression is one of bliss, peace, completion.

And there, on the cover of the magazine, Nita and her two boys in close-up. She is wearing a bright red dress and lipstick that match the red lettering of *Journal*. Her smiling face is turned to the camera. Her features are fresh and distinct, and her expression is open, joyful, suffused with a clarity of purpose. Mike is behind her, with his arms around her neck and his small hands clasped, his forehead resting against her temple. He is three years old. Steve, just a year, is in the lower-left corner, his chubby profile visible, his two hands pressed to his mother – one to her chest, the other linked with Mike's. They will never be more beautiful than this.

By the winter of 1954–5, my mother is pregnant again. To keep herself busy on the cold winter nights when my father is on the road, she joins the King's Players, the drama group at the local church where she and Jack and the boys attend Mass. In *Our Town*,

she plays one of the dead women in the graveyard, looking with such pity at the living, who don't appreciate what they have, the small miracles of every ordinary day. One of her few lines is 'Goodness! That ain't no way to behave.' My father goes to see her performance. For days after, whenever one of them commits some minor domestic offence, the other will exclaim, 'Goodness! That ain't no way to behave.' And they will laugh.

The photos of the boys are piling up. My mother saves them in shoeboxes in the closet and vows that winter, before the next baby arrives, to arrange them in albums. Their temperaments are apparent in nearly every photograph, and the difference between the two of them is striking. Steve is a wild-eyed rascal. There is an odd knowingness to his merriment: he appears in several photos to be

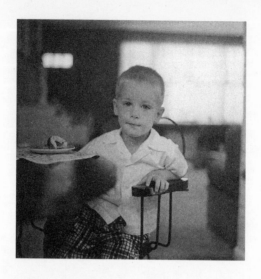

throwing back his head when laughing, like a little Buddha. He is stocky, solid, unbreakable. He looks as though you could roll him across the floor like a ball and he would come up smiling. Mike, in comparison, is physically delicate, as lean as Steve is round. His fair skin and blond hair lend him a radiance, as though he exists in a flash of sunlight. There is something precarious there, too, a softness to his features that is so pronounced he appears at times almost translucent. He is, quite simply, angelic.

With each passing year, the family grows a little more comfortable financially. Though my parents were raised to be thrifty, they are not immune to the pleasures of upward mobility. The unreliable Little Car, which carried them from their wedding to their honeymoon and through the early years of their marriage, is a thing of the past. They now drive a fire-engine-red Cadillac. Gone, too, are the days of dark, cramped apartments and the humble starter home in Haddonfield. By 1956, my father has landed a real coaching job – for the varsity basketball team at the University of Pennsylvania – and within a couple of years the family is living in a split-level in Broomall, with a big curved bay window overlooking a sloping front yard. My mother adores it. When you face the house you can see the four upstairs windows flanked by their wooden shutters, one window for each child she has now. The daughter she'd prayed for had come, in 1955. So unlike the boys, who are always punching each other and wrestling, Robin sits in her playpen for hours, quietly amusing herself. Another boy, John, was born in 1957, blond with big brown eyes and a gentle disposition.

Mike, meanwhile, is growing into a beautiful bright child, if sometimes a little pensive. His grandmother watches him one day, seven years old, walking home from the school bus. He is dragging his bag of books behind him instead of throwing it in the air and catching it like the other boys. Another day he gets hysterical when the bus driver changes his route and passes his usual corner stop. He's prone to nightmares, too, sometimes dreaming the house is on fire. My mother worries, but not excessively. All kids have bad dreams and fears of the dark and funny little things that terrify them that would never strike you as scary. Mike's fears and his idiosyncrasies seem no more ominous than those of any other child. Also, he has this smile. Sudden, unreserved and enveloping, it is more than a mere expression; it is the sum of him. An inner light that breaks through, hinting that underneath that strange gravity is a secret reservoir of joy.

My mother is ironing in the upstairs bedroom of the Broomall house when a neighbour phones to tell her that Kennedy has been assassinated. When she hangs up, she turns on the radio but keeps ironing, tears running down her face. It's a Friday afternoon in November; the older kids are still at school. She thinks to herself, *Who is safe?* On the news there have been images of violence. Marchers and rioters. People throwing stones and bottles. The police with their fire hoses and night sticks and dogs. And only that September the four little black girls killed by a bomb at the church in Birmingham, in the basement putting on their choir robes. Children. She thinks about Kennedy – young, vigorous, beautiful, *good.* She voted for him, of course. The New Deal made a lifelong Democrat of her. She stands there ironing and crying and saying to herself, *If a president can be murdered in plain view, who is safe?* She thinks about her little babies, of the country they'll grow up in. Not only the baby in the crib beside her – she and Jack have had a fifth, Timmy, born in the spring of 1962 – but the baby not yet born. The previous week, she learned that she is pregnant. Her mother thinks she's crazy. 'Aren't you ever going to stop?' she said. But Nita is delighted. She is praying for another girl.

Mike is fourteen the year I am born, just starting high school. Thin as a rail, with freckles and a brush cut he flips in the front with a bit of Butch wax. He is serious, diligent, conscientious. At school, he is made Sacred Heart Boy, the award bestowed on the boy who shows the best combination of scholarship, athleticism and good behaviour. He is also competitive, and in this he takes his cue from his father. His father is not in the business of raising quitters, pansies, Mary Janes. One of his mottos is 'A winner is a loser who just didn't quit'. When Mike goes out for track his first year in high school, he runs and runs until he is vomiting.

He and Steve play basketball at the hoop behind the house, practising their moves. Mike has a beautiful jump shot. He is what they call a pure shooter. A photo shows him with seven other boys and my father, some Saturday afternoon, the blacktop still puddled with recent rain. My father, who stands under the basket, is leading the boys in a passing drill. Mike is smiling broadly, preparing to catch the ball. For some reason, as though we might not recognize him, my mother has written MIKE above his head on the photograph, with an arrow pointing down.

Another photo from a couple of years earlier shows a different face, one less open. He is posed against a grey, bare-branched, winter backdrop, a pack of baseball cards in one hand, wearing baggy denims, Converse and a T-shirt from Puerto Rico showing zany tourist scenes. It's in the posture, and the expression: a kind of cool is beginning to flower.

He is building his world – day by day, year by year – his inner world, which will move with him through the years like a thousand stories of himself until it is ravaged by the future. Or maybe not. Maybe nothing that follows, nothing that he will ever feel or see or believe to be true (that little brown women are poking pins in his

38

eyes) can destroy that world that once was his, the landscape of his past. What the rest of us will do is reinterpret that past. We will say there were signs – the separateness, the sensitivity, the bouts of introspection inappropriate to his age – but this may have less to do with him than with a desire to console ourselves. For some reason, we must believe that there were clues and that we saw them. That it was a secret he couldn't altogether keep from us.

Four

Years ago, I tried to write a novel about Mike. In November 1994, I boarded a plane at Shannon and flew to JFK, en route to my mother's beach house in Ocean City, New Jersey. My mother had decamped to Florida for the winter, and so for a month I would have the house to myself. The purpose, ostensibly, was to work on the novel. It was going to be a family saga, spanning decades and tracing the arc of my brother's life against a backdrop of the changing social landscape of America, and when it was finished, I would understand what it was I had felt about Mike all these years, and just what his illness had meant to me, and to the family.

I already knew that I had long felt guilty about him – for having wished when I was young that he would vanish, and, when I was older, for never having made an effort to see him when I was living not far from him in Portland. But I had not, on a conscious level, felt guilty about the fact that he was ill and I was not. What I'd felt all those years was relief – at having escaped a fate that seemed, to some unknown degree, stitched into our genes. The fact that Mike had schizophrenia meant that all his siblings had a greater chance of developing it – 7 to 9 per cent versus the approximately 1 per cent chance within the general population in the US. Throughout my teens and most of my twenties, I had looked at him and felt the uncanny connection of blood and been grateful for the randomness that had left me sane.

But by the time I'd reached my late twenties, I had begun to look over my shoulder. In July 1992, two years before the escape to my mother's house, I had written in one of the notebooks I kept, *I am afraid, suddenly, of everything*. I was living in the west of Ireland then, I was just about to get married, and I knew things had to change. *I* had to change. On our honeymoon in Puerto Rico, along with vowing to take up knitting, study French and learn to play the piano,

I swore to *Drink less, read more*. Over dinner, my new husband and I toasted our commitment to being better people, both individually and together. The band played a song for us and we danced in our slow, clumsy fashion, full of love and of woolly notions of the future and our own self-improvement.

The next evening, the everything I was afraid of gathered itself into a roiling panic in a bar in San Juan. One minute, all the people around me were laughing and chatting and enjoying themselves in a perfectly familiar manner. The next, they seemed to swell and throb, as if filling with some menacing energy they were unable to properly contain. They looked like Robert Crumb creations. I started to sweat and shake and found it difficult to swallow. The tapas I'd ordered suddenly looked obscene, like genitalia gone wrong in a nightmare. Objects were pulsing as though seen through a desert heat. My husband took me back to the hotel, where I lay down and waited for whatever it was to pass.

I had never had a full-blown panic attack before, and the onset of it had been so like the onset of a psilocybin excursion the previous month that I wondered if the attack was some sort of flashback. The mushrooms had been taken on a whim one lunchtime in a pub. Tossing them into a mix that already included a hangover, pre-wedding anxieties and whatever other ghouls were flitting through my mind resulted in my rushing home to cower under the bed-clothes for hours. Upon surfacing that evening – peeking my head out from under the blankets like some cartoon character – I told myself I had enough trouble managing my mind without such self-inflicted challenges. I recorded in my notebook that I would 'never again underestimate the beauty of reality', a resolution that, along with taking up knitting and learning the piano and drinking less, was quickly forgotten.

The first years of marriage were, for me, like the honeymoon writ large. Too much drinking, a twitchy anxiety, excessive self-consciousness with no resulting insight. I schlepped messily from one day to the next.

New Year's resolutions, 1993: *Work harder, drink less, and* [once again] *learn to knit.*

Though there were brief periods of calm and order during which I glimpsed that life could, perhaps, be lived in a happier, more productive and less confused way, I had no idea how this state of affairs might be brought about. A friend said to me one night, in a moment of scornful drunken truth-telling, 'You're only playing at life.' It was true. I felt both darkly unhappy and insufficiently serious.

In 1994, my husband and I bought a house in the Irish countryside, on the side of a mountain and overlooking a bay. That summer we worked on our house, and in the evenings we ate dinner outside at the table in the front garden, candlelight and wine, the indigo sky spread out around us. For a time, we felt lucky. We walked on ice, or on air, and the things we had toasted that honeymoon night seemed once again possible: that we might yet be better people, that we might yet create something shining and true.

But whatever it was that was wrong with me kept dragging us down. I didn't know what to call it, and all I could do, it seemed, was watch myself unspool. My emotions and my thoughts were growing alien. On the one hand, I often felt as though the medium of my existence were an ooze of instinct and emotion on which I could get no purchase. The emotions themselves were warped and melodramatic – arising out of that strange blend of chaos and monotony that alcohol engenders – and seemed as though they were being manufactured at a point so deep inside me it was impossible to access. On the other hand, my mind could churn obsessively, moving in ever-smaller circles around an ever-shrinking number of themes, overlaid with the sizzle of anxiety. (When I think of an anxious mind, I think of flies frying on an electric fly killer.) Other times, thoughts would arrive with an exaggerated slowness, like railway carriages that had been disconnected from one another, bumping past at slow intervals. What should have felt seamless – the rolling, unbroken flow of perception – was fractured into frames. I watched my hand reach for a glass and saw it stutter, as though under a strobe light. Other times, it wriggled shakily, independent of my commands, like a still-fighting fish on the end of a line. (Eating soup was out of the question.) The shake in my hands felt like evidence of some inner tremble, as though something at the core of me had got very cold and was radiating its icy weather.

I told only one person about the wriggling-fish sensation: a Canadian neighbour who had ended up on the side of the same mountain when the lover she'd followed to Ireland left her. She told me that once on LSD she had seen her arm floating completely free of her body. In a way, this made me feel better – for although my friend was eccentric, she wasn't crazy; in another way it made me feel worse, for she had been on acid at the time, whereas I merely had a hangover.

The poppies in the back garden took on a hallucinatory menace, and there were days the long, flat-topped mountain behind us loomed like a tidal wave. I had begun to dream dreams in which I was drunk and could not find my place, could not remember how to eat, sit, behave. My various resolutions had boiled down to one, and it was repeated nearly every day: *Drink less*.

All of this I recorded in my notebooks. That sanity was feeling 'very slippery as of late'. That I was afraid this 'aimless, rambling fear' would 'devour' me. That walking, talking and other ordinary elements of daily existence had acquired an 'unbearably strange' cast. One day in a bank in Dublin, I broke out in a sweat, my heart palpitating, as I tried to sign my own name to withdraw money on my own credit card. My signature was so shaky and bore so little resemblance to the one on the back of my card that they refused to believe I was who I said I was; incapable of arguing, I hurried away. The split I had begun to experience – the sense that I was watching someone acting in my place – had reached the point where, in 'pretending' to be me, I felt guilty of attempting to perpetrate fraud.

By the time I boarded the plane at Shannon in 1994 to take me to my mother's empty house, my prevailing panicked feeling was *Stop the train, I want to get off*. As much as I imagined I was getting away to write about my brother, my more pressing need was to pull back from the brink. For I had begun to fear that I was losing my own mind.

It had all started rather agreeably, I thought, my relationship with alchohol. Although there were blackouts from the start, and I sometimes did things I was embarrassed of, and nicked vodka from my mother's liquor cabinet and blamed it on Mike when she noticed, and though I had watched my brother Steve hit bottom the year I turned seventeen, none of it worried me, and my own drinking I enjoyed.

Everything changed in the summer of 1984. I was nineteen years old and had moved for a couple of months into the upstairs apartment of my grandparents' house on Central Avenue in Ocean City – just blocks from the house to which I would flee, ten years later, in an attempt to recover myself. Becky, my best friend from high school, had come from Oregon to join me. We were filled with good intentions. We would get waitressing jobs and save all our tips and be flush by summer's end. We would live on something called to (pronounced *toe*) soup, made from a health-food recipe Becky had brought with her, which would, she promised, cleanse us of toxins and keep us svelte in our bikinis. We would swim and exercise, get up early and ride our bikes on the boardwalk as the sun rose over the ocean. We would relive the innocence of my mother's teenage summers here.

Things turned out otherwise. We did get jobs waitressing, but I was fired from mine a couple of weeks after starting for spending too much time talking to Becky when she dropped by. After that, I got a job checking beach tags for minimum wage. From ten till four, I walked up and down the beach, asking people if they had tags – a tax the city had recently imposed on bathers. It was mind-numbingly dull but would've been a pleasant enough way to pass the days were it not for the daily hangovers. They had begun to spill into one another, with no break between for mental regrouping. My capacity to process the muddle and mayhem each night brought was breaking down. One morning, as I dragged myself the four blocks to commence another day of walking up and down the beach, I began to cry. *I can't do it*, I thought, *I can't do it* (as though 'it' were something quite demanding). I got as far as the shack on 9th Street where we picked up our tags for the day, and told them that I didn't know what was wrong with me but that I couldn't work. At least it was the truth.

As for Becky, she had landed herself a plum job that promised serious tips, at a posh seafood restaurant on the docks where the employees nipped into the walk-in fridge to speed-drink Heinekens and gobble jumbo shrimp on the sly. But midway through the summer, she was riding her bike down the street when someone opened a car door and knocked her off. She hyperextended her knee and was laid up for weeks, unable to work but quite capable of sitting in a deckchair drinking beer with the air of an aristocrat celebrating her immobility.

By then, we had acquired a gang. Becky and I did not so much 'make friends' that summer – an activity that would have struck us as square and lacking in the requisite 'randomness' (we believed that what seemed random was, in fact, laid on for our existential instruction) – as sweep people up in the centripetal force of our combined personalities. (Becky was the hub and source of our energy, though; without her, I felt myself go flat.) Aside from John 15th, so called because he worked on 15th Street and could thus be distinguished from John 17th, there was Wendy, who drove a red convertible and held down two waitressing jobs – one in Philadelphia and one in Ocean City – which enabled her to rent the fourth floor of a beach house on 17th Street. It had a porch where we always ended up dancing late at night and off which we miraculously managed never to fall. Wendy's boyfriend was John 17th, who looked like a handsome version of Andy Warhol and had an effete and goofy charm. John 17th was in law school in Philadelphia. He had a quasi-real job up there, which had something to do with documents. (I was regularly astonished that people we had spent the weekend getting wrecked with should subsequently apply themselves to life with a clear head; it struck me as a kind of disloyalty.) We had also made friends with two cousins of John 15th – decent good-looking college boys who seemed a little bit corrupted by us, one of whom we nicknamed, for reasons too inane to remember, Sybil. Finally, there was Paul, a young man who worked at the same restaurant Becky did and with whom Becky had, within hours of meeting him, fallen obsessively in love (it was mutual). Paul was clever and sang in a band and drank as much as we did, but he was also a grafter and held down two jobs to pay his college tuition. He had a habit of stealing bikes. He would ride around with Becky on the handlebars yelping with joy, and then ditch the bike wherever was convenient.

The members of our menagerie fell regularly in and out of love with each other, and it was always hard, the next day, to remember what had actually occurred, what had been only suggested in garbled stage whispers and what had remained mere fantasy. Anyway, it hardly seemed to matter. Possessiveness was frowned upon. Experience was all. We played to death Jimmy Cliff's *The Harder They Come*; its mix of plaintive alienation, spiritual questing and boppy American-style can-do spoke to us as we pinwheeled our way through the summer, teary and fractured and prone to such elastic and confusing loves.

At the beginning of the summer, Becky and I had agreed with my grandparents that we would find other digs for three weeks in July, as they had long-standing tenants for that month whom they didn't want to let down. We took a room on Moorlyn Terrace, a few blocks from my grandparents' place but otherwise a world away, for there we lacked even the civilizing ballast of elderly people living underneath us. The room was the size of a small bedroom, with one bed and a mattress that pulled out like a drawer from under the bed, and a kitchenette in the corner that we never used. There were clothes and beer bottles everywhere, and we climbed over them, and each other, to reach the door, which was the only thing, other than the beds, worth reaching.

One night a girl our age named Sheila arrived at the door of our room. I knew Sheila from beach tagging, though not well. I'd met her on one of my first days on the job. It had started to rain, and so everyone got to go home. Sheila had invited a bunch of us to her parents' house – a beautiful beachfront family home – to play drinking games. As the afternoon wore on and the big oval dining table grew crowded with empties, any pretence of drinking according to the rules of a game was abandoned and I recognized in Sheila a kindred spirit. She was crazy, she was *out there*, and I looked forward to having buckets of fun with her.

But the night she showed up at our little room, she was crying. Her face was red and splotchy and she was babbling, in terrible distress. She was saying something about an abortion, something about rape. It hadn't happened recently but for some reason – maybe she'd run into the guy again? – it had come back to haunt her that night. Becky was calm. She talked to Sheila at the table while I lay on the bed watching them, amazed at Becky's compassion, her show of solidarity. I was glad she was there because although Sheila was, technically, my friend first, and Becky knew her even less than I did, that night I wanted nothing to do with Sheila.

By then, I was coming unmoored. It had started one day a few weeks earlier when John 15th took Becky and me drinking at a place called Los Amigos in Atlantic City. I had met John in the spring when I'd applied, unsuccessfully, for a job at the Port-O-Call hotel's restaurant, which he managed – the same hotel where Mike had worked his teenage summers. John was twenty-six and knew all the bars worth going to. As it was raining, and the tourist season hadn't really kicked off, nobody had to work. So off we went, over the bridge to Somers Point and on to the Atlantic City Expressway.

At the start of that day, life was fine and fun and I felt clean and fresh inside, so full of confidence in the smooth unfolding of the future that it couldn't even qualify as confidence: I just didn't know there was any other way to feel. Nothing happened at Los Amigos, nothing other than that the three of us got drunk, which was a pleasant enough way to pass a rainy day at the shore. And yet something did happen. Because one minute, John 15th and Becky and I were three carefree people sitting at the bar, eating salsa and chips and drinking Dos Equis and shots of tequila, cosy in each other's company, and the next thing I knew it was the following morning and fear had entered my life. For the rest of that summer it shadowed me, so that I looked back on that afternoon, crossing the Somers Point bridge, full of anticipation and ease and a blissful ignorance as to the darker corners of my own mind, as the point at which a part of my life ended and another began.

Several weeks later, towards the end of summer, I rode to Philadelphia one sunny day with Wendy in her red convertible, drinking cold beer and wearing a new wide-brimmed red hat. We were going to a concert in the city, where I would pass out on the grass, forget everything I had paid to hear and lose my lovely red hat. (So many things we lost that summer: watches, beloved books and articles of clothing, favourite cassettes, money.) I remember that ride, though, and the heightened intensity of the colours as we zoomed up the expressway, and it was almost – *almost* – like before, when the days were rich and bright with the promise of everything and nothing in particular.

But it was not as before, and the approximation served only to make obvious what I had lost. Something pure and uncomplicated had been leached from the world, and what I saw when I looked at it now was a hoarding, a two-dimensional display behind which there was only emptiness and the dark. I felt confused and jaded and strangely old. Something had been stolen from me, and, at the same time, I had come into possession of a weighty and unwelcome secret, one I had no idea what to do with.

Ten years later, back in our island beach town and with hardly more clarity about myself than I'd had the day I lost my red hat, I sat on my mother's deck overlooking the Atlantic, immersing myself in the literature of schizophrenia. I read E. Fuller Torrey's *Surviving Schizophrenia: A Family Manual*. I read a memoir by Lori Schiller called *The Quiet Room*, in which she describes in harrowing detail her hellish years of schizophrenic psychosis (she was eventually helped by the antipsychotic clozapine). And I read Mark Vonnegut's memoir *The Eden Express*, in which he recounts his own descent into madness, and his emergence. (Years later, I would see in a letter that my grandmother had read this same book in 1978. She told my mother, *I am reading the Eden Express and it is so real. I feel Mike's problem is 'Biochemical' as mentioned often in the book. At 14 he was skinney, irritable, unfriendly. He has really carried a burden all these years. It is not the disposition but an illness. Can't you bring this up before his 'Shrink'.*) In my suggestible state, what I was concluding from all my reading was that insanity lay on the other side of a very thin pane. Hadn't I lain on my mother's sofa, eyes closed, trying to quell the panic as I felt my body take on strange proportions? Didn't my heart race for no reason? Didn't I unplug the phone, because other people's voices had assumed an unreal quality? Hadn't little menacing faces taken shape in the paisley pattern on the bathroom wallpaper?

There were good days that November at my mother's house, too. Moments of calm, uncomplicated clarity, stark departures from the inebriated chaos of the previous months, when I would look at the wallpaper and see that, yes, there were squiggles that looked like faces, just as there are clouds that look like bearded men, but that was all they were – anthropomorphized curlicues – and I would chuckle with sad compassion for myself and feel smugly sane.

Still, I was in no shape to try to enter, imaginatively, my brother's psyche. Nor, despite my inner refrain of *Stop the train*, was I quite ready to disembark. After a few weeks at my mother's place, I returned to Ireland, with considerable apprehension – for I knew that I would rejoin the madness – no further along with my novel and no wiser about my own dilemmas.

I wasn't the first in my family to have sought refuge, at a time of distress, in Ocean City. When, in the mid seventies, still reeling from a series of psychotic breaks, Mike wrote to our grandparents, *I asked Mom if ever we could make a wish about where we would live it would be in Ocean City*, he wasn't talking about all of us moving east together and making a new life for ourselves. He was talking about going back in time, to a moment from which a bright clear future radiated. To a vantage point from which he might catch a glimpse of himself he could recognize. To the feeling, perhaps, that possessed him at eighteen when, walking the few blocks from the house to his summer job at the hotel – a little cocky, a little unsure, very much in love – he wrote to his girlfriend Lara, *I think about you a lot but especially when I'm walking to work in the morning and the sun is just coming up over the ocean . . .*

Between 1966 and 1976, my family had moved from Pennsylvania to North Carolina to Oregon – there were five houses in ten years – and so whatever collective sense of continuity that exists in our lives is rooted largely in Ocean City, the place where my father first saw a photograph of my mother, and where they went with their children every summer from 1950, when Mike was born. For many of those years, we stayed in a turn-of-the-century Victorian on 12th and Central, the house my grandparents Fanny and Tony bought in the early 1960s when they retired, the same house in which Becky and I would live during the summer of 1984.

Compared to the more modern ranch-style houses my family tended to live in during those years, the Victorian seemed grand and timeless to us. A set of wide, uneven steps led up to the wraparound porch from which thick pillars rose. The downstairs half of the house, where Fanny and Tony lived, had a heavy, old-fashioned feeling to it, with dark wood and heavy oriental rugs. The air was still and the radio played low in Fanny's bedroom. It never felt as summery as upstairs, where the sunlight and the breeze penetrated freely, and the furnishings were cheaper and provisional – a white tin kitchen table rimmed in red, pull-out sofas, the carpet made for heavy wear. In the upper kitchen, the walls sloped halfway up and were painted a pale turquoise. Black linoleum with white streaks covered the kitchen and bathroom floors. An imperious old claw-foot tub occupied much of the bathroom.

The house was in the middle of the long, slender island, between the bay and the Atlantic. A few blocks north of it lay a slightly dilapidated area, which looked as though it had been carved from the Deep South and set down there. Then the numbered grid ended, opening out into the Gardens, where the streets meandered in a pretty but disorienting way and the houses all had front lawns; it felt more like a posh suburb than a beach town. At its south end, far from the congestion of downtown and the boardwalk, the island had an exposed, windswept quality. There was less development. It was empty and lonesome and beautiful. It also seemed impossibly far away from our house, and a minor homesickness floated over us whenever we were there.

As children, we kept to the few streets nearest the house, riding bikes before dinner round and round the blocks and down the alleys that ran through the middle of the blocks. From the alleys, you could see the backs of houses – something impoverished and makeshift in that view of them – and catch the smells of fry oil and fish from the seafood takeaways. In the evenings, we'd sit on the porch with Fanny and Tony doing not much of anything at all, just watching the street and talking, and this in itself – this not-doing – seemed to belong to another era.

When Mike arrived, unannounced, on the doorstep of this house in June 1975, he was covered in scabies and boils. He had left Oregon several weeks before, having been discharged from a mental hospital. He'd been sleeping rough for some of the time since. My grandparents were on their own in the house – the rest of us were in Oregon and would not arrive for our summer visit for a few weeks – and they took Mike in without hesitation, and applied themselves wholeheartedly to his care. They managed to get him back on the medications he had been on in Oregon. They monitored his symptoms and sleep patterns. They stocked up on insecticides, steroid creams and antiseptic soap to treat his skin infections. When he passed the scabies on to them, they didn't complain.

A brief period of stability followed. My grandmother brought Mike books from the library and he read till late at night and during the day played LPs on Tony's record player.

He seems very contented and domesticated, my grandmother reported.

But in a letter home, Mike didn't try to hide his distress.

Dear Mom, Dad, and Everyone,

This letter is about the fact that I might not be able to come out to Oregon soon if I don't get a job at the Port-O-Call. Please don't consider this a rebuff to your hospitality or a bad idea about you but I just don't know what is happening right now or in the reality around me. Please think about me and say a prayer for me at the church on Sunday. Please be good and don't be too worried about me because I really like you a lot and I want to see you all soon.

Within a couple of weeks, he did manage to get himself some shifts as a bellhop at the Port-O-Call, the hotel where he had worked over several summers as a teenager. But by the time my mother

arrived in Ocean City a few weeks later, Mike's condition had deteriorated again. The day she invited Father Flynn to visit – an old family friend, with whom Mike had served his first Mass as an altar boy – Mike was lying in the upstairs bedroom, gaunt and sometimes rambling. Father Flynn pulled up a chair next to the bed and Mike cast a vague look in his direction, nothing that indicated recognition. My mother, perhaps in an effort to boost Mike's self-esteem, or simply to connect her son to the here and now, explained to Father Flynn that Mike had been doing some odd jobs at the hotel up the street; but Father Flynn thought surely not, not in this state. Mike started to speak, but he was babbling – like a toddler still learning language, Father Flynn thought. Father Flynn said prayers right there beside Mike's bed, administered conditional absolution and the Sacrament of the Sick.

My mother stood next to the window. She saw boys passing below with surfboards on their way to the beach, young couples, families, small children festooned with inflatable toys, and thought, *That was us, a thousand years ago.*

Though it seems it might have been more dispiriting than consoling for Mike to return to a place so replete with reminders, his desire to come back here makes sense to me. With the reality around him grown twisted and uncertain, there was nowhere more likely to offer a restoration of coherence. For this is the still point. This is where the past resides.

I miss you both very much and often think about the summers that I spent in Ocean City and how nice it would be to do the same thing again.

In other letters from the mid seventies he repeats this wish *to do the same thing again*, to return, not to his own parents' home (which was itself cracking in two by then, casting the shared past in a disorienting light), but to the home of his grandparents, whose lives are as set as if in aspic. Morning Mass at Saint Augustine's, lunches at Harry's across the 9th Street bridge, long afternoons sewing dresses on the Singer, watching the Phillies on the box. Pepperidge Farm and Shake 'n Bake, pound cakes made from scratch. Tony rustling up the *arroz con pollo* (he'd *die* without the odd plate of rice). Each winter the spell in Puerto Rico, each spring the return, preparing the apartment upstairs for its succession of tenants, the town swelling with summer residents and day-trippers. Ticking off the days till our arrival.

Ocean City is so exciting in summer just watching the tourists and neighbors. Then my loves coming to us . . .

Then the few stragglers in September, college kids down from Philadelphia for a weekend. And then the quiet, the nights closing in, hunkering down for winter. The slate sidewalk in front of the house going slippery with ice, the lamps lit by four. Our grandparents' living room with the big Bakelite phone, and their huge unambiguous love for us and the small containable geography of the island. How solid and true it all was. Compared to the false floor Mike was standing on, the cosmic span of his mind's unsettling capacities, this world of absolutes must have looked like heaven.

Five

In the summer of 1966, just after Mike's sixteenth birthday, we move south, to Winston-Salem, North Carolina, where my father has taken the job of head basketball coach at Wake Forest University. Our house is a six-bedroom split-level with a big backyard bordering a golf course. My mother loves it, especially the family room downstairs, with the sliding glass doors opening on to the shaded backyard. It is where we go for relief from the Southern heat. *I think we have the coolest house in town*, she writes to her mother, *plenty of big shade trees. It is very pleasant always.* After the move, my mother and Fanny exchange letters about three times a week. My mother's, breathless with discovery and full of details about family life, are breezy and light, while Fanny's tend towards anxiety, advice, the latest ominous dream she's had and jags of comical irreverence.

Life is different in the South. There is a moralistic edge to things, alongside something genteel, decorous. The racism is more overt. A billboard outside Fort Bragg proclaims, *Welcome to Fayetteville, Home of the Ku Klux Klan. Fight Communism and Integration*, while another near Raleigh reads simply, *Welcome to Klan Country*. There are no bars in Winston-Salem, and hard liquor may be served only in private homes. On the other hand, this is tobacco country, the only state in America with no cigarette tax. In spring you can smell the tobacco blooming in the fields.

It's Baptist country too, and my mother discovers there are two kinds of Baptists: those who hold hands to say Moravian blessings and drink juice with dinner, and the more free-wheeling variety. *Saturday night . . . the swingin'est, dancingest party I've ever been to. Much fun! They have a mansion and most of the guests seem to be millionaire doctors, but very regular, and most warm and sociable.*

It is amazing how many Southern millionaires my mother finds 'regular' folk. There is something good in everyone she meets. Next door are a paediatrician and his wife (*a real regular girl with a good sense of humor*), and next to them a Catholic family, the wife from Venezuela (*very spunky and cute*). The neighbourhood kids call round for us. The invitations from other couples pour in – to dinners and cocktail parties and cook-outs. My father is a local celebrity. Basketball fans are hoping he will turn the team around. His last year at Penn, his team had won both the Big 5 and the Ivy League championships.

The worst my mother can say of anyone is that they are a 'lemon' or a 'dud'. *The maid turned out to be a dud. I nicknamed her 'Let's Pretend', as she was a towel folder.* Mostly, her letters describe the nicest people, the best filet mignon, the 'plushest' country club. Even the grocery store is laudable: *brand new, very clean and beautiful.*

The only thing missing from the idyll is Mike, who will arrive in Winston-Salem at the end of that summer after finishing work as a bellboy at the Port-O-Call in Ocean City. In his absence, I have taken to calling my Raggedy Anne doll 'Mike' and commemorating my brother in song. It is the year Dionne Warwick releases 'Message to Michael', and I sit playing on the floor of my room, singing a garbled version of it:

Take a message to Michael, message to Michael
Tell him I miss him
Every day
I play blocks

My mother, too, is eager for his arrival.

Dear Mike –

We all miss you very much. It just isn't a family without you. Your room is really nice – cozy and beautiful. With a place like that to study, a boy would be sure to get straight A's!

   Can't wait for you to get here. I know we will be happy here.
   God bless you.

Love, Mommy

Everyone at Bishop McGuinness, the Catholic high school Mike and Steve will attend, knows that the sons of the new Wake Forest coach are coming. Hopes are high. The school's basketball team has been playing so badly recently that the cheerleaders made up cheers for losing.

By early October, Mike has a girlfriend, his first. Not just any girl, but an older girl, a senior. The first time Kathy looks at him she blushes. He is boyish and pretty, with beautiful long eyelashes. He strikes her as young for his age, as though he hasn't been around girls much, and she is charmed by his naivety. It happens on a school hayride. A horse-drawn Conestoga wagon, an autumn night. The Southern air still dusky-warm, boys and girls together in the dark. She can feel he wants to kiss her but isn't sure how to make his move. Though she isn't shy, she plays it cool. *If he wants to kiss me*, she thinks, *let him*. He does. And when the hayride is over, he looks at her and says solemnly, 'You make out real good.'

My mother approves. *Mike's girlfriend is a real swinger, but a nice girl. She has a musical combo, and they play for all the dances at school . . . This girl has the pierced ears, dark glasses, and crazy haircut, but cute as can be . . . big brown eyes & stringy blonde hair, & really looks a little like me. The world is moving too fast, huh?*

Kathy adores him. He is patient, funny, romantic. Gentle and soft-spoken and, in spite of his brains, not prone to boasting. They play records at our house – the Animals and the Turtles – and in the afternoons do their homework together. In the downstairs rec room, they make out on the sofa, alert to the sound of anyone coming down the stairs. Kathy loves being at our house, there are always so many people around, so much life. Her home is a less happy one. Her father is an alcoholic.

Kathy is a bit of a badass, and she knows that's part of what Mike finds attractive. She is one of the gang (Steve is, too) who sneak booze into that year's Christmas party in the cafeteria. The 'party' consists of the screening of a film chosen by the nuns. That year's film is *The Long Grey Line*, a 1955 drama starring Tyrone Power as an Irish immigrant at West Point. The evening ends badly when a girl named Sally rats on them. The offenders are made to sit in the unheated school eight hours a day for three days during Christmas vacation, copying in longhand from the New Testament. Kathy has eluded capture, but when the student body begins to dissolve into factions – the goodie-goodies against those who were caught, those who were caught against those who weren't – she turns herself in and gets suspended from the cheerleading squad. The nuns, in an apparently progressive attempt to heal the divisions the episode has created, allow the students to meet privately in one of the classrooms to discuss it. At the meeting, Sally keeps saying, 'They did this . . .' and 'They did that . . .' Finally, a girl named Betty stands up and says, 'As a member of The They . . .' The 'private' meeting, as it turns out, is a sham – at some point, the kids hear crackling over the intercom and realize the nuns have been listening all along – and the only thing that comes out of it is the formation of this gang of harmless baddies known as The They. Its members adopt nicknames. Steve is the Pope. Kathy is Big Mama.

Mike is not a member of The They. He is a model student, a lover of reading and studying and, anyway, not much of a joiner. Although everyone likes him – and he *is* dragging the basketball team out of the cellar (twenty points one night, twenty-two the next) – he doesn't really have close male friends. He is intense and introspective, active at school while remaining slightly aloof. Kathy notices his aloofness but doesn't think it creepy. She puts it down to personal reserve. My mother notices, too, and attributes it to adolescence, telling her mother:

> *Your letter to him was lovely. He is saving it on his top bookshelf.*
> *I don't know whether he intends to answer it, or it is just a sentimental*
> *attachment. I love where he said – 'I even miss you sometimes.' He is not*
> *as cold as he seems, I guess – just tries to appear 'cool', as the kids say.*

By February, things with Kathy are strained. She is argumentative, difficult, a flirt; two other guys – Eddy and José – are hovering on the perimeter. Her home life is taking its toll on her moods. Mike is getting fed up, though he hasn't lost his sense of humour. For Valentine's Day, he makes her a big card – affectionate, needling, ironic – and presents it to her just before a basketball tournament in Charlotte. He draws a red rose on it, underneath which he writes:

You look OK
You smell like a rosé
I'll see you in Charlotte
Along with Eddy and José

The break-up with Kathy is conducted according to a high-school script of awkward utterances, public melodrama and parental cameos. After one of the games, Kathy accuses him of having his eye on another girl. He denies it but admits he's finding her difficult. That night, she and a friend drive to the corner of Mike's street and Kathy gets out of the car to wait for him. She needs to talk. But when he comes around the corner, instead of slowing down, he guns it and speeds past towards home, leaving her standing there, crying. The next day, my mother calls Kathy's house and tells her mother that Mike and Steve won't be riding to school with Kathy any more. And that's the end of that.

In March, Kathy's father dies. At the wake, she can see Mike and Steve coming towards her in the line. Steve gives her a hug and whispers, 'I'm so sorry, Big Mama.' Then she hears her mother say Mike's name and she holds out her hand to shake his and says, with all the formality she can muster, 'Thank you for coming.'

'Oh, cut that out,' he says, and puts his arms around her and holds her very tight.

In the brief interlude between ending with Kathy and beginning with Lara, Mike dates Donna, a black girl in his class. It takes nerve in 1967. Blacks live in East Winston, nowhere near the golf course that edges our backyard. There are still signs on some of the drinking fountains – for Coloureds and Whites.

Mike and Donna don't last, possibly because he has already set his heart on Lara. Born in South America while her father was in the service, her family fluent in Spanish, Lara is an exotic creature by Bishop McGuinness standards. She is also intellectual and deeply serious and has the same cutting sense of humour as Mike. They compete with each other, both in their sarcasm and in their studies (career aptitude tests at school show they would both make good psychiatrists), though Lara is more rebellious than Mike. She, too, was involved in the Christmas party scandal – as a result she got an F in Conduct, was kicked out of the National Honor Society and suspended from the cheerleading squad. For a while she managed to keep it from her parents, leaving the house on game nights wearing her cheerleading outfit.

If Mike still has that delicate beauty that captivated Kathy, he is no longer wide-eyed. Encouraged, perhaps, by Lara, he has begun to think about the world beyond sports and girls. In the March 1967 edition of the school's *Signet* newspaper, Mike publishes a poem titled 'Something Ignorant', in which a Green Beret lies in a trench in Vietnam as lead whizzes overhead, thinking of the protests back home, caught between a knowledge that the killing is pointless and the loyalty he feels to his fellow soldiers.

> . . . Cruel and senseless were words that came to mind,
> Trying to think in this din of slaughter.
> 'War,' he thought, 'was something ignorant
> in the human heart. A defect for which each man
> Must, himself, pay the ugly price of peace.'

*

In the summer of 1967, Mike sits behind the bellman's desk in the Port-O-Call in Ocean City, writing letters to Lara, who is in Mexico with her family. He is back at his summer job and staying at his grandparents' house. His letters are a mix of self-mockery and self-congratulation. He tells Lara he is learning to surf, and details the fortunes of the two basketball teams he's playing for, itemizing his own stats. Despite the fact that his picture sometimes appears in the *Ocean City Sentinel* – clipped devotedly by his grandmother – he assures Lara that he is too modest to send the clippings.

Occasionally, he and the guys from work get six-packs of Budweiser and hit the rides at Wildwood. At weekends there are parties and concerts and dances, but Mike doesn't dance with anyone. He tells Lara he hasn't met a girl who could hold a candle to her. These are good times and the money is rolling in, but the Kid – as he likes to refer to himself – can't wait to get back to Winston-Salem, to see his girl, to start driving his father's new Firebird. Sometimes he throws a bit of rudimentary Spanish into his letters. He watches the bullfights from Mexico City on TV, but says it's not a sport at all because the bull doesn't have a chance. Like a fool, he says, he keeps rooting for the bull.

September 1967. He is entering his final year of simplicity, when the world will for the last time revolve around him, around the number of points he scores and the envelopes lying on the kitchen table when he comes home from school – solicitations from colleges up and down the east coast. His life is catalogued in detail in my mother's letters – she fed him steak for dinner, he wore yellow socks to school – just as it was in his infancy. It is as though he is at the centre of a small industry dedicated to his future flourishing.

Mike drives Lara in his white '59 Olds, purchased for $175, to the Dixie Classic Fair. Swine judging, cake baking, rides for a quarter. At a mock slave auction at school, he buys her for four dollars – this, just three years after the Civil Rights Act and only months after major race riots in Detroit and Newark. In early November, Winston-Salem sees its own unrest. My mother writes to Fanny:

Our race riot began Thursday night after the funeral of a colored man who had resisted arrest while drunk & was killed by the arresting policeman. So they wrecked downtown stores & set a few fires . . . We haven't felt any effects except that there was an 11 pm curfew for everyone last night, the high school football games were cancelled, some stores closed early, & the liquor stores are all closed until further notice . . . The national guard has been on duty downtown since Thurs nite & everything has quieted down now. Jack's parents called last night & we were at a cocktail party at Forsyth Country Club, of course . . .

A week after the riot, the kids go on a hayride. Forty of them come back to the house afterwards and the downstairs family room rocks with music and dancing. My mother makes six batches of cookie bars and sets out bowls of potato chips and pretzels. With the party in full swing, she and my father creep out into the dark backyard and watch the kids dancing through the sliding glass doors. Who is she by now? How does she feel? Not just about this moment – with her hand on her husband's back in the dark, the life they have created together framed and illuminated before them – but in general? Three times a week, she taps it all out on her typewriter.

Dear Dearies . . .

Dearest Dollies . . .

Dearest Mommy and Daddy . . .

I am very happy, feel wonderful, & am busier than I have ever been, but happy-busy – planning dinner parties, football weekends, bridge dates, religion classes, etc . . . everything is wonderful – Jack & the children all well & happy, & doing well in school, Jack ready to start basketball practice this Monday & most eager, & me with my usual half dozen projects in the works . . .

She edits the Wake Forest Faculty Wives' newsletter and decorates our living room in gold and black, the school's colours. She appears in the papers with some frequency. She is the 'lovely blonde wife'. The 'statuesque blonde'. The 'Wife, Mother, Sometime Referee and Full-Time Fan'. She is the helpmate, the complement, the enthusiast. A *Winston-Salem Journal* article reveals that she is seldom without her Wake Forest button – 'I pin it on my skin when I take a shower,' she jokes – while the *Raleigh News and Observer* notes that she feels 'extra fortunate in being able to share so much of the agony and glory of the game' with her husband.

And how does she describe herself?

As a 'frustrated journalist and a frustrated athlete'.

As someone who 'can't seem to help getting involved with people'.

As a woman who tries to combine 'what's in style with what's right for my age'.

As a person who 'enjoys most things but in the back of my mind I think I should be in the Peace Corps'.

The Peace Corps? Does she mean that? Is she filling every minute of her life with activity in order not to notice an emptiness at the core of it? Does she read *The Feminine Mystique* and feel a gnawing, thwarted potential? Is she ever tempted, like millions of housewives across America, like her own mother (who has been on the sedative phenobarbital for years), to turn to pharmaceuticals?

Probably not. If she feels a lurking unease, it is not related to any lack of self-fulfilment but rather to a flitting guilt about her own happiness. The feeling that her world is snug and inviolate, that she is insufficiently concerned with the luckless multitudes. But she is not, in general, one to sit around wringing her hands about all the other lives she might be living. In answer to one of her mother's particularly plaintive letters, she writes, *Please enjoy yourselves – life is a frame of mind – enjoy whatever you're doing at the moment – peeling potatoes or partying*.

Rarely does she allow her philosophical side to show. When she does, it is always coupled with a sort of disclaimer. Who is she to be thinking such deep thoughts?

I know I sound silly but my New Year's resolution was to communicate more fully with my fellow man. I think it is the most important thing in this life, whether it be on a boardwalk bench at 13th Street or in Ponce, PR. What do any of us have but each other?????

I am off on a philosophical kick, but this is Ash Wed. & this resolution is to do one kind deed for my fellow man. Today was the birthday of the basketball captain, so I baked 3 dozen cupcakes for him & the team.

It's not that she doesn't have her worries. She is concerned about the draft. For now, Mike is safe under the student deferment clause, but the law could change. *The talks with Hanoi look good*, she writes, in a rare reference to the wider, scarier world. She worries about the unpredictability of the country, the way anything seems possible, in the worst sense. Kids with funny clothes and flowers painted on their faces, that's not a big deal. But there are other things that disturb her. Black flags of anarchism. The clenched fist of militance. Abbie Hoffman burning money. The loosening of public morals. She types a paper of Mike's on the New Morality. *It will curl your hair. I hope he doesn't believe all this stuff he wrote!* Language is changing. Coloureds become Negroes become Blacks (her mother still calls them 'boogies'). She worries about the direction the Church is taking: *I read yesterday that birth control is no longer prohibited by the Church in Spain, & you can buy the pill in any drug store without a prescription. Si, si, senor!* And yet she is not, by nature, conservative. Change is exciting. She likes the guitar music at Mass and even though she misses the Latin, she was thrilled to hear 'This is my body' in English, admitting, *It seemed almost bold somehow*.

Occasionally, she takes a night chaperoning at the 'Attic', a hang-out at Wake Forest where students drink coffee, play bridge, listen to music. There are the clean-cut kids from Wake and the 'kooks' from the North Carolina School of the Arts, what one of her neighbours calls the Tip-Toe School. My mother enjoys them all. She's a people person. Homosexuals and hippies. Supernaturalists (she has signed up for an ESP class). The maid who dips snuff and goes fishing on her day off. Coloured people, generally. Even Southern racists. When Jack has young black recruits to the house for dinner, it doesn't pass without comment from the neighbours. Nothing vicious, just a quick clutch at the heart accompanied by an exclamation of *There-goes-the-neighbourhood!* or some such witticism. But if the boys can deliver, who cares if they're green? Charlie Davis scores forty-one and a neighbour comes to the house the next morning waving a small white flag and it's all a good laugh.

The tension persists, though. Some of the college's basketball fans object to my father's recruitment of black players. One woman takes the trouble to write to my father:

Sir:

It has become disgusting to watch Wake basketball on TV. Wake now has the aspect of one of the negro oriented 'slum' colleges out of Phila, NYC or New Jersey. A typical photo in the paper showed three negroes on the

court at once . . . the situation and those responsible for it are utterly
contemptible and a disgrace to the old North State.

But my father comes from nothing and he thinks you can earn your place at the table whether you're a spic or a Mick or a wop or a Negro. Such distinctions have no place in the country he went to war for. (He tells his children to ignore those 'Colored' and 'White' signs on the drinking fountains.) Mike feels the same, though his sentiments arise from his absorption of the civil rights ethos in the air. After a game in the small town of Wentworth, when the opposing team's fans kept heckling McGuinness's black player, Mike tells his mother he was disgusted by their ignorance.

He does everything right, she writes.

A week after Wentworth, Mike sets a school record by scoring forty-six points in one game. Big headlines in the Sunday paper. His coach couldn't be prouder. Danny, whom all the kids call by his first name, teaches English literature at the school and took over the team last year from a dictator they called GI Joe. Danny is only twenty-three. He has long hair and a nineteen-year-old wife who wears miniskirts. My mother calls him 'the flower child'. *Parochial school education sure has taken on a new look!*

Mike loves him, and the affection is mutual. Sometimes he and Lara stop over to see Danny and Sharon when they're going out on a Saturday night. Mike is relaxed at Danny's house, he can hold his own with adults. But Danny senses in Mike – despite the apparent confidence, despite his being the school basketball star and having a beautiful and intelligent girlfriend – a sensitivity and a deep vulnerability. Mike is somehow both a part of and apart from the team.

By December, they've won five of seven and people are talking about the Catholic League State Championship. In a game just before Christmas, Mike pulls down twenty-nine rebounds for another school record. (Though he's still skin and bones, he'll mix it up underneath with bigger guys.) For Mike, and for Lara, too – she is co-captain now of the cheerleading squad – the games are everything. When the team travels to weekend tournaments, the cheerleaders and the players stay in the same hotel, on different floors. Mike and Lara pass notes to each other out the windows – the where and when of the evening's assignation.

They reach the finals of the State Championship. My parents drive to Charlotte to see the game, Mike's last in high school. There is a photo from that night that will end up in the school yearbook. Mike with Conrad Williams (the black boy who'd been heckled at Wentworth), co-captains of the team, conferring with a referee before the game. Those legs that go on for ever and the old short shorts; black Chuck Taylor high-tops and socks up to his knees; a short-sleeved warm-up jacket with a racing stripe down the side. Mike is looking over the referee's shoulder towards the camera (he knows he's being photographed), his expression bored but determined. His head is cocked slightly to one side, his hair, as always, swept perfectly across his head.

They lose. The season is over. At the annual basketball banquet in the school cafeteria the following Sunday, Mike is named Most Valuable Player. Two weeks later, Duke offers him an academic scholarship. It's a big honour, though he is unsure about taking it. He wants to play ball but is not big enough, or maybe good enough, for Duke. In the end, he can't turn down a scholarship from one of the best universities in the country. He will try to make the freshman team.

In the Bishop McGuinness 1967–8 yearbook, there is a photo that since the advent of teenage angst must have appeared in virtually every high-school yearbook in America. It shows a row of lockers shot at an angle in a darkened and empty corridor, in that dead hour when the school is deserted. The light is shadowy, the mood desolate and profound – a reflection of the melodramatic teenage impulse, the excessive sentimentality that infuses the last days of youth. There is also, because this is a parochial school in 1968, the clichéd, inspirational Latin:

Venimus
Vidimus
Vicimus

Beneath the portrait of every senior is a caption meant to sum up the individual's character – a few words chosen by the yearbook's editor. Mike's is a quote from Arrowsmith: 'Sharp wits, like sharp knives, do often cut their owners' fingers.' The portrait shows him still in possession of a delicate beauty: smooth skin, thick lashes. (So different from how his father looked at this age, standing on the deck of the 1326 in the South Pacific, with his slab-thick physique and cocksure look.) He hasn't decided yet what he'll study at Duke. He's told Danny he might like to be an architect. He has toyed, too, with the idea of studying math. Most recently, he's said he may major in psychology and minor in history. Whatever he chooses, he is sure to apply himself wholeheartedly. His scores for the college entrance exams were in the 96th percentile. His report cards consistently show first-class honours. His list of achievements is impressive: Student Council vice-president, Key Club president, inclusion in *Who's Who Among American High School Students*, Glee Club, Publicity Club, associate editor of the school paper, co-captain of the basketball team, member of the National Honor Society.

His photo appears frequently in the yearbook. Whether the shot is posed or informal, his bearing is the same: proud, contained, infused with a tentative composure that promises to one day ripen into solid self-possession. He is a tad vain. Never a hair out of place. (That style, a left-to-right sweep with no perceptible parting, requires effort to appear so unintentional.) He isn't one to smile, but neither does he look unhappy. What he looks like is someone who knows more about himself than perhaps he should at this age, someone who has acquired an ironic distance on the roles he is playing – the scholar and the athlete and the first-born son upon whom dreams are pinned – which is not to say he isn't keen to play them.

Before he goes north again to his summer job, our mother throws an end-of-the-year party for his class. The girls arrive early with food and coolers full of Coca-Cola, and she helps them decorate the back deck. *We strung Christmas lites thru the trees & it was like a fairy-land. They danced & had a ball & were perfectly behaved . . .*

It is also a goodbye party for Lara. Though she too will be going to Duke – like Mike, she's gotten an academic scholarship – her family is moving to Memphis. They will leave the following day. There is a photo from this party which shows a group of them – including Steve, Mike, Lara and Conrad Williams – on the deck. It is unposed, though whoever took the picture has clearly placed Mike and Lara at the centre of it. Lara is wearing a modest, long-sleeved white dress, her thick hair held back by a band. Mike wears a short-sleeved button-down shirt and slacks hitched too high on his waist (his squareness underscored by the guy beside him, lithe in a pair of hip-huggers). He is watching Lara, while Lara, smiling broadly, has cast her eyes heavenward. If you were to imagine what was behind their respective expressions, you might guess that Mike has just made some irredeemably corny pun and is enjoying his girlfriend's chagrin. And yet the look on her face is so indulgent, so *happy*, it's obvious that whatever he has just said is emblematic of everything she loves about him. They have spoken about the future. They have spoken about having children together.

From where he sits in the hotel lobby, he can see the boardwalk and beyond that the blackness that is the ocean and the night sky. It's a quiet evening in June, before the summer season has really kicked off. A kind of restlessness rises off him during the dead hours. To pass the time, he will make small talk with the guests, then catch a bit of the Phillies game on the new colour TV in the lobby. He will write a letter to Lara. He will tell her that his shift is dragging tonight, that when he visited Duke last week it was more beautiful than ever, that he misses her more every day.

I think about you a lot but especially when I'm walking to work in the morning and the sun is just coming up over the ocean and I think about what you wrote in my yearbook . . .

He is still a straight arrow. Some kids try to get him to smoke grass, but he isn't up for it. Apart from the occasional beer at Somers Point after the basketball games, he is clean-living. Indeed, he has dedicated himself to the 'Spartan life' this summer so he can make the freshman team at Duke.

Lara's summer is different. She starts working on Eugene Mc-Carthy's presidential campaign. Riding in a station wagon with a few others through the back roads of Tennessee one day, the car covered with blue and white McCarthy stickers, she runs into trouble. Three guys in a pickup start following them, then ramming their car, shouting 'nigger-lovers' and trying to run them off the road. Finally, they have no choice but to pull over, and the guys in the pickup pull two of Lara's friends out of the car and start roughing them up. The incident makes the papers, with everybody's names. After that, Lara's parents' yard in Memphis is vandalized.

She writes to Mike about it. They are of one mind about such things, such people. His letters, over the summer, are sprinkled with references to politics and race. Though Mike doesn't get involved like Lara does, he is beginning, almost shyly, to take positions. He is reading the Kerner Report, produced by the presidential commission on the race riots of the previous summers. The report blames the riots on the poverty, unemployment, slum housing and poor education created by white racism, and the existence of the ghettos on the white institutions that have created and sustained them. Mike refers to his grandmother's bigotry and tells Lara that he is becoming more 'pro-Negro' every day. Nixon and Humphrey scare him. Not to mention George Wallace and his running mate Curtis LeMay, who likes to joke about the harmlessness of nuclear weapons.

But it isn't just the stirrings of political consciousness that separate the letters of this summer from those of 1967. There is something more – in the tone, traces of uncertainty. Nothing unusual, just the kind that accompany the true end of childhood, the jumping-off point, when he can look over his shoulder and see up close the world he is about to lose. He doesn't know, of course, how total the loss will be. He doesn't know that he will never, in any true sense, go home again.

Six

Duke is a world unto itself, an oasis of privilege. In 1968, the year Mike enters, it is about 90 per cent white, and rich; the city of Durham – eighty miles east of Winston-Salem – is 40 per cent black, and poor. 'Durham rhymes with germ,' goes the Duke joke. The school is set on nine thousand verdant acres, seven thousand of them managed forest with miles of hiking, biking and horse-riding trails. But Duke is no summer camp. It is an intensely competitive institution, consistently producing its share of Rhodes scholars and annual entrants into the top tier of the nation's professional classes.

Approached via a heavily wooded avenue, the campus proper is a combination of the genteel and the austere. Quads open one on to another in a graceful unfolding. Neo-Gothic classroom buildings and residence halls are built in the local Hillsborough bluestone, which ranges strikingly through seventeen shades, from slate grey to creamy brown to rusty orange. The centrepiece of the campus is the chapel, its 210-foot tower straining towards the heavens. The sober austerity of the architecture is softened by the profusion of cherry blossoms and flowering dogwoods. When it rains, the grass shines a luminous green. My mother declares it *the most beautiful place in the world*.

Like many of America's finest universities, Duke is still, in the autumn of 1968, an essentially – if precariously – conservative institution. Fraternities and sororities are still fashionable. Kids still listen to the Four Tops. Girls are housed on a separate campus. Mike is still, upon his arrival there, a clean-cut kid in a button-down Oxford and dress slacks hitched too high. He is assigned to House P on Kilgo Quad, Room 109, on the West Campus, and allocated a room-mate named Matthew. Immediately, there are tensions. Matthew is unathletic, uncool, lacking in the requisite machismo. Nita calls Matthew and Mike 'the odd couple', and supports the idea of

Mike switching room-mates. Fanny is more objective: *Of course the mate may ask to be moved also as Mike can be very uncommunicative and does everything when he wants to and you have to love him to take it* . . . Burdened by his own insecurities, Mike is uncharacteristically hostile, belittling Matthew in front of other guys.

He and Lara are off. It was her decision. Since the last time they saw each other, she has changed, become much more political, for one thing (that incident in Memphis left its mark). She is no longer the girl she was the night of the party on our back deck. The break comes almost immediately after they arrive at Duke. Mike is caught up in his new life, though, and doesn't seem unduly affected. Basketball try-outs are over and he has made it, one of seven walk-ons who will join the four scholarship boys on the freshman team. For the next several months, four or five hours of every day will be taken up with practice, scouting reports, game films and games. This is a world he knows. It is his bridge from adolescence to whatever lies beyond – a narrow path he can keep to through that first year of quasi-independence.

He quickly establishes a circle of friends, one of whom, Kevin, becomes his room-mate. (As Fanny predicted, Matthew has gotten himself relocated.) Although Kevin is more politically minded, involving himself in civil rights discussions in the dorm – it isn't just abstract theory: the dorm maintenance man is head of the Durham branch of the KKK – Mike and Kevin are inseparable. They talk about girls and studies, they play Frisbee and listen to the Moody Blues and Creedence Clearwater Revival.

Mike is upbeat and funny, popular enough to be wooed by a number of fraternities. To the surprise of our father, who was a Sigma Chi, he decides to pledge Zeta Beta Tau. While the Zebes, as they are called, tend to come from Philadelphia or New York, and their accents are more familiar to Mike than the slow drawl of the South, they are not his demographic. It is a Jewish fraternity, and Mike will be the Zebes' first Catholic. They are intellectually sophisticated, left-leaning, slightly avant-garde liberals – a frat for guys who are too cool to be in a frat. They are clever, sarcastic and cynical – cynical to a point, at least, because they also want to get into med school.

Maybe Mike pledges ZBT because Kevin is pledging. Or maybe ZBT's outsider status appeals to him. As for the Zebes, they are pleased that this tall, good-looking basketball player wants to join their band of eggheads. They all know who his father is, too. Jack now has his own TV show. Every Sunday afternoon at two o'clock, he talks basketball, running film clips to illustrate plays and giving his picks of the top teams in the country. He has also done a Coke commercial, which is airing that autumn.

The guys don't go into Durham often – for pizza, maybe, or to the Waffle House off East Campus. Mostly they play bridge or hearts in the dorm. Drink beer, smoke a little pot, watch *Star Trek*, Johnny Carson, Knicks games on Sunday afternoons. Or they watch the news, not much of which is good. The Selective Service announcing another increase in the draft call, and casualties in Vietnam mounting: 14,589 in 1968. For US forces, it is the deadliest year of the war so far. Students are exempt from the draft for as long as they're at college, but nobody knows how long the war will last.

In February 1969, a headline in the *Duke Chronicle* reads, 'University in Turmoil'. Black anger, fuelled by the fact that the apparent victories of the civil rights movement have failed to bring real change to the lives of most blacks, is spilling over from the inner cities on to college campuses. Just days before, Black Week had concluded on campus – a programme of art, drama and soul food sponsored by the Afro-American Society to help 'educate the White masses'. The president of Duke had supported Black Week but now finds himself up against a more militant agenda, as seventy black students barricade themselves inside the Allen Building, rename it Malcolm X Liberation School, and issue a list of demands, including the establishment of an Afro-American Studies department and an end to merely token representation in university power structures.

The occupation doesn't last long. About ten hours after it begins, the students, threatened with legal consequences, begin to exit the building. As they do, a couple of thousand students who have gathered outside swarm around them. Some will say it was a show of unity, to protect those coming out from being targeted by police. Others will say it was just general mayhem. Whatever the case, the police begin firing tear gas into the crowd to disperse the students. The images are all over the news. Nita writes to reassure her mother.

> *Before I go into anything else, I'll tell you that Mike is fine. He called us after the game Sat nite to let us know that he's not in jail or in the hospital. He was out on the campus with the rest of them, I'm sure, but not too active, as Duke ruled last summer that any student on scholarship who was involved in a protest could have his scholarship taken away . . . Of course his sympathies were with the blacks on most issues – he's such a crusader.*

Mike isn't quite the crusader his mother believes, but his consciousness of racial and social inequalities is deepening. He has applied for a summer job with the Experiment in Self-Reliance in Winston-Salem, coaching 'underprivileged' kids basketball and baseball for $2.60 an hour. *I told him he'd be drooling for the Port-O-Call in a week, but he's at the age where he wants to improve the world – and I admire him for it.* His private life, meanwhile, looks to our parents like an extension of this liberal impulse. After a courtship earlier in the year with a 'coloured' girl ended in friendship, he begins dating a Japanese girl. *Jack said he probably fought her father in 1945. I think Mike is trying to erase all the color & nationality & religion lines all by himself – a real crusader.*

Halfway through the basketball season, the box scores tell the story, and it is unspectacular. Though he may have recognized the milieu – the floorboards buffed to a high sheen, the raucous locker-room banter and the pre-game pictography of Xs and Os – he himself has been relegated to the unfamiliar role of bench-warmer. Every day he hustles, busting his tail at practice. He still has the sweet jump shot. But he's not big and strong enough to play forward, not quick enough for guard, and way too skinny to be taken seriously. Most games, he hardly gets in long enough to break a sweat. By spring, he knows that his playing career is over.

The single photo of him that will appear in the Duke yearbook

over the course of his four years there is taken during a basketball game his first year. He is at mid-court, far from the action, his stance flat-footed and tentative, as though he's just come off the bench. He looks small, breakable and astonishingly young, younger even than in many photos from high school. It is the last picture taken of him in which he looks like a boy. That summer, in family photos taken at the shore, he has the aspect of someone straining towards gravitas. Posture erect, hands clasped behind him, he assumes a rigid formality incongruous with the holiday mode. He has grown sideburns and a moustache, and his hair is a tad moppy. And, though his pants are still hitched too high – he never does get the hang of the hip-hugger – they are now faded, bleach-stained jeans. He is inching, finally, away from us.

In November 1969, he starts dating Susan. He is her first true love. He is *it*. She believes she could stay with him for ever. His buddies at Duke think she's gorgeous, and they envy Mike's good luck with girls. It's the combination of refined good looks and rugged athleticism,

the wicked sense of humour and the slight aloofness – a suggestion of depths a girl might yet gain access to. In the photos of him with Susan and their friends, he is angular, square-shouldered, skinny as ever. But something in his expression has changed: the naive presumptions of youth are slipping away. The neat moustache grown over the summer is longer and a bit droopy. His hair, which had been short at the sides and sensuously thick on top (a style that could've travelled well through many eras), is now almost shoulder length, lank and unflattering, still parted at the side and a bit bulbous around the ears. It gives his head an unattractive bell shape. He has finally graduated to flares – jeans and corduroys – and scuffed ankle boots. He is growing, literally, blurrier around the edges, losing the sharp definition that pressed Oxfords and neat khakis afforded. It's in the poses, too, a looseness. At the ZBT house, guys and girls drape themselves familiarly over one another. They lie on floors and beds, or sit lotus-style rolling joints. In the background, cheap furniture houses small armies of LPs. There are amplifiers, turntables, wires snaking everywhere. Ironic decor includes a wall-sized confederate flag. On Mike's own wall: a picture of Freud on which someone (maybe Mike himself) has written:

To my good friend Mike
Best regards, Sigmund

He is free now. From the long hours in the gym, the discipline and the rigorous supervision. But greater than the freedom is the loss. The game provided an identity, a place of privilege. He was someone who belonged to something, to other people – for the team is like an organism, self-protective and cohesive – and suddenly he belongs to nothing. The days can yawn with unfilled time.

Drugs are everywhere, whatever you want, but for now it's mostly just hash. He gets blasted with the guys and they go to the General Sherman Motor Inn on Route 85, where you can get chicken for seventeen cents. Mike is still pretty straight, though, still getting As and Bs, still making the Dean's list. He has declared his major in psychology. Susan is studying religion. A straight-A student herself, sweet and a little naive, she goes to church each Sunday and plays golf. She is cute rather than beautiful. She is like Lara-lite, Lara drained of intensity and complexity. Lara is still at Duke, but lives off campus in Monkeybottom, in a shack with no electricity, out where it becomes farmland. Most of the neighbours live in shacks, too. They work in the tobacco industry and make their own corn liquor and they get along just fine with the college kids who live there. The kids have a band doing a travelling rock-opera thing, and Lara is part of the 'happenings' they perform – people dancing, people perched in trees, people in costume doing . . . whatever.

Mike still hangs with the same guys, though he spends time with Susan's friends now, too. More of a peace-and-love crowd than his own, who prefer to play intramural basketball or talk politics or smoke dope and play catch on the quad outside the dorm. He can talk about all sorts of things: girls, sports, psychology, politics. When he goes home the odd weekend, he argues with our father about the war. (Steve is impressed: our father is formidable.) But our parents could hardly be more proud. Easter weekend he brings Susan home to meet them. Nita thinks she's great – *just right for him.* Jack is so impressed by the pair – their academic success, their interest in world affairs (even if he doesn't agree with their conclusions) – that he imagines them in the White House.

As summer approaches, Mike toys with several ideas for employment. He could go back to the hotel in Ocean City. Or there's a job at a trucking company in Winston-Salem. He also considers going to Alaska to lay railroad ties for a hundred dollars a day. In the end, he decides on DC for the summer. He moves into a shabby townhouse with Bill, a friend from Duke, and takes a dull job with the Veterans' Administration processing papers. Unlike Bill, who never touches a drug, a drink or even a cigarette, Mike is smoking a lot of dope. By that summer, he is leading a double life: giggly pothead and straight-laced son.

Sometimes, the two worlds collide. During a break from his job at the VA, Mike takes Susan for a visit to Fanny and Tony's place in Ocean City. His grandparents aren't sure what to make of them. Mike – all dishevelled and with a spacey grin – is not the boy he was the previous summer, and she with the love beads and the uncombed hair down to her behind. The damage-limitation is left to Nita.

I know he & Susan embarrassed you by their appearances; I should have warned you about their clothes. She has some lovely things – she put a dress on for Church here, & to fly home. But I guess it is part of their rebellion against materialism – they don't want to dress up . . .

Mike and Susan are good kids, Nita knows, not into any of that really radical stuff, blowing up ROTC offices or running safe houses for Black Panthers. Whatever happened to peace and love? *That* she could sympathize with. You see the pictures of children in Vietnam with their napalm-burned skin, or the stick-thin peasants shot dead and strewn across the road, and you have to think the protesters are right. But now it's all gone violent here, too. There are bombs in police departments and courthouses, in the US Capitol building, a Senate office. There are students setting fire to their own school buildings. In Isla Vista, California, they burned down the Bank of America. Some poor kid who wasn't even one of the troublemakers got killed accidentally by a policeman. How farcical and tragic it's becoming. And the three who blew themselves up in Greenwich Village. They'd built a bomb packed with nails. They were going to plant it at an officers' dance at Fort Dix. Nita knows people who weren't sorry to see the kids die instead. She wouldn't wish it on any parent.

Thank God with her own it's just the crazy music and the hair. Steve and John, both teenagers, have grown theirs almost to their shoulders. They put on the headphones and listen to albums downstairs in the rec room (she can't understand what's on the covers, let alone the lyrics), which, despite the shelves full of sports trophies, now feels more like a dusky, subterranean hang-out than the bright family room it once was.

Seven

When I got the email from Matthew – Mike's ill-fated room-mate from those first months at Duke – I was at an Internet café in the Serbian enclave of Gračanica, in Kosovo. It was late 2005, and I had just begun to correspond with people from Mike's past. I had ended up in Kosovo through a reconnection with my own past. In the winter of 2004, for no particular reason (I hadn't given him much thought in years), I had done a Google search for Paul, who had been my old friend Becky's boyfriend in Ocean City in the summer of 1984. I knew that he had gone to law school, so I thought I might find his name attached to a law practice somewhere. I found nothing other than a single legal paper that led me nowhere.

That same winter, as yet unbeknownst to me, Paul was working with a woman who was from the town in the west of Ireland where I had spent ten years. Paul mentioned my name to her and, because the town is small, she knew of me. Paul did his own Google search then, and so it was that one evening only four weeks after the night I had tried to find him, his name appeared in my inbox.

Paul still played in a band and still loved singing and drinking beer, but he had long since given up bike-thieving and was now a human-rights lawyer with the UN in an ugly little town in Kosovo called Gnjilane. In a few months, he was getting married to his Serbian girlfriend. He invited me to the wedding in Belgrade, and it was there that I met William, a UN colleague of his. I went to Kosovo soon after to visit William, and thus began our relationship, and, for me, two years of living between Kosovo and Dublin.

Gracanica was the third place William and I had lived since I'd begun staying with him. Our first place, the year before, had been a six-bedroom house in the west of the province with a wraparound front porch and ceramic lions perched sentinel on the various pillars. There was a long pergola from which fat purple grapes hung, and in the garden there were peppers, tomatoes and cabbages. From the upstairs balcony, I could see farmhouses with red-tiled roofs, and fields of corn yellowing in the heat. The crest of the hill in front of the house overlooked fertile, carefully tilled land, surrounded by a ring of rolling blue hills. Tiny human figures moved under the benevolent warmth of an autumnal sun. If you didn't know better, you'd think, *God's Country*.

Those six weeks I'd spent with William at what we called 'the palace' had been my first extended visit to Kosovo. William had thought I would love the house, that it would be the perfect place for me to write. Instead, perched there, isolated and huge and exposed, it filled me with foreboding. Every day, when he was at his office, I worked at a makeshift desk in the living room, amidst a disconcerting stillness broken only by occasional visits from the landlord, who spoke no English and was sometimes drunk. He would appear at the door and rant at me in Serbian, then complain later to William that I wasn't 'a lady' because I never asked him in for a cup of tea. Our driveway had become an unofficial local dump, and a spreading field of rubbish pushed towards us from the road. In the sunny upstairs bedrooms, fat sluggish flies congregated and every day the floor was strewn with the dead. Mostly we just kept the doors closed, but a few times I swept them up and the piles filled my dustpan.

The countryside was often beautiful, but the built landscape was garish and surreal. Massive hypermarkets had sprouted on the outskirts of cities, providing the cheap furnishings of provisional expat lives. The petrol stations gleamed aggressively; plonked down along the pitted rural back roads, they looked like the sites of unspeakable deeds. Monstrous four-storey homes were springing up everywhere, often painted pink or purple or lime green, and new, huge and empty-looking hotels dotted the landscape, as if a population explosion and a tourism boom were expected at any minute. Alternating with the clusters of gleaming glass and luridly coloured concrete were groups of burned or firebombed houses and churches, and sometimes just a lone one, hunkering darkly in a field.

Woven into the fabric of my days was fear. It wasn't Kosovo, as such. Kosovo was creepy, but the war had been over for a few years, and though hostilities were still strong, foreigners were not a target. It was something in me, a feeling of impending doom that I could neither shake nor find the source of.

Anxiety is essentially the condition in which fear is fearing itself. Kierkegaard likened it to a Grand Inquisitor, who attacks when we are weakest and never lets us escape, 'neither by diversion nor by noise, neither at work nor at play, neither by day nor by night'. Anxiety might start with tangible concerns – money, work, whether the object of one's affections is really gone – but at a certain point, the worry detaches itself from its real-world causes and becomes an indistinct and enveloping dread that takes all the nourishment it needs from itself, so that the very act of thinking feels like a kind of poison. (If alcoholism is the condition that keeps telling you that you don't have it, anxiety is the state of mind that keeps reassuring you that you are in its grip.) It is a closed loop of debilitating chatter in which one can become terrified of one's own thoughts.

I had arrived in Kosovo in an anxious state of mind. A couple of days before I'd left Dublin, I was eating dinner and became convinced that something had lodged in my throat. My throat felt as though it were closing. I went *aaahhh* in the bathroom mirror and ate bread and drank vats of water, while my dinner companion tried to calm me by reminding me that my breathing was unobstructed. She talked me out of going to A&E. As I walked home alone, the panic came in waves. *Was I still breathing?* I stopped and stood and a woman passing hesitated, on the verge of asking if I was all right. Our eyes met and I nearly said, *I can't breathe.* Then, afraid of hyperventilating, I inhaled slowly. The woman said nothing and we both walked on. The following day, my doctor looked down my throat and couldn't see anything. But I knew something was wrong. By the time I got to Kosovo, I was monitoring my swallowing obsessively, frightened that my throat was about to swell closed.

Schopenhauer writes that when we are in an egoistic frame of mind, our intelligence concentrates itself on imagining the countless dangers and hostile phenomena surrounding us. In such a state, the mind becomes fixated on self-protection and anxiety is the keynote of our disposition. The business of starring in the drama of one's own imminent demise in the absence of an obvious threat leads to a strange sense of self-importance as well as a sterile isolation. For the anxious mind is incapable of companionship. It is only ever with itself. I sat there in the big empty living room of the palace, a nervy hum in my head, and wondered what the pay-off was for all this negative grandiosity – for our habits of mind always involve a pay-off, even if it is destructive, like the reinforcement of some injurious view of ourselves. The nearest I came to an answer was the idea that free-floating fear necessarily posits – whether consciously or unconsciously – the existence of a safe elsewhere, a harbour where one might feel permanently, psychically, at home. It is the belief in a kind of afterlife on earth. Seen in this light, anxiety could be construed as a kind of hope.

In his memoir *In the Dark Room*, Brian Dillon draws parallels between hypochondria and addiction:

> By a devious logic, the hypochondriac turns his or her feeling of not getting enough from life into an extravagant demand, simply, for more. More life. Nothing of the everyday can match the exhilaration of rebirth that seizes one when the imagined disorder fails to become real . . . But the ruse is compromised, counterproductive. The high doesn't last, and when, inevitably, the ordinariness of things begins to press too hard again, ever more elaborate fears are called for.

When I quit drinking in 1996, the feeling of rebirth had been so phenomenal and full of grace – the splendidness of the natural world so freshly apparent and the release from misgiving so absolute – that in the years that followed, in moments of sadness or ennui or self-doubt, I thought perhaps I might start drinking again so as to be able to enjoy, upon quitting again, the rebirth of wonder.

The drama of my closing throat came to its conclusion one night when I prevailed upon William to take me to a doctor, a Serbian friend of his. The doctor took a quick look at my throat and said, in his stilted and matter-of-fact English, 'Ah. Your throat. It is burned totally red from stomach acid.' I rejoiced at having a diagnosis and, as soon as I began taking the medicine he gave me, the swollen feeling eased, along with the intermittent panic. But whatever space it had left vacant quickly filled up, if not with the fear of something else, then with an awareness of itself as a space that was waiting, needing, to be filled.

Peace of mind came to me, not because I understood much of anything better than I had, but because in the months to come I got used to Kosovo and because, at my insistence, we moved from the sinister kitsch palace to a cosy granny flat in a hilly area south of Pristina. By then it was early December. The first snow had not yet fallen but would any day. A white furry frost covered everything; not the sparkling frost of a crisp early morning, but something thicker and heavier. About a hundred feet away from wherever you stood, the trees, the shrubs, the ground itself went blurry and then appeared to simply drop off into nothing. It was the world as I had never seen it. It was lunar and mythical and I loved it.

People thought it strange that I was willing to make half a life there. There were virtually no foreigners in Kosovo save soldiers or those in the aid business. But we had, William and I, in our little flat in the hills, a strangely happy existence. All around us life churned in its curious mix of the fascinating and the banal. We were surrounded by uneducated herdsmen and peasant farmers but also by power-brokers and diplomats, human-rights specialists and about-to-be-indicted war criminals. Amidst the quiet rhythms of rural life, history was being made, and I was eager every day for the news.

Our landlords were a Serbian couple with three children. They treated us like members of the family, insisting that we eat with them, giving us jams they'd made from fruits in the garden, and huge jars of sweet red pepper paste. We took the children on Sunday drives and at night sometimes helped them with their English homework or took them for pizza in Gracanica. When the electricity went, as it often did, William and I would lie on the wide sofa in our flat and talk softly. In the most unexpected place, I had found a home. It was love, of course. I realized that one evening when

I went to meet him in Pristina. It was getting cold, and there was a steel-grey late autumn sky, fabulous in its austerity. In the taxi, I felt enveloped in the warmth of knowing I would find him in the harsh, unfamiliar city – the city so suddenly emblematic of a whole wide ungracious world, in which he was the harbour. I was waiting at a café called Valentino's when I saw him outside – the crisp white shirt and the woolly blazer and the smooth brown skin against all that roiling steely sky. He had bumped into someone he knew and was standing chatting, and as I watched him I felt such a strong sense of being at the heart of my life that I knew the idea of him and the idea of home had become one. We huddled together then in the warm café, drinking watery hot chocolates, and he told me he thought he might have a chance for a job elsewhere and we were excited at the prospect of it.

By late 2005, William had been in Kosovo for a few years and many of the people he'd started out working with were gone. One night we dined at a favourite restaurant of ours called Boston. The owners were excessively animated, happier than ever to see us. The portions were overlarge. We were the only customers in the place. When the electricity went, we ate by candlelight amidst the blood-red decor. 'It's over now,' William said, meaning the mission, the great post-war influx of money and aid workers. The foreign presence would limp along for years to come, but it was true, there was something decidedly autumnal in the air that night. It felt like the tail end of a monstrous party, and the owners of Boston, who had done well out of the last few years, were trying with a sort of desperate glee to keep the party going.

By then, we ourselves were on shaky ground. William had been transferred to a municipality a slight distance away from where we'd been living, and we'd decided it was time to come down from our sweet eyrie and move to Gracanica, a decision we almost immediately regretted. The electricity situation in the village was a nightmare, and where once the blackouts had been occasions for quiet togetherness, they had now become a reason to fight. When we had power, it came at about 120 volts rather than 220, which meant that it was permanently twilight in the house and we were afraid to run appliances.

We had two gas cooking rings, a gas heater we had trouble igniting, and two inverters, which stored power in batteries. We had bought a stabilizer to raise the voltage to 220. And we had recently bought a small generator with a cord you had to yank to get the engine going. When the electricity went the first night we had it, William walked out to the porch to start the generator. I could hear him grunting. Then I heard him curse and he came inside with the broken cord hanging from his hand. That night we sat depleted on the sofa.

The social highlight of my days was going to the Internet café on the main street in Gracanica. There were ceramic jugs and bowls for sale that had been made by a local NGO, and a few scarves and a single poncho made by a women's co-op. There were clusters of always unoccupied sofas and tables. In the corner was an espresso machine I had never seen switched on. Though everything looked new – microfinanced perhaps by some EU grant – the place had the half-abandoned air of somewhere in the midst of a closing-down sale. It was run by a young man named Dragan who was savvy enough to be doing something more challenging than standing morose guard over his one Internet-linked computer.

It is sometimes reassuring to discover unlikely connections with odd people in unusual places – it gives the world a kind of warmth and it concretizes the story of one's life, which can otherwise feel vague and inner – and such was the case at the Internet café in Gracanica. For in this random moment in time, in this precarious and unhappy place, Dragan and I discovered something about each other that bonded and consoled us. Dragan had a habit of wearing NBA gear (often a purple and yellow velour LA Lakers tracksuit), a fact that led me to ask if he was a basketball fan and prompted him to reveal, with justifiable pride, that he was a cousin of one of basketball's biggest ever stars, the late great 'Pistol' Pete Maravich, whom my father would certainly have known from his own years in the NBA. Dragan linked me to my father, and thus to my life; and I, I suppose, linked Dragan to the world beyond the garbage-strewn claustrophobia of this grey, embittered enclave. We talked basketball whenever I was in, and we were talking yet again about Pistol Pete and my father and the NBA the day I opened Matthew's email.

Matthew began by apologizing if anything he was about to tell me would upset me. And then he told me about those couple of months in House P on Kilgo Quad, about the harassment and the bullying. Of course, I felt ashamed of Mike's behaviour. In high school, Mike had fumed over the heckling of a black teammate, and I had assumed that meant that he believed that people of every stripe should be treated with dignity, that he was by nature liberal and fair. I had never imagined him a bully. But what struck me more powerfully was the second part of Matthew's email, in which he described a single meeting between himself and Mike during their junior year at Duke.

In the spring of 1971, the two of them had found themselves standing side by side waiting for the bus that ran between Duke's East and West campuses. By then, it had been almost three years since they'd spoken. Matthew had seen, in that time, the changes in Mike. He had noticed, because we tend to notice what becomes of those who have played a part in our first impressions of a place, that Mike's group of friends had changed. He had seen him growing thinner, stragglier, acquiring the telltale spaciness of someone who was 'experimenting'. None of this set Mike apart from many other young men on the Duke campus. It was just what Matthew noticed. Matthew, too, had changed: his hair was to his waist and he was decked out in full hippy regalia.

They were nervous in each other's company, though Mike was friendly enough. He sized up Matthew's outfit and told him he looked cool. He asked how things were going. Matthew couldn't quite believe the interest was genuine, he thought perhaps Mike was looking for an opening to ridicule him. But when he gave Mike an abbreviated update on his life, Mike said, with no detectable sarcasm, 'Well, that's great, you've really become a good man, a success, and look at me, I'm such a mess.'

Matthew wondered if Mike was offering him a sort of blanket apology. He had no idea what kind of a 'mess' Mike meant. He had noticed by then, though, that Mike's edginess was of a different order than simple social awkwardness. In fact, he didn't seem well. He mumbled, he rambled a bit, there were long hesitations between phrases. He mentioned acid, said he felt like he hadn't really 'come back' from his LSD experiences. Matthew wasn't sure how to respond: it wasn't the kind of disclosure he was prepared for. The conversation petered out. The bus arrived, rescuing them from the moment. They shook hands, an incongruously formal gesture, and stepped onboard.

By 1971, when Mike had begun to experiment in earnest with LSD, the drug had joined the ranks of Schedule 1 drugs under the Controlled Substances Act. Since the days of the grass-roots acid scene, with its earnest, shamanistic impulse, LSD had acquired a lot of baggage, both literal and figurative. The stuff was full of additives, at times more like industrial sweets than the near-sacrament it once constituted. Horror stories circulated – of kids stepping blithely out the windows of high-rise buildings, going blind from staring stoned into the sun, thinking they could stop cars with their bodies. There were rumours that LSD caused chromosome damage. The president of the American Medical Association had reported that latent psychotics were disintegrating under the influence of just one dose, and that long-term LSD use was creating a psychopathology.

Bad trips were said to be proliferating. What the psychotherapists called 'set and setting', the web of factors that framed and infused the LSD reaction – not just ideas about the drug itself, but the immediate environment and the larger cultural matrix – had grown fraught. By the early 1970s, the air was tense with the friction of rising militancy. The act of tripping, meanwhile, had become steeped in expectations. Acid was God, *now*, in the form of a piece of blotting paper the size of a fingernail, and it was not perhaps surprising that a generation raised to rely on labour-saving devices should take to it. Tripping was something of a litmus test, revealing how evolved you were. Labels attached themselves to the experience, namely good and bad – the sense of boundless benevolence and the pretty shapes and colours called *good*, and the pitch-black figures sprouting teeth in improbable places and the abyss-underlying-all very *bad* indeed.

Sometimes you got lucky. Sometimes you found yourself afloat in a perpetual present, where the division between self and others dissolved and what prevailed was a state of pure empathy, the root of all compassion, where there was no room for anything within you but this lava-lamp ooze of love. Other times you weren't so lucky. Sometimes the loss of the self was less an instance of prelapsarian liberation than a terrifying reduction of integrative capacities. You found yourself face to face with the death of your ego – that puffy confection of opinions and preferences and feelings you had vainly regarded as *you*. Timothy Leary claimed to have never recovered from that initial 'shattering ontological confrontation' of his first acid trip, which had left him permanently unable to take himself, his mind and the social world seriously. With his head running down his shoulders, he'd considered having himself committed.

Mike would have absorbed some of this zeitgeist. The question (because tripping wasn't only for fun, he wanted to find out what made him tick) was whether he was strong enough to trip freely of all the baggage, without denying it, without clinging to or cowering from it in terror. It wasn't easy: the drug was interacting with the neuroses and insecurities of a twenty-one-year-old consciousness. But the answer, sometimes, was an unqualified yes. There were good times. Not just the funny things, like getting pulled over on I-40 and apologizing to the cop for speeding, only to be told he was going thirty-five miles under the limit. There was beauty in it, too. Sunday afternoons that stretched into infinity. Playing catch in the dunes on the Carolina coast, the football spiralling, slowly, against a pale blue sky. Seeing simple things with a different dimensionality. Watching the leaves fall in the Duke forest, turning and hanging and hesitating. Those endless moments, moments that contained everything worth knowing.

In a letter home, January 1971, Mike wrote:

I feel much better psychologically than I felt over Christmas. I have real optimism that 2nd semester will turn out well for me. I hope the new year is good to all of us. Mom, I may end up applying to law school rather

than psych grad school. I doubt it but you can keep your fingers crossed if
you want. Bobby Kennedy will not die in vain!!!!

Despite the ironic bluster in the Bobby Kennedy reference, there is an odd tone of lament in these lines. No specific disturbing incident seems to have occurred – not that my parents remember – and no subsequent mention is made in any letters of what was troubling him over Christmas, yet Mike wrote as though the new year might bring an end to some sad period he had passed through. Why wouldn't the second semester turn out well? His grades were still excellent. He still played bridge and basketball with the guys from ZBT. He seemed happy with Susan.

But that spring, around the time he told Matthew that he was a mess, he began to phone home on Sunday evenings, saying he felt depressed. When my parents asked why, he was vague. Probably he didn't know why. The strict certainties of his upbringing undoubtedly had splintered. (What had happened to the spirit and presumption of his seventeen-year-old self? What had happened to 'the Kid'?) He wasn't sure who he was, or who he wanted to become, and the day was drawing nearer when he would be expected to step out into this disordered world and make something of himself.

Maybe the depression had something to do with the drug, or what it left in its wake. That grey, jangled coming-down zone, where the world looks bleak and flattened out and the mind feels edgy, as though in the grip of an uneasy conscience. Even aficionados like Baba Ram Dass talked about the post-acid despair: '. . . you came into the kingdom of heaven and you saw how it all was and you felt these new states of awareness, and then you got cast out again, and after two or three hundred times of this, began to feel an extraordinary kind of depression set in . . .'

Or maybe it wasn't vague despair but actual recurring perceptual disturbances that were unnerving him: geometric forms, flashes of colour, trailing after-images, halos around objects – all redolent of the experience of tripping; or flashbacks, which can involve feelings of depersonalization or detachment, anxiety and panic, an altered sense of reality, the resurgence of certain thought loops.

. . . look at me, I'm such a mess . . .

Another possibility is that Mike had entered the 'prodromal stage' before the onset of schizophrenia. This can last from a month to several years, and may involve perceptual abnormalities (but not yet full-blown hallucinations or delusions), difficulty concentrating, a preoccupation with odd ideas, decreased emotional response, rapid mood swings, odd behaviour, sleep disturbances, social withdrawal and depression.

Even if Mike could have articulated what was happening to him, my parents would have had trouble comprehending it. Their son was young, healthy, intelligent. He was enrolled in one of the finest universities in the country. What could possibly be troubling him? When he spoke of feeling depressed, alienated or anxious, what they heard were the whinings of pampered late-modern adolescence. Neither of them had any experience of depression, and it was not the buzzword, the common cold of feeling, it would later become.

By late spring, Mike had ended it with Susan.

Susan and I have called it quits for a while and this has been somewhat depressing during the last week. The whys of the story are too many to express here. I'll tell you when I see you.

Nobody remembers the reasons he gave. Susan herself didn't understand. She was heartbroken. She'd thought they were happy together. Although she had noticed the occasional gloom, and sometimes what seemed a lack of openness, she hadn't believed there was anything seriously wrong. But it isn't always those closest to us who see things clearly, or see them coming.

During the summer of 1971, a summer spent doing odd jobs, putting nameplates on seat backs at a football stadium and a few weeks as a counsellor at our father's basketball camp, Mike took a weekend trip to Ocracoke, an island off the Carolina coast, with three friends, Richard, Jason and Lorraine. They took Jason's VW van over on the car ferry, camped that night and dropped acid on the beach. With the purple and white waves breaking, they waded into the shallows, kicking up glitter-storms of phosphorescent flagellates.

The next day they weren't in the best shape, and decided to come back a day early to the mainland. They caught the last ferry and parked the van on a sand spit, where they meditated in a post-acid funk before heading back to Durham to spend the night at Richard's mother's house. When they got there, they were still surfacing. Richard's mother fed them. After dinner, when the others were out of earshot, she took Richard aside and talked to him about Mike. Later, Richard told Jason what his mother had said. Jason didn't put much stock in it. He hadn't noticed anything strange. And that night, certainly, they were all a little fried. But Richard's mother had seen manic depression in someone close to her and she had an idea of what psychosis looked like – apparently, even in its latency.

What she said was, 'Mike's going to be the next one to flip out.'

Eight

In 2007, Mike was living with eight other mentally ill people and a social worker in a small two-storey house outside of Portland, a few blocks off of 99 East, the boulevard that runs south from the city. The house sat in the shade of Douglas firs, so that even on sunny summer days it seemed enveloped in a slightly gloomy chill. But it was clean and pleasant. The neighbourhood wasn't a bad one, though it had its share of mischief and nastiness. There was a time, Mike told us, that when he walked from the house to the bus stop, kids would shout at him and throw stones.

I had arranged to pick him up at noon. Tim had lent me his car for the day. I was nervous. Though I saw Mike every couple of years, it was always in the company of my mother or one of my brothers. This would be the first time I had been alone with him in over thirty years.

When I arrived, a man sitting in the living room introduced himself as Gerry and told me cheerfully that Mike was still in bed. 'You gotta wake him up!' Gerry said, with unbridled enthusiasm.

I went down the hall and knocked on Mike's door. I said, 'It's time for lunch.' He called back to me in a muffled voice. He sounded like he was under a mound of blankets.

While I waited in the living room, I scanned the books on the shelf, a strange mix of subject matter: *The Everyday Guide to God* and *The Book of Mormon*, as well as Lee Iacocca's autobiography, Robert Hughes's history of Australia, several dime-store novels and a guide to child-rearing from the 1950s called *Parents and Children*.

I turned to Gerry. 'So did you celebrate Christmas?'

'Oh, yeah!' Gerry cried. Gerry was chubby and friendly. It wasn't clear what his problems were. Other than a genial gormlessness, there was nothing obviously wrong with him. 'We have a tree,' he said. 'It's a fake tree, though. Mike wouldn't let us cut down a tree.' He laughed.

'Really?' I smiled. I felt a surge of pride.

'Yeah.' Gerry shook his head and chuckled again, as though Mike were a rascally kid you couldn't but love.

Mike came into the living room – eyes downcast, slouching, shuffling. (It's called the 'thorazine shuffle'; he hadn't been on thorazine for years, but loxapine, his current antipsychotic, can cause that same slow, sedated gait.) His expression was dull. His layers of clothing looked like work to wear. I wondered, not for the first time, what he lived for. What got him out of bed every day, motivated him to walk down to 99 East, often in the rain, and board the bus that took him to Shari's for his bottomless cup of coffee. I wondered whether he had ever thought of suicide. Among people with schizophrenia, it is the number-one cause of premature death. It is estimated that 60 per cent of males with the illness attempt suicide at least once. Ten to thirteen per cent die of it.

Mike mumbled hello, as though we'd seen each other only yesterday, when in fact it had been almost two years, and said, 'Isn't Timmy coming?'

'Just me,' I said. He grunted with what sounded like disappointment, though on the phone the day before he'd sounded perfectly happy when I'd told him I was coming alone.

'Is that okay?'

'That's okay,' he said.

We got into Tim's car and headed down 99 East, its succession of strip malls made drearier by the weather. It was one of those numbingly dismal Oregon days: low skies and an enervating drizzle. We crawled through the traffic lights, flanked by the mishmash of a downmarket suburb: mattress shops and car dealerships, Burger Kings and Frog Thai and Hookah Island, low-slung windowless taverns and Portland's ubiquitous strip clubs. All the cars and concrete. The dull gleam of wet tarmacadam. Exactly the sort of cityscape Mike detested.

'Oregon didn't used to be like this,' he said.

He breathed heavily beside me, a result of three decades of smoking and his excess weight. Though he wasn't looking at me, I felt acutely self-conscious, under inspection, as though I were taking a driving test. I asked him about the Christmas tree and whether there was anyone else in the house who backed him up on getting a fake one.

'No,' he said, with a dismissive mutter. 'I was the only one. The rest of them are all retarded.'

Over the years, wherever Mike has lived, he has always managed to find a diner or a coffee shop where he felt comfortable and welcome. For the past several years, it had been Shari's. As we were shown to our table, I could see the other customers staring – Mike has the unmistakable bearing of the mentally ill – but the waitresses at Shari's have always appeared genuinely well disposed. They greet him by name, and don't seem to mind that his acknowledgement of them is less enthusiastic. They are like nurses with a curmudgeonly but endearing patient.

'How *you* doin' today?' asked Cindy, with that inflection peculiar to the American service industry. She led us to a booth next to a large window. Before she could even give us menus, Mike had ordered. He would have his usual sixteen-ounce steak. Aware that any delay would only draw out the encounter (already, in the car, I had struggled for things to say), I dispensed with my usual agonized selection process and told Cindy I'd have a BLT. We both ordered iced tea.

'You got it,' she smiled, pocketing her order pad and turning efficiently on her heel.

Cindy, I noticed, had not given the slightest indication that she and I were of one world and Mike was of another. It was an act of solidarity with Mike, a small gesture whose decency left me humbled.

It seemed to have the opposite effect on Mike. He said, 'Some of the waitresses here are retarded.'

I gave him a look.

'You don't believe me?' he said. 'They've had operations.'

It was a theme: the inferiority of the people and things that provided the furnishings of his life. The waitresses were retarded. The people he lived with were retarded. He derided the books at the house as 'simple'. He had barely acknowledged Gerry's cheerful

'See ya later!' What he admired was self-containment, the kind of cool aloofness for which he himself was once known. He told me he'd been watching a Japanese woman on the bus the other day. 'She was very calm,' he said. 'Nothing disturbed her. You know Zen means the ability to keep still.'

Remembering his comment in the car, I asked, 'Did you like Oregon when you first came here?'

'I hated it,' he said.

'Why?'

'The pain in my legs was so bad. Because they were shooting them with drugs, with needles.'

For some reason, though I was almost certain Mike had never done heroin, I thought immediately of that rather than medication, of 'they' as people he might've been homeless with rather than doctors administering injections.

'What drugs?' I asked. 'Heroin?'

'Heroin,' he said, 'all kinds of drugs. Everything.'

I nodded, a little confused.

He got up to go for a smoke. People with schizophrenia smoke a lot. It may be a form of self-medicating, as nicotine is believed to have a minor salutary effect on certain symptoms of the illness. When he came back, I was staring out the window, in what I realized was a studied pose. Always this desire when in his company to appear imperturbable and deep. Anything to prevent him from lumping me in with all those retarded people. There were things that hadn't changed in thirty years. I felt as transparent before him as I had when I was twelve and he'd turned his condescending gaze on me and laughed out loud when I walked by.

'You look lonely,' he said, and sat down.

We talked about time.

He told me, 'I don't believe it's 2007. I think some time has passed but not that much. I think it's about 1978.'

He insisted, though, that he was living in the present. 'I never live in the past,' he said. And then added, somewhat lyrically, 'How can it be yesterday for you?'

In spite of his insistence to the contrary, he had always seemed to me very much like someone living in the past. He still looked like a hippy. For the past fifteen years, with few exceptions, his hair had been below shoulder length. He spoke like a hippy, too. Not just the idiom – talking about people's *trips* – but the grand abstractions and the language of the moral high ground that went with being eighteen in 1968. His persecution complex, softened by medication or time, now found expression in assertions of his estrangement from the conventional world the rest of us inhabit.

'I hate television,' he said to me, 'I hate all the things you people like.'

I had always assumed that Mike retained the hippy mantle because it linked him to the period when his identity was last stable. I had assumed he kept his hair long because it was one of the few forms of control he could exercise over his own life, and that he listened to Portland's 'classic rock' radio station out of nostalgia. I had imagined that his conversation often dwelled in the distant past because the last thirty years didn't contain many memories worth revisiting. But maybe, in a manner more literal than I'd imagined, he was living in the past.

In his book *Awakenings*, Oliver Sacks writes about several survivors of a sleeping-sickness epidemic in the 1920s – people who had been left with a post-encephalitic disorder that resulted in decades of catatonia – and what happened in 1969 when they were administered a new drug called L-DOPA. Upon 'awakening', many patients behaved as though they were much younger than they were, as if, Sacks writes, 'their personalities, their process of personal growth and becoming, had been arrested at the same time as their other physical and mental processes'. One woman, Rose R, referred to events in the mid 1920s as though they had just happened. Her mannerisms and turns of speech were obsolete ('she gave the impression of a "flapper" come suddenly to life'). Rose R could date specific events that had taken place during the decades of her illness – like Sacks's other patients, she had not actually been asleep for forty years – but said she couldn't imagine what it was like to be older than twenty-one because she had never really experienced it. 'I've registered it all – but none of it seems real. I know it's '69, I know

I'm 64 – but I feel it's '26, I feel I'm 21. I've been a spectator for the last forty-three years.'

In 1989, something similar, if less dramatic, happened in relation to schizophrenia when the antipsychotic drug clozapine became available. Despite its significant health risks – it could cause a lethal depletion of white blood cells – clozapine, for reasons still not clearly understood, proved a miracle drug for a small percentage of sufferers who had not responded to existing antipsychotics. In a file of my mother's labelled 'Mike', there are still clippings from 1989 issues of *Clinical Psychiatry News* ('Clozapine Held Major Advance in Treatment of Schizophrenia') and *Psychiatry Today* ('Sandoz Introduces Clozaril – A Breakthrough Antipsychotic Agent'). She had circled certain paragraphs – those pertaining to the drug's potential and to its risks. Earlier that year, Mike's doctor had written to my mother to update her on how Mike was doing. By way of backing up her assessment that his current condition was the best we could hope for, the doctor had cited a chart of Mike's from a hospitalization some years previous, which stated that a combination of psychotropic drugs and lithium had only managed to control his illness rather than bring about any significant improvement. But clearly my mother had not given up hoping for something more than mere symptom control.

Mike was a candidate for clozapine, and it was offered to him. But he refused to try it.

Halfway through our lunch, he was gazing out the window at the rain.

'Now *you* look sad,' I said.

'I'm not sad,' he said. And then, 'It's just there's a lot of duplicity in the world. People who can't be honest about what their trip is.'

'What are you talking about? Who are you talking about?'

'I can't say specifically.' He looked me in the eye. He is, unlike a lot of people, perfectly capable of the level gaze. 'There just is.'

A moment later, he mentioned having a headache, and when I asked him if he'd like to take something for it, he said, 'I don't take drugs. I've never taken drugs of any kind.'

This was a lie. I didn't believe that he had forgotten all the recreational drugs he'd taken years ago or the prescription drugs he had taken as recently as that morning. But I didn't argue. Despite his disdain for many of the niceties of human relations – the duplicities that grease the wheels of social convention – there was an expectation that we not call him on his own fabrications, or delusions.

He said to me that day, 'I haven't seen my birth family for a long time.'

'What do you mean? Mom was just here. You're seeing me now.'

'Jack and Anita aren't my parents,' he said. 'They kidnapped me. You were kidnapped, too. We all were.'

I smiled, barely.

'What?' he said. 'You don't believe me? The police know all about it. You should look for your birth parents.'

Later, I would report his claim to my siblings. We would try to break it down into its constituent parts of feint, delusion and seeming mockery, and we would ask ourselves, *Is he better than we think he is, or worse?* I would also report to my siblings Mike's answer when I asked him if he ever wished he could live in North Carolina again.

'Yeah,' he said, matter-of-factly. 'I want to retire there. I don't like Portland because everybody's trying to show that they're big time. But I don't want to let Clackamas County Mental Health down. There are a lot of people here who need my help.'

Did he really believe he was working for Clackamas County Mental Health? Or was he testing my willingness to play along with what I regarded as his delusions? To suggest the latter may be attributing a clarity to him that he did not possess, but it is often the case that his stranger declarations seem to be accompanied by a slight smirk. It is one of the things that makes him unsettling company.

'Mike liked being outrageous,' an old friend of his told me. 'That was part of his charm.'

'A good deal of schizophrenia is simply nonsense, red-herring speech, prolonged filibustering to throw dangerous people off the scent, to create boredom and futility in others.' This was written by R. D. Laing, whose approach to people with psychosis – his commitment to taking seriously a patient's existential position and regarding his or her expressions as valid descriptions of experience rather than mere symptoms of psychiatric disorder – was revolutionary. Laing has fallen out of favour, but many of his writings on the inner experience of schizophrenia are consistent with accounts written by people who have the illness. None of the obfuscation he refers to above is simply for the purpose of amusement. Laing believed that a deliberate use of obscurity, pretence and equivocation – to the point that 'the schizophrenic is often playing at being psychotic' – was a survival strategy necessary in even the most ordinary exchanges, because to be understood was to be threatened.

> [The schizophrenic's] outward behaviour is a defensive system analogous to innumerable openings to underground passages which one might imagine would take one to the inner citadel, but they lead nowhere or elsewhere. The schizophrenic is not going to reveal himself for casual inspection and examination to any philandering passer-by. If the self is not known it is safe.

Mike's statement about his birth family may well have been delusional chatter. It may have been a red herring. Or it may have represented truth at a metaphorical level. A way of saying that he felt so estranged from us, or so different from us, that he could not conceive of us as family. What are we to him, anyway? A sporadic audience. Reminders of what he has lost. We are people who show up out of the blue, drive him to lunch at Shari's, make strained conversation and then drive away again down 99 East, past the strip joints and the mattress shops and all the dreariness, melting back into our lives.

Nine

For his final year at Duke, Mike is sharing a big rented house on Chapel Hill Road in Durham with five other guys. Most of them are from ZBT, though the frat itself has disbanded. Following a successful drive to do away with voting potential members in or out – an unfashionably elitist practice – it just fell apart, gone the way of other so-called traditions that had become embarrassing anachronisms. The set-up at the house is loose. The place is mostly empty. Furniture is considered bourgeois, as are locked doors and private property. One day Mike lets a tramp in and feeds him. Then, out of some socialist impulse or simple inattention, he leaves him alone in the house and the tramp robs them.

Mike and Kevin, inseparable those first two years, have grown apart. Nothing awkward about it, but Kevin is straight, he's into politics, while Mike enjoys drugs – hash, mushrooms, acid and morning glory seeds (buy them at the local hardware store, toss them into the blender and off you go). He has become a vegetarian, and he and his friend Jason take up kundalini yoga, attending classes at the nearby Friends Meeting House. Kundalini combines body postures, controlled breathing techniques, meditation and mantras to awaken energy in the base of the spine and channel it upwards through the various chakras, or energy centres, to the top of the head. By stimulating the higher centres, practitioners are said to develop enhanced intuition, clarity and creativity, ultimately achieving a union between individual and infinite consciousness.

Kundalini is intense and dynamic, and the boys are warned about Kundalini Syndrome, which is believed to arise when kundalini energy begins to flow abundantly in a person who has not developed or maintained a clean energy system. Symptoms are said to include psychological upheaval, stress, depression, lack of concentration, depersonalization or derealization, and mood swings. Mike pushes it. He still has that competitive, athlete's mentality. When they do the bellows – rhythmic shallow breathing intended to be done for very short periods – he boasts, 'I did that for fifteen minutes!'

There are no more phone calls home complaining of depression, not that my mother will remember. The only other worrying omen comes from her own mother. Fanny dabbles in cards as well as dream interpretation, and fancies herself a bit of a clairvoyant. In a letter to my mother in the autumn of 1971, about six weeks after Mike's trip to Ocracoke, she writes:

> I hope Mike is happy and well. Last Tuesday Oct 19 I woke up at 12 pm and could not go to sleep again until after 3.30 which is unusual for me. I did not dream but wide awake thought of him in an accident and hurt his head. I know he must be all right or I would have heard from you . . .

Just after Christmas, Mike and Jason take a trip to New York to visit friends. On New Year's Eve they are watching television at midnight as the ball drops in Times Square. And drops again. And again. Mike flips. It's ridiculous! Absurd! He goes on and on about it. As if you could replay 'now'. What's wrong with people, anyway? The city in general has disconcerted him. In a letter to our parents when he returns to school, he writes, *New York was really strange. It convinced me that I don't ever want to be really wealthy. Money breeds a certain state of mind that I don't want to get into.* He no longer mentions grad school, or any plans at all, other than a vague desire to travel. In this he's not unusual. Nobody in his gang discusses careers. They hardly even discuss the future, that's part of the deal. They're all reading *Be Here Now*, Baba Ram Dass's illustrated guide for making the journey from the worldly to the spiritual. Ram Dass is one of the original dropouts. Prior to his awakening in India, he had been Dr Richard Alpert, a Harvard professor with a Mercedes and a Cessna 172 and a nagging feeling that it was all rather meaningless.

Mike has begun to wonder what forms dropping out might take. Is it enough to shed possessions or is the only proper drop a move to, say, the Himalayas? Does one drop out of society, or is it a state of mind, a question of letting go of attachments? Dropping out in a small group – a group-drop – is fine. Go to Colorado or New Mexico and live in a geodesic dome. Take up subsistence farming, resurrect the barter system. Whatever it takes to free yourself from the trappings of institutions and illusion.

This idea of the individual in conflict with a crazy world is not confined to counterculture discourse. Contemporary literature, including several of the psychology textbooks on Mike's curriculum, poses related questions. What is sanity? Is mental illness just one more piece of propaganda the system has cooked up to keep us down? Thomas Szasz had blazed the trail in 1961 with *The Myth of Mental Illness*, in which he argued that so-called mental illness is nothing more than a 'convenient myth', a manifestation of the struggle with the question of how to live. A few years later, Abraham Maslow's *Towards a Psychology of Being* argued that sick people are made by a sick culture. 'Clearly, what will be called personality problems depends on who is doing the calling. The slave owner? The dictator? The patriarchal father? . . . What shall we think of a well-adjusted slave?' For R. D. Laing, to be well adjusted is often an 'abdication of ecstasy'.

Mike is twenty-one years old. He is losing his bearings, in the midst of all this. While the feeling of being always on the brink of something – a mind-bending insight, a radical renunciation – is all terribly invigorating, it makes for a strange place to get lost. Does he have any idea what is happening? Does he think about the books he's read and the late-night conversations he's had and believe that what feels like the fracturing of his psyche is actually the path to enlightenment?

If, in the beginning, he feels exhilarated – if the grass shines an incandescent green and flowers quiver on their stems as though they might, at any moment, speak, and his whole being is flushed with the erotic charge of revelation; if the world looks lush and slightly liquid, as though after heavy summer rain, or like it does in the first stages of a trip before everything starts to melt; if the sunsets grow impossibly vivid and the seventeen shades of Hillsborough bluestone proclaim their subtlest distinctions, and the whole material world seems enraptured with itself – it wouldn't be unusual.

There is sometimes a honeymoon period. Before the enveloping light hardens to an unforgiving glare and those ecstatic objects start to menace with whispered messages.

So far, only a handful of people have noticed anything amiss: his old room-mate Matthew; his friend Richard's mother that night in Durham; and now Kathy, his old high-school girlfriend who first kissed him on an autumn hayride. Kathy didn't go to Duke, she stayed in Winston-Salem and went to Wake Forest. But she and Mike bump into each other occasionally at parties, weekends he is home. Last year, around the time Mike started phoning home complaining of depression, she noticed that his underlying sweetness was becoming overlaid with something false and stylized, like he was straining to detach himself from who he had been, and with unconvincing results. She wrote it off as an unfortunate pose. But now, she finds the oddities more pronounced. He jabs at her with his finger, 'Hey! What's up? We had some good times, huh? Yeah! We had some fun!' She says to herself, *Who is this guy?*

It's hard to know what to think, though. Everybody is acting strange, everybody is changing. Talking shit. Stoned off their heads. Even Sally, the girl who ratted on them for drinking in high school, is a hippy now. But Mike is different in a different way. His personality is unfamiliar. He doesn't talk about studies any more, just snaps his fingers and says, 'Hey! I'm just havin' a good time! There's some good drugs!' There is something manic, Kathy thinks, something false in his insistence on all the fun he is having.

It is 16 June 1972, the day of Mike's graduation. He has brought our mother and father and our sister Robin to his house in Durham. There are mattresses on the floor, dirty dishes everywhere, barely a stick of furniture. Robin, who is seventeen, thinks it's a cool crash pad, but to our parents it just looks filthy.

Mike's only plans for the future are to use the graduation money his grandparents have given him to drive across the country with his friend Rob, one of the boys he's been living with. After that, who knows? My mother doesn't disapprove exactly, but she does hope the aimlessness will be a brief phase, that he will soon start putting his considerable intelligence to good use. She looks at him and she does not see much trace of the boy they brought here four years ago. But then the world is not the world it was.

After the ceremony, they take turns snapping photos, arranging themselves in alternate groupings of twos and threes (*Okay, now you take one of us . . .*). It may be the weather – the day is unseasonably grey, with low clouds and a wind that is lifting Mike's lank hair – but there seems an absence of celebration about the pictures. There are no crowds, no caps tossed in the air, no friends arm in arm. There are just four people in a field on an overcast day in June. The grass is yellow in patches and worn away in others. In two of the photos, you can see the side of a car, as though they are in a makeshift parking lot. The photos might have been taken just as they were about to get into the car and drive away when somebody suddenly realized they hadn't taken any pictures. Not one of the four looks entirely present, or even like they quite belong together. The clothes don't help. Nobody's afraid of colours or patterns now (my father in tan, blue and red, Robin in a purple and white mini), so everybody clashes. They look insufficiently formal, without looking convincingly relaxed.

Mike is as thin as ever. His skin is pallid, his posture stiff and his expression stoical and distant. He never quite smiles, the barely discernible lift at the corners of his mouth hinting not at happiness but rather an ironical tolerance. In one snap of him with his mother, he has his arm around her shoulder, but his fingers are curled inward like a loose fist against her arm, as though he cannot quite bring himself to embrace her. In contrast to his father's wide tie and ample lapels, his attire is conservative and dated: a skinny tie, neat-fitting grey suit coat and peg-legged dress pants, leftovers from the late sixties. He has not shopped for formal wear in the last four years.

My mother is still beautiful. Her hair – it may even be a wig, she did have that phase – is slightly mussed, a layered, thick-on-top style. An early summer tan is set off by her casual ivory-coloured sleeveless dress. She has assumed a look suggestive of a good time, of evenings drinking pina coladas in conversation pits and late-night parties boogieing half self-consciously to the hits.

It could be the fact of her smallness – sandwiched between her strapping husband and her tall son – that has imbued her with a look of vulnerability. Or it could be age (she is forty-six now), the slight tiredness the eyes have begun to assume. Or maybe it is actually how she feels. Because despite her smile, despite her always upbeat missives to her mother, her attitude-is-everything approach ('It ain't what ya do, but the way that ya do it'), all is not well. She has recently become aware of certain *inconsistencies* in her marriage. Stories underneath the surface. Her husband has been unfaithful, and with someone she knows.

She is hoping that she and Jack are about to put all that behind them. Mike isn't the only one packing up. We, too, are leaving. We're leaving the house beside the golf course, leaving the big family room with the sliding glass doors, the dozen dogwoods that flower each spring and the little creek that floods its banks in winter. We are going west. My father has gotten a job in the pros, coaching the Portland Trailblazers. He'd been thinking about leaving Wake Forest for a couple of years. Both Portland and the Philadelphia 76ers had contacted him about coaching jobs. Initially, he'd opted to stay on at Wake; he thought they might really do something there. But as time passed, he got increasingly sick of recruiting. The last straw came when he went up to see some high-school hotshot in New York. He was about eighth in line to talk to this kid, and the kid was sitting there, messing with a ball, doing little tricks, and he said, 'Hey, Coach Jack, what's Wake Forest gonna do for me? Whatcha'll gonna do?'

After a pause, my father said, 'You know what we're gonna do? We're gonna stick that ball right up your ass.' And he got up and walked out.

The first thing he did was call Philadelphia and Portland. Philadelphia was talking to somebody else by then, since he'd said he wasn't interested, but the Portland job was still open. Portland had the worst record in the league last season, and so has the number-one pick in the upcoming draft. The potential is there to turn it all around.

For my mother, the move is a chance for a fresh start in a place where they have no history and know no one – where, when she goes to the local supermarket, there won't be anyone she's afraid to bump into.

The week after graduation, Mike and Rob and a little white terrier named Samantha set off on their cross-country road trip in Rob's '69 four-wheel-drive Jeep Wagoneer station wagon. The first night of their trip the car blows a universal joint near Notre Dame campus in South Bend, Indiana. They walk to the campus, where a forty-year class reunion is in progress, and convince someone to let them sleep that night in the dorms. Then they party all night with a crowd of sixty-year-olds. It's an auspicious start.

The car repaired, they head west along Route 80 – Illinois, Iowa, Nebraska – then south-west into Colorado. When they reach the Rocky Mountains, it is mid July, though there is still plenty of snow. A photograph taken one morning shows Mike standing beside the remains of their cooking fire, two white tin plates at his feet, the

ground a bed of pine needles and patches of stiff grass alternating with snow cover. He wears horn-rimmed glasses and a red bandana rolled into a headband. His mouth hangs slightly open, giving him an uncharacteristic air of dimness and abstraction. In the foreground sits Samantha, staring straight into the lens, loyal and sad. Sleet is falling. The photo has that curiously ominous look common to pictures taken before a person disappears, death by avalanche or a fall into a crevasse.

Although they have no gear apart from a light tent and their backpacks, Mike and Rob intend to go to 14,000 feet. At some point on the way up, Rob is taking pictures of mountain sheep and Mike walks ahead. When Rob hollers to him, Mike keeps going, over the top of the ridge. Rob calls and calls, then tries to track where Mike has gone but it begins to get dark, and Rob and the little dog make their way down the mountain. At the patrol station, the rangers tell Rob they've had no news of anyone matching Mike's description. Though there is nothing they can do until the following day, the rangers call my parents to tell them that their son has vanished in the Rockies.

We are already in Portland, and my father books the first flight out to Denver. Racing to the airport the next morning, he rear-ends a guy at a red light, jumps out of the car, gives the guy his name, says, 'My son is lost in the Rocky Mountains, I gotta go . . .' then jumps back into the car and zooms off. At the airport, he hands the car keys to a cop – there are perks to being the new coach of the Trailblazers – and the cop parks it for him and promises to look after the keys.

When he arrives, the rangers have already gone out in the helicopter to look for Mike, and Rob has spent the morning walking back and forth across the ridge where they'd been the previous day. My father wants to go up in the helicopter, but the rangers tell him to sit tight, that there's nothing he can do. Later that day, Mike ambles into base camp. He spent the night outside at zero degrees Celsius with no gear. Come morning, he followed the streams because he knew they led down, but ended up on another range. Finally, he managed to find a road and hitch a lift back to base camp. He is shaken and cold, but fine.

The episode is a foreshadowing of things to come, the nights and weeks that will be spent not knowing where he is, fearing the worst every time the phone rings. But for the moment, it is nothing more than a wacky story my father will tell upon his return to Portland. It is the kind of story he likes – in the retelling like an action movie, or perhaps a television ad for some suitably masculine product. The dash to the airport, the forgiving fellow motorist and the supportive cop (well-wishers accumulating along his route), the rescue search against the dramatic backdrop of snowy peaks. Finally, the affectionate exclamation – 'God damn!' – that the sight of his son evokes, an exclamation that manages to encapsulate his relief, his annoyance and his admiration. His son is possessed of a daring spirit, and of that, at least, he approves.

For the moment, we are all just one anecdote richer.

Mike and Rob continue on their way, towards Mesa County in western Colorado, where they lie on the ground at night watching the Perseid meteor shower. They are very different people – Mike thinks Rob is too wrapped up in money and he doesn't like how

Rob listens to baseball games on the radio out in the middle of this quiet wilderness – but they both love exploring. If they see a road that looks like it leads somewhere interesting, they follow it, sometimes just to find the end. Pitch their tent wherever.

After making their way across to California, then up the coast and into Oregon, they arrive in Portland in August. In a letter to Fanny and Tony written from our new house, Mike sounds relaxed. He raves about the trip and tells them about some great hot springs he and Rob have discovered south of Portland. *I'm probably going to live in Oregon for a while starting in the fall so I'll be near the family. I'll get a little house of my own and a not too strenuous job and work for McGovern's election.*

But he doesn't stay in Oregon, nor does he get a little house of his own or work for McGovern's campaign. Instead, after a few weeks of Frisbee and swimming and general loafing around, he and Rob take off again. They head south, to the Santa Cruz Mountains in California, where they spend a couple of months living in a rented trailer. During the days, Rob goes dirt-biking for hours in the Redwood forests while Mike hikes. In the evenings they have dinner in town and drink pitchers of beer. Occasionally there are women, floaty and fresh-faced, drifting through the days just like they are.

Eventually, they continue down the coast and then cut east across the state to Death Valley. By now, Rob is feeling ready to go back east, to start thinking about real life again. Mike has little interest in real life, in applying himself to anything conventional, or in the crowded cities of the eastern seaboard. He doesn't want to go home to Oregon either. He tells Rob he knows some people – maybe in California, maybe Nevada or Arizona, nobody will remember – and he asks to be dropped there. Rob feels a little odd just leaving Mike like that, but what can he do? The time has come to go their separate ways. And so, in the early winter of 1972, they part. It is the last time they ever speak.

Ten

They have come a long way from their beginnings, from the basement apartment in Bala Cynwyd with the Paoli local thundering past, from Tuesday nights with Milton Berle and fifty bucks a game in the Eastern League and counting quarters at the Stop 'n' Swat in Somers Point. Oregon is worlds away from the grime of Philadelphia, and nothing like the South, where underneath the good manners and the sleepiness lies something old and hard and resistant, the entrenched divisions of race and class. Some people call the Northwest God's Country, for its storybook beauty: the pristine lakes and crystal-clear streams, the lush valleys and thick forests and snowy peaks. To my mother, it must seem the perfect place for a fresh start.

We live in a five-bedroom ranch-style house of wood and red brick, high on a bluff, in an affluent suburb of Portland. The house is not in the same league as those in the über-rich neighbourhoods that flank downtown Portland, where the old money reside in their stately colonials and the new in their modernist *Architectural Digest* dreams. Nor is it as coveted as the property that fronts on to the lake. But it is, in its own casual way, wonderful. Glass doors and ceiling-to-floor windows overlook the huge backyard, from which we can see the lake in the distance, ringed by Douglas firs. Just beyond the grassy verge a steep slope and a trail lead down to a watertower, though from the house our land appears, like a flat earth, to drop off into space.

The yard is perfect for games of Frisbee and whiffle ball and flag football, for make-believe camping on summer nights. There is plenty of space for our new toys: a tyre swing; a pet bunny in a wire coop Tim has rigged up; a sit-down mower that makes whoever is behind the wheel feel like a farmer. In the crook of a tree outside the kitchen window, my father builds a tree house where on warm afternoons we play games of gin rummy and drink pitchers of iced tea. There are brick patios front and back, and smaller private ones off two of the bedrooms. Purple wisteria climbs a trellis on the westward-facing patio.

Inside, along with some cautiously groovy new furniture, are the leftovers from our previous life: the black and gold sofa and chairs, the heavy wood credenza. In the cellar there is a bomb shelter, though no one seems quite as worried about bombs these days, and instead of stocking it with canned goods and bottled water we play creepy variations of hide-and-seek there, lying like corpses on the high wooden shelves.

That first summer, we pile into the fire-engine-red Maverick and drive to one of the easements on the lake. Thick, linked logs mark the boundary of the larger of the 'pools', and we swim out and mount them like horses, our legs dangling in the opaque water, our feet flinching from the occasional swipe of a passing fish. The older kids stand on the logs, spinning them underfoot in a contest to topple one another. In the shallower pool, enclosed by a wooden dock, we sink our toes into the mucky floor, then slither towards the surface, hoisting ourselves like amphibious creatures on to the sun-warmed boards, which sway slightly in the spanking wakes of speedboats. In late afternoon, when the sun moves behind the trees, the sparkling green surface of the lake goes a slick black in the shade, the grass on the bank grows cold under our feet, and the whole small world takes on the darkened aspect of a fairy tale.

We still go to Mass each Sunday. My parents like the one with the folk singers – a wan, long-haired trio strumming away to the left of the pulpit. They embrace rock 'n' roll, or at least a hokey pop strain of it, my father with his jazzy renditions of 'Bad, Bad Leroy Brown' and my mother belting out Helen Reddy's feminist anthem 'I Am Woman'. Some of their new friends are on their second marriages (hard to believe that until recently divorce constituted a genuine scandal), and right next door to us live a middle-aged lesbian couple. Bette and Nancy are the classic butch–femme pairing. Bette is a keen sports fan and often wants to talk to my father about last night's game.

'Hey, Jack,' she rasps (her throat raked by cigarette smoke), 'you guys played a helluva game last night!'

'Hey, Jack, those goddamn refs robbed you!'

Nancy, meanwhile – gentle, soft-spoken, matronly – floats delicately about (is she carrying a tray of just-baked cookies?), like a figure in a photo spread from *Good Housekeeping*, circa 1950.

Although still relatively conservative, my parents love the two women. My father, particularly, gets a kick out of them. He's always had a soft spot for people like Bette, people with a bit of *oomph* in them, who aren't afraid to be who they are. At parties in the backyard, by the light of the tiki torches, he dances with her to 'Tie a Yellow Ribbon Round the Old Oak Tree'.

In their own little ways, my parents are loosening up, opening themselves to new experiences. Nita dabbles in yoga, standing on her head in the middle of the living-room floor. They go whitewater rafting on the Deschutes and waterskiing on the lake, where their new friends live, with their speedboats and their split-level waterfront decks. They have begun to vacation in the Virgin Islands. They bring back snaps of themselves, arm in arm on the beach or stretched on chaises longues, their skin tanned to a purply-black.

On the one hand, these are halcyon days, shot through with light. Photos from our first months in the new house look as though they have been bathed in some solution that renders objects soft around the edges. My parents – she in a flattering white blouse and slacks posing by the white rhododendron, he leaning jauntily in the front doorway, a carpet of peach-coloured blossoms at his feet – appear happily surprised at where they've found themselves.

Well, their expressions seem to say, *would you get a load of us*.

And yet these are the last months of a blissful ignorance; the time before the seriousness of Mike's problems became apparent, before my parents' own troubles grew intractable. So much would change in the next couple of years that hindsight lends those days a precariousness, suffusing them with an innocence we were very soon to lose.

Mike is with us the Christmas of 1972, our first in the new house, having made his way back to Oregon from wherever Rob had dropped him. In a letter to Fanny and Tony early in the new year, he writes:

> I'm home now and things are going pretty good. I'm thinking of staying in Portland at least for the winter and get a civil service job or some kind of important post ha! ha! How's things in Puerto Rico. I'd like to be there basking in sun and listening to your famous jokes Fanny. Today we took down the Christmas tree which is always a sad occasion. I really enjoy be at home now don't worry about me I'm doing fine now.
> Happy Birthday Fanny!
>
> I love you both
> Mike

Despite the lapses in punctuation and syntax, and the seeming randomness of the subject matter, the letter is coherent. The 'worry' he is attempting to dispel arises from the fact that he has shown no interest in applying himself to a career. It is an attitude that our parents have attributed to the spirit of the times. They do not yet suspect that Mike's bouts of apathy and low moods, and his sometimes esoteric mutterings, are anything more than the affectations of a spoiled generation unwilling to pull itself up by the bootstraps and get a goddamn job.

Our grandmother links his apparent indolence to a temperament unhelpfully prone to introspection. Around this time, she writes to our mother:

> Mike takes the world too seriously. He must remember we had nothing to do with its creation and was just dropped down here as part of it. You don't fight it – just join it in the most comfortable manner.
> He must build up his body because _that_ we have to suffer or enjoy – resulting from the care we give it. High thought and yoghurt will only get you misery from a weak body and a youthful burial, leaving only sadness behind.
> He has not changed from seven years old in Haddonfield when I watched him walking home from the school bus dragging his bag of

books behind him instead of throwing it in the air and catching it like
the other boys.

He thinks too much but when Mike does smile it is like the sun shining
over Norway after six months of darkness. The people all love it and go
crazy for a while. Tell him to try to be happy if only for his own sake.
We all love him so much.

With his new job, my father is once again enjoying local celebrity, if
not always of the most welcome kind. That first year is difficult.
Though pro basketball is not yet the multi-billion-dollar industry it
will become, the stakes are higher than at Wake Forest and the pressure more intense than what he's used to.

Things get off to a bad start. The number-one draft pick has been
squandered. My father wanted Bob McAdoo, but was overruled by
the Blazers' owner. Instead, Portland drafted LaRue Martin.
McAdoo, who was drafted number two by Buffalo, will be that season's Rookie of the Year; he will go on to be a league MVP, a
five-time NBA All-Star and a Hall of Famer. LaRue Martin will be
none of those things. Instead, he will come to be regarded as the worst
number-one draft pick in NBA history.

The losses pile up. Tim and I go with our mother to all the home
games, and after each game we wait with her and the other wives
and girlfriends in the lobby outside the players' dressing room. The
women chatter away, about clothes and babies and their men who
are always on the road, but each time one of the men emerges, a
solemnity descends, and the room quietens in deference to defeat.

On the way home, the four of us often stop for a late-night snack
at a diner called Sambo's, where pictures of a little black Sambo
adorn the walls and nobody thinks twice about it, any more than
we do about the figure of Aunt Jemima on our maple-syrup bottle.
The young waitresses at Sambo's know who my father is and treat
him with a mix of proficient feminine sympathy, as though they are
nurses, and bashful flirtatiousness. The brazen sensuality of the
navy skipper (now heightened by his sideburns) is still in evidence.
We sit around a semicircular table under fluorescent lights – a
morose little foursome in our velour cowl necks, polyester blends,

113

crocheted sweater vests – Tim and I eating our French fries in silence while my parents make muted conversation between themselves. On the rare occasions the team wins a game, the mood is lighter, and my father might flirt back with the waitresses or sing a few bars of 'Raindrops Keep Falling on My Head', drumming his thick fingers on the table-top as though it's a piano, and listing from side to side in time with the tune.

Sportswriters phone our house. Sometimes my father refuses to take their calls, waving his hand 'no' as my mother tucks the receiver into the crook of her neck and mouths a name. Many people say he is doing a bad job. The boys in my third-grade class taunt me about my father's supposed incompetence, repeating, I suspect, what they have heard their own fathers saying. I feel guilty when I go home after school, as though I have failed to defend his honour. But I also feel thrown to the lions.

Although the Blazers win only twenty-one of eighty-two games in my father's first season, it seems to me that his air of authority doesn't desert him. Wherever we go, men recognize him and treat him with a respect he seems to take as his due. A slight catch in the air greets his appearance, as though the molecules have instantaneously rearranged themselves. I can feel it with the guys at the gas station, with traffic cops and maître d's and local businessmen – this near-obsequious regard. When I am with him, I bask in the glow of his celebrity. In contrast to him, other men strike me as pale specimens of masculinity.

That spring, Mike packs his things and hits the road. For a while, nobody thinks much of it, assuming it is just more of the restlessness and lack of industry that he will soon grow out of. But after a couple of weeks we stop hearing from him. Then we get a call from Danny, Mike's old high-school coach in Winston-Salem.

Mike phoned Danny to say that he was travelling the country. 'Like Kerouac,' he told him – he knew Danny had a soft spot for Kerouac. He asked if he could come and stay. Mike used to visit Danny whenever he was home from Duke, and Sharon and the kids loved him, so Danny said, 'Yes, of course, come.'

The first few days Danny and Sharon didn't notice anything odd, except that Mike wasn't bathing. He played with the kids, went to the store with Sharon, entertained them all with tales of his travels across America – the crazy characters who picked him up hitching, the bear that almost ate him in Yellowstone. But after a week or so, he started acting strange – going to the nearby park at night, coming back wired, jittery, talking about 'Arabs' and sex, stories Danny and Sharon didn't know whether or not to believe. One night he told them a particularly weird tale, about going home with one of those 'Arabs'. When Danny asked him if he thought that was a good idea, Mike just looked at him and said matter-of-factly, 'It was neither a good nor a bad idea.' Mike was never aggressive with anyone, but his inhibitions in certain areas – mainly sexual – had simply vanished. Otherwise, he was perfectly coherent. This was what Danny and Sharon found so strange, the bizarre behaviour side by side with lucidity. Not knowing what to do, they phoned my parents, who sent money for Mike to return to Oregon.

The local high school is close enough that Robin, just turned eighteen and in her final year, can walk there from our house. One day, soon after that phone call from Danny and Sharon, she is coming into the driveway after school when our father comes out the front door to meet her. She can see that he is extremely shaken, not quite in possession of himself. He gives her a hug and tells her he loves her very much – not his usual greeting when she arrives home from school – then leads her inside to where her eldest brother is stretched out on a bed.

The last time Robin saw Mike, he was just an ordinary hippy, heading off on his Kerouacian rambles. Clearly, something has changed. He is skinnier than he has ever been, and yet he does not look physically ill. Whatever is wrong with him is more complicated than that. He stares at the ceiling, like she isn't even there. She doesn't think she's ever seen anyone like this up close, certainly not anyone she knows. It scares her. She has no idea what to do, and nobody has explained anything to her. At some point, when her parents are out of the room, she sits on the twin bed opposite and attempts to make conversation with him. Small talk with Mike has never been easy for her – she finds him aloof and somewhat intimidating – but she tries, asking him where he's been on his travels. Even as she says it, she can hear how silly the question sounds.

He stares at the ceiling while his sister fidgets. Finally, he says, 'Robin, your words are meaningless to me.'

It's a Friday. My parents don't want to take Mike to a psychiatric hospital, but they do want him to see a doctor. The only one they can get hold of that weekend is an acquaintance of theirs, a young psychiatrist who has long hair and wears love beads. When they bring Mike to his office the following day, the psychiatrist talks to them, then to Mike alone, then to all of them together. He asks Mike some questions.

'If you saw a letter on the ground with an address and a stamp on it, what would you do?'

'I'd put it on the windowsill so it wouldn't blow away,' Mike says.

'If you were standing with a group of people at a bus stop, what would they be talking about?'

'Me,' Mike says.

There is no test that provides a definitive diagnosis of schizophrenia. Diagnosis is made on the basis of an interview with a clinician, who assesses the presence or absence of certain symptoms and the period of time over which they have persisted. Aside from the psychotic symptoms – hallucinations (typically auditory) and delusions (fixed, false beliefs) – there are also the so-called negative symptoms (a diminishment in normal thoughts and speech and an absence of normal emotional expression) and the disorganized symptoms, which include confused thoughts, memory problems, and difficulty concentrating, following instructions and completing tasks. The long-haired psychiatrist diagnoses schizophrenia that day.

Despite the doctor's explanation, my parents have no idea what it means, really, this ugly word, the word that from this day forth will define and describe and circumscribe their son. There is a terrible unceremoniousness about it, this upending of their reality, the way they are expected to just absorb the news.

Late that night, my mother sits on the built-in bench in the kitchen, the big plate-glass window behind her and the blackness beyond, her stomach churning as she asks herself again and again, *What is happening?* Apparently, Mike has done some drugs, serious ones, the ones that make you think you're Jesus or that you can fly. Are they what's done this to him? Or was it something she and Jack did, something *she* did? The concept of the schizophrenogenic mother has not yet been entirely discredited. She doesn't exactly fit the bill (overprotective, dominant but rejecting), but it will be many years before she is free of the fear that some action, or else a more consistent feature of her mothering, was the cause of his illness.

Mike, not surprisingly, does not accept the verdict. He keeps insisting his parents are the ones who need help. The weekend isn't easy. While my mother makes dinner, Mike walks around the kitchen barking like a dog.

Soon stabilized by the antipsychotics, Mike spends his time playing the harmonica, meditating and reading books by Maharishi Mahesh Yogi. I turn them over and look at Maharishi's photo on the back, his fleshiness and glinting eyes and luxuriant grey beard suggestive of a sensuality I find creepy. Mike has a bushy beard, too, and heavy black horn-rimmed glasses. He sleeps on a big blue waterbed, and sometimes we sit on the bed together in the lotus position and he tries to teach me the harmonica.

I am nine. I do not know what to think about either him or his trouble. It is, after all, adult trouble, and if the words *paranoid schizophrenia* have filtered down to me at all (or been communicated in some solemn family conference), they have not been accompanied by any in-depth explanation; we are living in an age in which adults have not yet begun to burden children with well-intentioned attempts to put life's dreadful phenomena into age-appropriate language. My thoughts and feelings about Mike are shaped by a mix of intuition, overheard or handed-down bits of information and misinformation, guesswork, fear, fascination and the instinctive bond of siblings. In my world of unknowing, half of me adores him and the other half feels vaguely repelled.

By June, he is well enough to get work as a freelance gardener, work he will continue through that summer. He begins a vegetable garden of his own in our backyard. He toys with the idea of getting his teaching certificate, though at the moment there are more teachers than jobs. But while his future remains uncertain (*His plans for the fall are still indefinite,* my mother writes, *but he is happy, tan, healthy – no booze, ciggies or pot . . .*), everyone, including him, still assumes he has one, that the madness of late spring was a drug-induced breakdown from which he will emerge.

Dear Fanny and Nony,

Greetings from the rain capital of the world, Portland, Oregon. Today I was out trying to make a few bucks for summer travel so it decided to hail for ten minutes and then rain the rest of the morning. I just hope it doesn't frost and kill the garden I'm growing. We've got asparagus, lettuce and spinach coming up with some tomato plants. Mom and Dad came home last night they're all tan and relaxed. They brought me a Mickey Mouse T-shirt for my birthday. Nothing compared to what you gave me thank you thank you thank you thank you. It's been so long I don't know what else to say except that I'll put the money to good use this summer. Dad's talking about renting a house boat and sailing up to Canada from Washington. I'm more for back packing and beaching in California myself. We'll compromise somehow. Not much else to say except I think about you both a lot. John and I may be coming east this summer. We'll see you somehow.

Love,
Mike

The letter, written less than two months after his first serious trouble, shows no signs of psychological disturbance. Though clearly eager to be on the road again, he sounds very much a part of the family. Recently, we have added to our brood: a dog, whom Mike picked out from the pound and to whom he will remain lovingly devoted for the twelve years of her life, often preferring her company to that of humans. For reasons unknown, he christens her Munka. She is a mongrel, not proud or intelligent or beautiful, but excessively affectionate. Unable to contain her joy when one of us arrives home, she waggles her whole bottom and pisses with excitement, the voluminousness of the stream in direct proportion to the intensity of her affection, its force and duration greater if you've been out of town.

Mike grows lean and fit working on his gardens. Sometimes he takes me along when he goes to one particular client – a sweet elderly widow who lives in a mock-Tudor house on the lake shore. She feeds me petite sandwiches at an ornate wrought-iron table overlooking the water, and while Mike works I swim in the lake and loll on the dock, pretending that this is where we live. He and I have a way of being alone when together that seems to suit us both. From his point of view, our affinity may be based on the fact that I am the only one in the house young enough to be ignorant of what his recent diagnosis means.

He has given me two souvenirs from his recent travels. One is a small, rust-coloured coral square that has been etched by natural forces with what looks like cuneiform, so that it might be an ancient tablet in miniature. The other is a segment of pocked coral, its surface inlaid with dozens of tiny fossilized sea urchins. No one in my family has ever deemed anything so small, so unimproved upon, worthy of cherishing. Taking my cue from Mike, I regard both of these objects as exotic treasures and display them on the shelf in my bedroom.

Our moment of affinity turns out to be brief. By the following year I am old enough to be embarrassed by his oddness, to want to distance myself from whatever is wrong with him. At the same time, I fail to take it seriously. Some days after school, my best friend and I skulk around, spying on him through windows, excited less by his fairly ordinary activities than by our secret vantage point, and a feeling of superiority we don't begin to understand. He is like a caged creature brought back from some exotic isle, the only adult in our midst who might actually do something not just odd but totally bizarre, noteworthy enough to be entered in the little logbook in which we keep a record of all the silly doings of our lives. Sometimes we ring the front bell, then dash into the rhododendron bushes and watch as he comes to the door, first puzzled, then spooked, then annoyed.

We are trying, in the colloquial sense, to drive him crazy. It is nothing personal; we like to play this irritating game with lots of people, just as we like to hide things people need and rifle through our parents' personal belongings and call strangers picked at random from the phone book. Or, if it *is* personal, it is only so in the sense that we, being children, naturally visit our tortures upon those in whom we detect vulnerability. I know that there is something strange about Mike, but I have no idea that his problems are related to a periodic inability to distinguish between what is real and what is not. And so we ring the bell and run away. We knock on the windowpanes, then press ourselves, out of sight, against the outer wall.

My failure to grasp the gravity of his condition might be partly accounted for by the gap in our ages. Because there are enough years between us that I can't remember him being any other way, he seems to me more an eccentric uncle who's come to stay than a once-brilliant brother unravelling before me. And I still assume – so unconsciously it doesn't register as an assumption – that nothing truly calamitous can ever befall our family.

The 1973–4 season begins promisingly for my father. In October, the Blazers have the first winning month in their history. NBC says that it looks like they will make the play-offs. Then the losses begin. As the season progresses, rumours swirl as to whether, and when, my father will get the axe. Tim and I go to all the home games with my mother (Mike is seldom with us, either away from Oregon or else preferring to stay home alone). When my father emerges from the dressing room after yet another trouncing, we follow him and our mother down the long grey concrete corridor towards the exit, the two of them arm in arm, my father's head down, my mother appearing to support him. By then the arena is empty and the few security guards remaining bid us goodnight with the muted deference of undertakers.

There is something tragically heroic in my father's bearing and mysterious in his ability – no matter how numerous or how humiliating the losses – to remain larger than life, deserving of our faith. There is a feeling of cohesion between the four of us. I am learning that people need each other more in adversity, but also that nobody loves a loser. I have a vague sense that there is some occasion I must rise to – that what is required of me is a form of loyalty I don't yet understand. I do what I can, though, to affect a doleful bearing that mirrors my parents' attitude of mourning, because I have also learned that while winning may be more fun, losing tells us more about ourselves, and, if handled well, has a complicated dignity all its own.

The team ends that season with twenty-seven wins and fifty-five losses and my father, with one year left on his contract, is fired.

Eleven

They meet as though on the other side of something, a space containing all that has happened in the six years since they were last alone together. See them sitting opposite each other, in a boarding house with furniture that reeks of cigarette smoke and some ineradicable dampness. Young, rail-thin, a little shell-shocked. Since the late spring days of 1968, of his pressed white dinner jacket and the pink flower pinned to the strap of her dress, since the talk of having kids together and the letters written those summers apart and all the other inexpressible wonders of first love, they have passed, each of them, through a dark wood.

There is no awkwardness, nothing phoney. No *isn't this great, I haven't seen you in years* kind of thing. Neither of them pretends that anything is clearer than it is. But there is an understanding between them. If anyone can understand him, it is Lara.

They haven't spoken since they broke up. He sent a few notes first term, and flowers on her birthday, but they never met – in four years, never once ran into each other on campus. She spent her junior year in Europe – supposedly studying French and theatre in Lyons, but really only showing up for exams. Instead of going to classes, she drove around Europe by herself in a car she'd bought in a café for next to nothing. She had wanted to learn by experiencing; *experience everything* was the phrase she was prone to repeating then. If it all led to greater self-knowledge, how could it be bad for you? She thought she was invulnerable, but she got burned, like a lot of people she knew. She wound up in jail, arrested for sleeping on top of a railway car in Yugoslavia, then had a terrible car crash in Spain and ended up in hospital. Back at Duke for her senior year, she lived off-campus, going to classes and choreographing dance pieces, but mostly trying to pull herself together.

She lives in Canada now, some kind of communal set-up, but is down in North Carolina visiting her parents – they've moved back from Memphis – when she learns that Mike is in town. He has come from Oregon. After passing the summer of '74 there, he once again upped stakes and made his way back east, his sudden departure taking everyone by surprise. *It seems I cannot worry anymore,* our grandmother writes. *I do not know what happened but I suppose it is True Faith, or I realize no matter what happens we live through it all.*

Lara finds him fragile, less physically present than before. (She herself has got thinner. Never heavy to begin with, she has lost some of her curves and acquired a litheness that is accentuated by her long, straight, unstyled hair.) She senses that he has cut himself loose from everything and everybody. Clearly, he feels like a mess. But it doesn't occur to her that he is going over the edge. For he is also lucid, self-aware, and unashamed of how things stand with him. He seems to view his situation in the context of an unfolding.

They leave the boarding house and walk, for hours, talking. She tells him about what happened junior year, how she learned a lot from it but that it had been dangerous. How everything looked different after Europe. She tells him that finding work you feel passionate about is essential. That's what she's trying to do in Toronto, learning photography and teaching dance, building a life around her work.

Mike has so many questions for her. He wants to know all about the scene up there in Canada, about her life, her friends, what they do, how they live. He is full of admiration. It sounds so much more progressive than anything he's seen down here. He has a job in Winston-Salem, washing dishes. She keeps coming back to the work thing. She can see he has nothing to care about, nothing to ground him and hold him together. When he was younger, basketball did that, and he's never found anything to replace it.

There is nothing he would like more than to find a more authentic way to live, like Lara has. He wants to be productive, not like a wage slave, but in a way that answers to some deeper need, that quells the anxiety that a multiplicity of possibilities provokes. Permission to question everything can be paralysing as well as freeing, and while he mightn't need the brackets of a nine-to-five, or the crutches of property or position, he needs, like everyone, some kind of limiting horizon, a frame within which he can embed himself. But after the turmoil of the past two years, what remains to organize his world? Medication. The cities he grew up in – lodestars by which he will try to orient himself. One or two friends who might still understand him. Family, possibly.

It is not an easy year. He travels as far south as Florida and as far north as Pennsylvania, unravelling as he goes. Dropping in and out of people's lives, never staying anywhere for long. He is doing everything that someone in his state of mind shouldn't do. No base, no routine, no support network or contact with doctors. Nothing to cushion his fall, should it come.

Susan, his old girlfriend from Duke, is living in Florida that winter. She has finished grad school at Vanderbilt and is teaching Transcendental Meditation from a house in Fort Meyers when Mike shows up at her door, filthy, smelly, looking like he hasn't washed his hair in a month. It's not cool. They were all hippies at Duke but they still took a shower every day. He doesn't seem mentally ill to her, more bum-like. Somebody at a loose end, without purpose. They go out to a little bar the night he arrives, he and Susan and the three others she's sharing the house with. They have a couple of beers and dance, but Mike isn't very communicative. He doesn't stay long at the house, only a night or two. It's their work space, they can't have this smelly guy hanging around when they're trying to teach TM. So he leaves.

For several weeks, we have no news of him. He is squatting in a big burned-out house in Gainesville, Florida, but no one knows that. I somehow fail to realize how scared my parents are, how real they consider the possibility that we might never see him again. How is it that I remain oblivious, when my mother is waking with a knot in her stomach every morning, when she has the Red Cross out looking for him and various police departments on the alert? Do I not even catch a whiff of the anxiety? Likely, I have begun to find his presence sufficiently unsettling that his periodic absences come as a relief. The details and the degrees of distress they occasion in others simply don't concern me.

Finally, my mother prays to God, 'If he's alive, let me hear from him tomorrow.' And the next day, like a miracle, Mike calls and says, 'Send me money.'

He doesn't want to come home, despite my mother's pleas, and instead begins to make his way back up the east coast, stopping again in North Carolina. For a brief spell, he lives at a crash pad near the Duke campus called African Violets, then in somebody's garage apartment in Winston-Salem. He spends some time with Jason, his old friend and former kundalini partner. He tells Jason he's been following Elton John on his US tour. He keeps repeating the lyrics from his favourite songs, convinced that Elton John is communicating with him.

He asks Jason to be his shrink, but Jason knows that whatever Mike's problems are, they are way over *his* head. Mike is a mess. Disoriented, agitated, sexually obsessed. Jason has to stop him from taking off his clothes in the supermarket dairy aisle. He thinks Mike has got stuck in the second chakra, the one to do with sex. When he looks at him, he cannot find the person he once knew. Mike has a scary energy, a crazed look in his eyes. He is the kind of guy, Jason thinks, that if he got on a bus you'd pull your kids a little closer.

Mike also drops in on our sister Robin, now in college in Charlotte. He calls her one night and says he's in town. She goes with a friend to pick him up at somebody's house and he stays with her a few nights in the dorm until she is summoned to the resident administrator's office and told that her brother's presence is upsetting the other students. He will have to leave. Robin gives him the news – softening the bit about the complaints – and he sets off again.

By early 1975, Mike is back in Oregon, back in the hospital. He receives electroconvulsive therapy. He hates the hospital. When he is discharged, he comes home to our house, where my girlfriend and I torment him, ringing the doorbell and running away, or spying on him through the windows. My father is still out of work. Our parents' marriage is showing signs of trouble, the kind of trouble my mother hoped they'd left behind in North Carolina. Not surprisingly, Mike prefers the open road. That spring, he gets on a bus and travels, once again, the 3,000 miles back to Winston-Salem. He goes straight to Lara's parents' house.

Lara's mother Kate comes home to find him sitting on their doorstep. He isn't looking good, and he is upset because he's left his guitar on the bus. He tells Kate that his memory is shot, because of the ECT. He says that his parents put him in the hospital and that it didn't help him at all. Drugs were easier to get there than on the outside. One day, he says, someone attacked him with a coat hanger, poking him in the eye.

When Lara's father Dave comes home, Mike presents him with some pipe tobacco he's brought as a gift. He mentions that he is looking for a job, and Dave says he'll make enquiries. Mike asks if Lara still goes to church, and when Kate says no, he says, 'Well, you should cry, that's what my mother does and it works.' It's a joke, and they all have a little chuckle. But the visit leaves Dave and Kate feeling very sad. Mike seems lost. His spirits are low. Though they have not seen him in years, there was a time he was like a son to them, a time Kate wrote in a letter to my mother, *We have really missed Mike. Dave compares all boys with Mike and finds them sadly lacking, but after knowing Mike I'm afraid we're spoiled . . .*

Dave manages to get Mike a job washing dishes at the Baptist Hospital in Winston-Salem. About a week later, he calls the hospital canteen to see how Mike is doing, but Mike has disappeared.

Neither Lara nor her parents ever hear from Mike again, although in among the letters my mother has saved is one from Mike to Lara, written a couple of years after their meeting in Winston-Salem, but never sent.

DEAR LARA,

YOUR TIME IS VERY PRECIOUS AND YOUR PRESENCE IS A BLESSING FOR ALL AS WE MOVE INTO A NEW YEAR IT IS VERY APPARENT THAT THE SCHOOL HERE IS IN A STATE OF FLUX. AND THE WHOLE IDEA OF GETTING A WORLD WIDE PHOTOGRAPH SEEMS A LITTLE SILLY BUT REMEMBER WHAT THE LORD SAID THAT THE ONLY THING WE HAVE TO FEAR IS FEAR ITSELF AND DON'T GET ANY FLAT TIRES IN MONTREAL. SO LOVE, MIKE

Twelve

In January of 1996, I recorded the following in my notebook:

*I dream that Mike is a child – golden & beautiful – he is swimming
towards a row boat, in which a young girl is standing. Maybe my sister.
He is almost drowning. She helps him into the boat, saves him, but once
on board, he falls & hits his head very hard on a wooden seat. His eyes
bug way out of his head. But the girl seems unaware. Then we are back in
a crowded place. I am insisting that he be taken in an ambulance to the
hospital – everyone thinks he's fine because he didn't drown, but I know
the future – that he will never be right again. So they take him. A woman
doctor examines him & tells us that he'll need to go on medication for
manic-depression now. I say to my mother, angrily, you never told me
about that accident. She says, you never knew he was a talker either. The
next scene is a woman talking about the group he'll be in (all crazies, etc).
So this is it for life.*

At the time of the dream, I was living alone in a rented gate lodge
in the rural west of Ireland, quaint but dark and cold, its walls damp
with condensation. I had left my marriage four months earlier and,
following a brief period of elation, during which I realized I could
do whatever I wanted, I proceeded to do whatever I wanted, to disastrous effect. Christmas was the nadir, a succession of nightmarish
days whose beginning was marked by the abandonment of my car
on St Stephen's Day on the main road running between Sligo and
Donegal. I had been driving home from town that evening when
my right leg – the one responsible for controlling the accelerator
and the brake – began to shake uncontrollably. I pulled over and
walked to a nearby pub. From there, I was ferried by a friend to a
pub closer to where I lived. Another friend, Dermot, picked me up
and brought me to his house, where he and his wife were eating

leftovers from Christmas dinner. He sat me down in front of the fire, put a plate on my lap and gave me a glass of wine. I ate with my fingers, as managing cutlery was out of the question. Leland was there, too. Leland and Dermot had known each other since the gritty old days, writing books in Dublin and in London, cities choked with coal smoke and teeming with disreputable and eccentric lovers. Now, they lived relatively settled lives by the sea in north Sligo. Since my separation, I had done a lot of drinking with both of them.

There were two pubs on our peninsula, about a mile apart, both peopled mostly by restless young men, who farmed cattle or fished, and old men – drunk, delusional, mostly kind – who were prone to random oracular outbursts. The atmosphere in both places tended to veer between a mute despondency and a desperate bonhomie, like barrooms out of Eugene O'Neill. Ellen's, the more respectable of the two, was a cold and darkish place which on a good night could overcome its desolation and blossom into something riotous and life-affirming, and to which people from Sligo town, twelve miles away, sometimes ventured for a bit of rural rough. It was run by a couple in their fifties who were as plain and peaceable in their way as Jordan – the proprietor of the other pub – was garish and profane in his. Jordan had once staged a short season of female mud-wrestling in the lounge area of his establishment; now, he contented himself with the occasional after-hours porn video on the box. In small doses, he was irresistible. Middle-aged but with a head of dark, licentious ringlets, he was like a wild-eyed Pan or Caravaggio's sick Bacchus gone florid-faced and fat. No one from town ever came to Jordan's.

The night I left my car by the side of the road, Leland and I went to Jordan's. We stayed till closing time, by which point I was begging her, 'Don't leave me alone.' She took me to her house and put me to bed on her sofa, and the next afternoon we returned to Jordan's and stayed again through the evening, and again she took me home to her sofa. At some point, in the midst of those days, there was a storm; ice coated the fields and the trees and the laneways. Even walking was treacherous. We were trapped on our glistening peninsula, a landscape lifted from fairy tale that under other circumstances might've thrilled me but which now intensified my claustrophobia.

There was nothing to do but ricochet between the two pubs, the poles of my narrowing existence. One day we cracked open the sloe gin. We had made it ourselves. In October we had tramped gaily up the mountain, filling our wicker baskets with the beautiful cobalt-blue berries, the excursion taking on a deceptively healthy feel. Then we'd plopped the berries into gin and watched, over the weeks, the liquid turn an unearthly neon violet, like some nectar of the gods. When we drank it that icy Christmas, it reduced us to tears.

After a few days, the thaw began, though the roads were still frozen over in patches. Leland and her daughter drove me, very gingerly, to my house. (My car was still by the side of the main road where I'd left it, though the police had phoned to ask me to remove it, a simple and predictable request that left me feeling like a sweating, breathless fugitive.) While they went for a walk, I took a shower. There was an eerie stillness to the place, and it was so cold I could see my breath in the living room. On the floor of the kitchen there were two dead rats.

Those Christmas days were the worst in a long year tainted with a sense of ominousness. I was sure something terrible was on the verge of happening, though I had no idea what it would be. I dreaded getting up in the mornings, half believing that if only I could sleep long enough, I might sleep through it, whatever *it* was. And yet when I slept deep into the day, I woke with a panicked awareness of lost time (for my absence brought home to me the frightening fact of my own contingency: life had gone on without me), of nights having passed of which I remembered little and for which I had nothing to show but this grim nervousness – too dark and complicated to be called a 'hangover'.

> Remember how long you have been putting off these things, and how many times the gods have given you days of grace, and yet you do not use them.

I read the aphorisms of Marcus Aurelius and, although I called myself an atheist, I felt a distinct sense of sin about this squandering of my brief moment on earth. I was reading less and less. My memory and concentration were terrible. My thoughts scrabbled anxiously over one another, like a spooked herd, or else they dripped so slowly there seemed large blank spaces between them, and I would stare at whatever was in front of me, as though life were a dull slide show and I was waiting, submissively, for the slide to change.

The one thing that calmed me was basketball. A few years before, I had joined the All-Stars, a 'ladies' team in town. I hadn't picked up a ball since 1985, when I had quit my college team in Philadelphia, forfeiting a scholarship worth thousands of dollars, an act of supreme self-indulgence justified only by the fact that I was falling apart. It was after those months with Becky in Ocean City when, instead of sharpening my skills in summer league, which was what I was expected to be doing, I had instead fallen into the cycle of all-night parties, returning to school that September in disarray – weepy, unfit and completely uninterested in the rah-rah of collegiate athletics. By December, I had left the team.

The All-Stars' coach was a bald, towering, pear-shaped English man whose primary piece of advice to us seemed to be, 'Breathe through your noses, girls! Through your noses!' Our team travelled to the towns and villages of the west of Ireland: Gort, Ballyhaunis, Ballina, Castlebar, Bunninadden, Ballaghaderreen. In Ballina, there were three sisters, each about four feet tall, who could shoot the lights out. They scurried around on defence like animals driven demented by a threat only they could perceive. There was an earthiness to them, a hunger; they looked like they'd just come in from birthing calves in the field.

There was a charm to those seasons with the All-Stars, to the cold gyms in the middle of nowhere and the fact that we travelled to them through the dark winter nights purely for the love of the game. (I thought of my father's first coaching job in the fifties at Germantown Academy in Philadelphia, where, because they had no gym, he'd found an unheated barn and had the boys wear gloves during practice.) I could almost believe we were headed for bigger and better things instead of just towards middle age.

By 1995, when the anxiety was spreading through me like some sort of fibrous growth, basketball was the one thing that could take my mind off my mind. It was a link to some healthier version of myself, a version I could still, just about, tap into. I would walk into practice filled with a vague paranoia – the sense that my teammates knew (knew what? I had no idea) – but once we started running, the chatter ceased, and for one or two blissful hours I was released from the dreadful internal cross-examination.

Eventually, though, even basketball wasn't safe. One evening in December, after a particularly heavy few days and nights of carousing, I was giving a friend a lift into town on my way to a game. She looked at me with worried amazement and said, 'You're playing in a basketball game tonight? You must have an incredible metabolism.'

I smiled nervously. I did not, I knew, have an incredible metabolism. I had the shakes and a hot pounding headache and a worrying slosh in my belly.

That night I had an out-of-body experience on the free-throw line. Standing there feeling both intensely anxious and cut off from the self who was experiencing the anxiety, I thought, *Who am I kidding?*

After that, I never went back to the All-Stars.

What scared me the most were hallucinations, for hallucinations meant madness proper – this I knew from what had happened to Mike. I could feel them lurking, in the hyperreal quality of the rats on the kitchen floor, in the way my mind felt porous, as though its filters were disintegrating, in the way the world some days resembled an old malfunctioning television set on which figures and objects appeared to be trailing ghostly auras.

I had known for years that drinking too much could leave me, in the morning, slow-witted and queasy, or, conversely, with a cock-eyed energy that, in the absence of refuelling, would lapse around 11 a.m. into a heavy-headed and metallic exhaustion. But no one had ever mentioned the paranoia that would take hold, that I would feel transparent and exposed, that the act of buying a loaf of bread could unhinge me. And so, just as the knowledge that excessive drinking caused shaking did not prevent me from attributing it to other causes (I looked at my trembling hands and worried that I was developing Parkinson's), so did I waver between an obtuse suspicion that alcohol might be linked to my psychological unease and a growing fear that I was starting to go the way of my brother.

I was not losing my mind, or not in the way my brother had. But alcohol had left my neurotransmitters in disarray – wreaking cognitive, psychological and emotional havoc. Neurotransmitters are the chemicals that relay or modulate signals between neurons – the brain's nerve cells. They play a huge part in determining how we feel each day and how we perceive ourselves and the world. Endorphins and serotonin are responsible for the sense of peace, joy and happiness we are capable of feeling. Dopamine plays a role in cognition, motor control, motivation, sleep, mood, attention and the reward system (food and sex both stimulate the release of dopamine). Norepinephrine is involved in alertness and arousal and underlies the fight-or-flight response – familiar to anyone who's ever had a panic attack. Acetylcholine helps to generate muscle movement and regulate the autonomic nervous system (a mostly involuntary system involving heart and respiration rate, digestion, perspiration and sexual arousal). GABA (gamma-aminobutyric acid) is the most calming of the neurotransmitters, inhibiting the brain's tendency to speed up. Anti-anxiety agents like Xanax and Valium work on GABA receptor sites, as does alcohol.

The reason you feel happy and relaxed after a couple of drinks is because of the way alcohol interacts with neurotransmitters, inducing a temporary euphoria. But excessive alcohol intake diminishes the brain's capacity to produce its own neurotransmitters. Eventually, you end up with depleted levels of serotonin (linked to depression, anxiety, insomnia and cognitive impairment), acetylcholine (impaired memory and nerve health, muscle problems and weakness), norepinephrine (poor memory and concentration, low motivation, fatigue, anxiety, depression, emotional instability, tremors and insomnia) and GABA. When GABA is depleted, we feel miserable and anxious.

The insistence on drinking again amidst the accumulated wreckage of all one's previous benders makes perfect sense when we understand that the beleaguered brain is seeking desperately to replenish its depleted store of chemicals. Never mind that they were depleted by alcohol in the first place – alcohol can temporarily jack them up again. About two drinks in, you begin to feel your mind's wrinkles smoothing. You are once again at home in the world, and you say to yourself, *What was all that fuss about?*

Several hours and drinks later, you wake, after a long blackout of a sleep, feeling anything but rested. All night, your brain has been trying to rebound from alcohol's depressive effects – overproducing glutamine, one of the body's natural stimulants. This increase in glutamine has prevented you from reaching the deepest and most restorative levels of sleep. In addition, because your body is metabolizing alcohol during the night, at some point before morning you have likely gone into withdrawal. Your sleep becomes shallow and disrupted; REM increases, as do dream or nightmare recall and heart rate. You greet the day exhausted, anxious, sweat-soaked. There is a large blank where the previous evening should be. And all that fuss is back in spades.

When I had finished showering and had dumped the rats outside and was gathering my things to go back to Leland's (still not willing to stay alone), the phone rang. I twitched, and stared at it. Every time it trilled into the cold stillness, it seemed the air would shatter like a pane of glass. The answering machine kicked in, and I heard my brother Steve's voice. I stood there in the living room and listened to him wishing me happy holidays, his tone easy and straightforward, an offhanded clarity that felt a million miles from me. He was a small point of light I could dimly perceive, sending a communiqué from another dimension.

That it was Steve's voice reaching into that eerie hour was fitting. He had passed through his own hell years before. Anxiety and panic attacks had started during his last year in college. By then, he could see what was happening to Mike and was terrified he was headed in the same direction. After graduation, he worked for a few years as a cop in North Carolina, then went into real estate. His drinking, already heavy in college, was taking over his life. Then, Christmas 1981, by which time our parents had divorced and Mike was settled in

Oregon – he was living in a group home but often came to our house – Steve arrived on our doorstep. He was twenty-nine and hitting bottom. He spent the next several months sitting on our living-room sofa in a cycle of drinking vodka and passing out, waking, drinking more, passing out. My mother watched helplessly as her second son fell apart before her eyes. Then one night she woke to the smell of smoke. He had fallen asleep with a cigarette. The next day she told him he would have to go. He couldn't be placing the rest of us in danger. She broke her own heart when she put him out.

That afternoon, drunk, Steve packed what few belongings he had and put them into a square battered suitcase, then asked me to drop him at the 7-11, a few blocks from our house. On the way to the store he said, 'Will you give me ten dollars?' His eyes rolled unfocused in their sockets, as though the bloodshot orbs had broken loose from their usual tether.

I refused, without a second thought. 'I'm not giving you any money,' I said. I was seventeen years old. I just wanted him out of our lives. I left him at the 7-11, standing outside the door with his back against the brick wall. For some reason, he wasn't wearing any shoes. As I drove off, I didn't even bother to wonder what would become of him.

A week or so later, he appeared on our doorstep again. Some time during those days away, he had had his epiphany: *There's something wrong with this picture*, he'd said to himself, as he foraged in a dumpster for food. At the time, he'd been sleeping under a fir tree behind a restaurant where he had recently been fired from his job washing dishes. He had then made his way to an apartment owned by a man who'd briefly employed him – cleaning out horse stables, the nadir of his working life. There, alone in the apartment, he had dried out, seen the DTs through with nothing to cushion his passage. And then he'd come home again, his drinking life over.

That August, I left for college in Philadelphia, and for the next three years, Steve and my mother lived together in an odd symbiosis of sparring and deep affection. He was grateful to her for what she'd done, for it had helped him to kick the booze, and she admired him for having kicked it. It took Steve some time to find his place again. He isn't easy. He is prickly, eccentric, often solitary. But he is also genuine, loyal and caring. Habituated to irony, he relies on a sometimes mordant humour to protect a too-soft core.

When he was in his mid forties and a law student living on loans, he won ten thousand dollars from NBC. Geraldo Rivera, during the Clinton–Lewinsky scandal, had claimed that criminal prosecutions aren't brought for lying about sex, and offered the cash to anyone who could prove otherwise. Steve did, and when NBC didn't pay out, he sued them for breach of contract and got the ten thousand plus eighty-six dollars for costs and postage. He gave a thousand to a charity assisting single-parent law students, and joked that having won a lawsuit against NBC, it might all be downhill from there.

Now he is a lawyer and a lecturer and is writing a textbook on substantive due process. Every few weeks, he donates platelets – the life-saving element of blood needed by people suffering from leukaemia and other cancers. Often, my mother looks at him and says, her voice tender, weighted with the whole of their shared history, 'I'm so proud of you.'

My own epiphany was somewhat less dramatic. It happened several months after that harrowing Christmas. The terrors of the holiday season had receded, and in their place had settled exhaustion and a droning despondency. There was also a strange feeling of homesickness, as though there was somewhere else I should be, could be. I felt I had lost something I was almost certain I had once possessed – something like the capacity for wonder. I could recall being seventeen and feeling free of fear and capable of uncomplicated happiness.

At the same time, I often wondered if everyone else wasn't, in fact, feeling more or less as I was. Maybe this grey stasis was just the way life was when you grew up, and nobody talked about it, the way nobody talked about death or menopause or the pain of childbirth. Maybe it was just one of the great unspoken truths of adulthood, and grousing about it would be an embarrassing breach of etiquette.

In *The Varieties of Religious Experience*, William James credits alcohol with stimulating in us those yearnings usually 'crushed to earth by the cold facts and dry criticisms of the sober hour'. James's notion that drunkenness makes us, momentarily, one with truth, and his simple, oft-quoted statement of fact – 'Sobriety diminishes, discriminates, and says no; drunkenness expands, unites, and says yes' – is framed by an acknowledgement that we are not designed to bear unlimited expansion. '[I]t is part of the deeper mystery and tragedy of life,' he writes, 'that whiffs and gleams of something that we immediately recognize as excellent should be vouchsafed to so many of us only in the fleeting earlier phases of what in its totality is so degrading a poison.'

If James had known what we know now of neurotransmitters, he undoubtedly would have applied this knowledge to his analysis of the human condition. But he viewed the drunken consciousness as part of the larger mystic consciousness, and it is likely he would have continued to recognize alcoholism for what it also is: a manifestation of the yearning for more, a misguided attempt to fill the void. For if the persistence of craving reveals anything, it is the sense of incompleteness at the heart of us.

That August, in what was to be my last proper binge, a group of us traipsed about together for two days and nights, and the exquisite release that one is always seeking but hardly ever finding – those moments when just the right note is hit and the fear and the cynicism and the knowing how it all turns out are simply forgotten – was given to me, like a parting gift, one final time. Dermot's publisher was over from London, along with the publisher's wife and his wife's brother. They'd rented a little cottage on the peninsula. Leland was there, and Dermot's wife, and two painter friends of ours from Belfast who lived nearby, and an Australian painter named Marcus who lived in Berlin and knew Wim Wenders. We all wanted to know about Wim, and Wim's name came up so often it was almost like he was there, too.

After pre-dinner drinks at Ellen's, Dermot cooked spaghetti bolognese – with Dermot, it was always spaghetti bolognese. We smoked joints with our meal, and as our bodies went limp, and we writhed with laughter we couldn't recall the reason for and struggled to remain upright, it seemed we had become the spaghetti that was heaped upon our plates. Later we played pool back at Ellen's, and afterwards I danced on Leland's kitchen table.

The following day, full of woozy cheer, we zoomed through the countryside – the English, being far more sober, the designated drivers – singing along with Hank Williams cassettes and hearing the literary gossip from London. The sea was everywhere. We played more pool, at Ernie's in Carney this time, and we bought a salmon in Rosses Point. We did the deal over a drink in a dark bar. That night we cooked a proper meal – or the English did – for Dermot always insisted on eating properly when we were on the razz.

The days were gloriously sunny and everybody fell waywardly in love with everybody else, and there were kisses around corners and proclamations of feeling, and there were tears and the gnashing of teeth. In the fields around us, the cattle lowed in all their oblivious and beastly majesty. On the kitchen table in the little cottage was a bowl of grapes, and I told Marcus that I had always wanted to be fed purple grapes while drinking wine from a pewter chalice – a fantasy of classical antiquity – and he complied. I put my head on his lap and he held above me a cluster of fat purple grapes and I took them, one by one, into my mouth. We had no pewter chalices to hand but made do. With the early evening sun streaming in the window and all the food and drink and friends I would ever need, I wanted the world to stop, right there. If we could just keep colluding in the dream, I thought, it would never have to end.

But the English went home and the Australian went back to Berlin, and we were left with ourselves and only our usual pool of unimpressive excuses. Everything crashed, in the way it always did, and all the ghouls lined up for their pound of flesh and the loneliness was as sterile and cold as steel.

One month later, when the fear of going mad had at last exceeded the fear of sobriety's diminishment, and I had finally grown both bored and exhausted of the enslavement, that part of life came to an end. Though it would take six months to be rid of the shakes, and though I sometimes felt like Odysseus looking down into Hades, the ghosts of my past swarming forth, on the whole I felt a sense of deliverance, and the relief was instantaneous. In those first weeks I had a clear image of myself standing in my living room (feelings had a way of externalizing themselves then, so that I sometimes saw myself before me, in quick illustrative cameos), a black suitcase in each hand, tired, chastened and looking oddly like a travelling salesman, as though after a long and arduous journey. I was Odysseus and Willie Loman both, and I knew, as surely as I had ever known anything, that I'd come home at last.

I also saw in my living room one night a pair of hands proffering a silver platter. The platter was empty, but it was perfectly clear to me that what was on it was my life: I was being handed back my life on a platter. At the same time, the hands were gesturing, for these images (I wouldn't describe them as hallucinations – I didn't believe that the hands and the platter were real – but as visions that felt partly spontaneous, partly conjured) adhered to the logic of dreams rather than the laws of the three-dimensional world. What the hands were saying, their palms facing outward, was that there was nothing required of me in the way of justification. *Here is your life*, was the message. *No questions asked*.

Later, of course, there were many questions and much guilt, and there were memories of acts that couldn't possibly be justified. But in the beginning, I just felt forgiven. I didn't even miss alcohol. When I was in the company of people who were drinking, I felt, as I watched them grow tipsy, as though I were on a dock watching a boat move slowly out to sea, its deck peopled with gay revellers (champagne, flappers, a beautiful frivolity), sailing off to somewhere I couldn't go. I stood, waving goodbye, and then I turned back to my life, like someone old and, though mindful of a form of loss, not at all unhappy.

In this state that felt oddly like an afterlife, in which my desires were, for the first time, in perfect harmony with the contents of my life, I began to read again. One day I sat on my bed reading Schopenhauer and I had the distinct sensation that I could actually feel my neurons firing and, what was more, could feel their delight. The joy was serene and well managed, for my concentration was intense. My whole brain was like a numb limb regaining sensation, and I'd never felt as lucid in my life.

Consciousness feels rightly affronted by attempts at its annihilation and will reassert itself, with claws. But if it degrades us beyond telling in taking its revenge, it is also capable of enormous acts of forgiveness. That September, the peninsula glistened under an Indian summer sun. The hills rose and fell in the distance, blond fields of mown hay alternating with green. Over the backyard a tangerine light hung in the late afternoons. My perfectly white cat bounded through the tall grass and the world reeled before me, ecstatic in its own right, unable to contain itself as the object of my rediscovery.

I took walks along the shore at sunset, when the mountains deepened to a cobalt blue against the horizon and the surface of the sea went silky, and I felt like a newcomer to some marvellous, uncharted country. Nights I stepped outside at midnight, and more than the stars it was the very act of looking up that was a revelation. For I had not realized until then how I had slouched, literally, through the days.

Thirteen

In the autumn of 1975, when my father's contract with the Trail-blazers has expired and money is getting tight, we leave our perch overlooking the lake and move to an end unit in a row of town-houses in a newish development a few miles away. The entire house is carpeted in a dull, slightly soiled-looking pea green. The kitchen lino is also green, as are the countertops and appliances. There is no backyard, only a slim strip of mulch on a slope out the back, which gives the impression that the house is sliding down the hill and into the creek below. It is an ugly and constricted place, the perfect venue for unhappy times.

I am old enough now to notice the news and sometimes to be haunted by it. I am fascinated by Patty Hearst, by the whole idea of being stolen out of your own life and turned into someone else. I look at the *Time* photos of 'Tania': in combat gear, wielding a sub-machine gun, behind her the seven-headed cobra of the Symbionese Liberation Army; grainy stills from the Hibernia Bank heist, Tania handling crowd control, her hair stylish, a trim peacoat that suits her; under arrest and smiling, a clenched-fist salute. Her mugshot on the cover, pencil-thin brows over racoon eyes, APPREHENDED stamped across it.

Charles Manson invades my consciousness, too. We gather around the set and watch *Helter Skelter*, the two-part TV movie about the Manson 'family'. (The Tate murders, I learn with horror, were committed on my birthday.) At the end, before the credits roll, it says that Charles Manson will be eligible for parole in 1978. People who live in California all want to come and live in Oregon–everybody knows that – and I am sure this goes for Charles Manson, too. I am sure that he will get parole and that he will come to Oregon and find my family and, with his mad shining eyes, kill us all.

*

My father still has not found a steady job. He is trying his hand at a few things, but nothing has quite taken off. The most promising was the plan to develop a 300-acre island owned by friends of his, two miles off the coast of Antigua, but nothing has come of it. Now, he's working on commission, selling time shares in Hawaii and Mexico from a rickety laminated desk in our green-carpeted house. But the country is deep in a recession, and between the economy and his own discomfort (the toadying of salesmanship doesn't suit him), it's tough. When he does sell, the company can be slow to pay out his commission.

Meanwhile, my mother has gotten a job. She had worked, briefly, in Winston-Salem: with her nest empty during school hours, she had taken a job in the L'Eggs division of Hanes Hosiery, makers of pantyhose packaged in plastic eggs. She was in consumer relations and complaint analysis, answering letters all day. She had a big beautiful desk that she said looked just like Nixon's. She didn't need to work, but she liked new adventures, and my father was all for it. Her mother, too, was supportive, accosting friends after Mass, coaxing them to buy L'Eggs. But some months later, when my mother, a little understimulated writing letters about pantyhose, decided to study for a realtor's licence, her mother struck a familiar tone of admonition and impending doom:

> I think you would be very foolish to change your job. You have too many responsibilities at home and you would be foolish to push your luck. Someone will suffer from it and you could ruin your health and have a breakdown or a painful facial tic. Do not be greedy or you will be punished . . .

Things have changed since then, and while her mother will never understand a woman wanting a career for its own sake – I never did like successful women – she knows well what it means to have bills to pay in uncertain times. Now, for three days and $150 a week, my mother takes photographs and writes articles for the biweekly newspaper in our town. It's the kind of work she'd dreamed of thirty years ago, back when she was writing for the college newspaper.

She covers city council meetings, Rotary Club luncheons and activities at the seniors' centre, and writes features on local citizens. Every day is different and the world is full of inspirational people – the paraplegic author, the octogenarian couple who raise money for orphanages in destitute corners of the world, the twelve-year-old fighting leukaemia. It keeps her own problems in perspective.

Whether her reports on Mike – unfailingly optimistic, almost always noting an improvement – are a reflection of her refusal to indulge in despair, evidence of her capacity for denial, or simply an attempt to shield her mother from the worst, isn't always clear.

He was so calm (and sleeping away these gorgeous days) that I cut him down to one pill in the evening. He has been really super – no more funny talk in the high voice. An occasional giggle at odd times, but don't we all want to laugh at the absurdities of life once in a while?

Neither is it clear from the letters whether my father shares her optimism, or her compassion – he has always been less forgiving of other people's frailties. What is certain that year is that as Mike's illness becomes more entrenched, my father is slipping away, belonging to us less and less. I am distressed not only by the splintering of our former cohesion (our four heads bowed as we walked morosely from the deserted Coliseum), but by the sense that my father's current ineffectuality – his inability to reignite his professional life – is somehow our fault. I see him as a being of a slightly higher order, deserving of a better life than the one the rest of us can offer. The boils that plague him, which he has caught from Mike, are merely the physical evidence of an unspoken truth: that our collective demoralization has its source not in him, but is a contagion the rest of us are spreading.

And yet, just as he is slipping away, I grow, paradoxically, closer to my father. He has been a distant and, because his work involved a lot of travelling, often absent figure. But this year, we play tennis together a few times a week at the club just up the street from our house. Though I am eleven and he is fifty-one, we have each just discovered the game, and have fallen in love with it.

'D'you want to hit some?' he'll say, and off we go. Sometimes we play games and he plays left-handed, to make it fairer, but mostly we just rally for the hour. Because he is so consistent, every ball as straight and clean as if it were being shot from one of those machines I sometimes practise with, I play better with him than I do with anyone else. The slight gawkiness I have begun to feel vanishes, along with whatever inner uncertainties might dog me. There are between us moments of grace and fluidity and fellow feeling that we will never manage to replicate in any other circumstances, the *tok-tok-tok* of our racquets on the ball like a dialogue between us, the back and forth of it ringing out clear and true.

In the room next to the room with the rickety desk, where the Portland Trailblazers and Vacation Internationale notepads are stacked – stationery that will follow us around for years after my father has gone (a triumph of parsimony over emotionalism) – is the sofa on which Mike lives. Mike's 'room' is meant to be a kind of family room, and so it has no proper doors. If we are coming down the stairs, or going into my father's office to watch television or out through the back sliding doors, we cannot avoid passing through it – spying him as he sleeps, giggles, talks to himself, or simply sits and does nothing, but always in his woollen skullcap, which he now wears even to sleep. A gloom surrounds him, moving with him through the house. His expression is often blank and impassive. He has developed a strange slumping gait. His long arms hang low against his outer thighs, and his head is inclined slightly forwards. With his beard, and his odd physical bearing, he looks like an evolutionary precursor to *Homo sapiens*. Any sense I'd once had of him as someone hip and fascinating has vanished. Most of the time I feel foolish in front of him, as though his random bursts of laughter are a judgement levelled at me. Suffused with the self-consciousness of early puberty, I feel seen through, fraudulent, my every normal act a pathetic capitulation to the arbitrary social conventions that his madness has somehow lifted him above. This sense of him as an unmerciful Greek chorus is one that will only intensify during my teenage years. Proper payback, perhaps, for the fun my best friend and I had at his expense.

And yet, beneath the sullen silences, amidst the nonsensical ramblings, there are pockets of rationality, hope and warmth. A number of his letters from that year mirror my mother's optimism – her belief that it can all, still, be put right.

Dear Fanny,

Wish I could hear your voice right now, but that would be a little bit impossible from so far away. Lines are hard to come with on such a time as right now but here goes. First, I want to thank you for the hospitality this summer as my career really needed a boost and my summer was fantastic . . . Really feel good this evening. My boils are slowly going away and my mind feels calmer than it has in quite a while. Mom and Dad are even counting on my progress . . . Please pray for me Fanny at church in the morning as I think we can make it. Just think if we all had jobs and were moving around in the city what the news would be like at dinner time. Maybe the world is getting warmer all around.

All my love, Mike

In the attempt to give his career a boost, there is almost nothing he isn't willing to try, or to undergo. Between bouts of sleep, his life is a constant round of odd (and short-lived) jobs, visits to doctors, to the vocational education centre and the local community college, tests for everything from his career preferences to his liver enzymes to venereal disease. Samples of his hair and blood and urine are taken. He enrols in judo, creative writing and bridge classes, not lasting more than a couple of weeks in any of them. His medication is changed, dosages are raised and lowered. He has recently been taken off Trilafon and put on Haldol, a dopamine-inhibiting antipsychotic he takes to control his delusions and hallucinations. It can cause stiffening of the limbs, aching muscles and joints, drowsiness and a mask-like appearance. It is likely responsible for his strange new walk and the blankness of his expression. Haldol can also cause muscle spasms and uncontrollable shaking. Christmas Day finds him on the kitchen floor, his long legs extended on the green linoleum, one of them trembling violently as he stares at it in horror.

Our sister is there, desperate to help him, but she has no answer when he looks up at her, terrified, and says, 'What's happening to me, Robin?'

I'll be happy to see 1975 go, my mother writes. *God said 1976 will be better.* For a little while, it looks as though it might be. Mike's letters are becoming ever more lucid. He seems genuinely interested in finding a job, not just washing dishes but something in line with his interests. He has an interview with social services. He is going to try for a position as a laboratory science aid, caring for animals used in medical experiments. My mother writes:

> *The last few weeks have been like a miracle. I don't know whether it's the new medicine, or finally his maturing, but he doesn't do the giggling anymore – just a real laugh at the right time, and the sunshine smile you always talked about. I do hope he'll get a job soon, as I know he is terribly lonesome all day. We go for walks on Sunday, and I play scrabble etc, with him. I really see God's Hand in his recovery.*

In April 1976, Mike is well enough to make plans to return to school. He has enrolled at Portland State University, where over the summer he will take biology, chemistry and math classes, required before he can embark on a two-year course to become a medical technician; apparently, all the tests he has undergone have not put him off the idea of testing the body fluids of others. At the end of a letter to his grandparents outlining his plans, he writes:

> *Today after church when the sun was out and we were on our way home Mom mentioned wouldn't it be nice if we could go for a walk on the boardwalk. I replied, that would be great and I'm sure the two of us each thought of our fun times in Ocean City . . . I wish I could come back but I've got my obligations here now for the next two years so it may be a while before I see you. Be good. All my love, Mike*

There is something poignant in the mention of his 'obligations', in the quiet sense of pride that comes through. The letter is like one he might've written at eighteen, minus the swagger. He spends the birthday money his grandparents send to buy the organic chemistry textbook he will need for the course, and he applies himself to the biology books my mother brings him from the library. The course will be hard and he is anxious to get a head start. His psychiatrist says that he won't need to see Mike again until the autumn.

He is a different person than you saw last summer, my mother writes. *It's like a miracle.*

My father has moved to a furnished office-apartment about forty-five minutes from our house in order to oversee the financing and development of an as-yet-unbuilt tennis club. He comes home for dinner a few nights a week, and sometimes we go to him and he gets a bucket of Kentucky Fried Chicken or takeaway burgers. In letters to Fanny, my mother explains my father's move in terms of his being closer to the job, and continues to project an upbeat persona.

Life is very peaceful and pleasant, believe it or not.
Spring is coming and I feel very happy today.
We are amazingly happy despite our little reverses. It will bring us out
of the fairy tale world back to reality.

But she is only pretending. The marriage is effectively over. My father is in love with someone else. After twenty-eight years with my mother, he has decided he wants a divorce.

There are only three of us kids living at home at the time – Mike, Tim and me. My parents assemble us in the green living room. Though the only line I can remember from the discussion is 'Your mother and I have decided to get a divorce' (or was it 'your father and I'? Who was speaking?), it soon becomes clear that the split is my father's decision. While my father tries to talk to Tim in his room – Tim, who tends towards the explosive, has flung himself on the bed in tears and thrown things around his room – my mother stays with me. I tend towards the implosive, and am hunched over, sitting on the edge of my bed, also in tears. My mother sits beside me and I say to her, 'Don't you love each other any more?'

With just a split-second's hesitation, she says, 'We love each other in our own way.'

And then I ask, 'What about Mike? Isn't anyone going to talk to Mike?'

I know that if my father is in Tim's room and my mother is in my room, Mike is downstairs on his own.

Did I really care? Did I really, at eleven, worry about how my twenty-five-year-old brother was coping with the news of our parents' divorce? He was way too strange by then, too distant and intermittently scary, to elicit in a child any instinctive tenderness. And yet, I can recall quite clearly sitting on the edge of my bed and picturing him as he sat on the edge of the pull-out sofa, down in the ill-lit family room, his leg wagging nervously, all alone in the dark after such an earth-shattering announcement.

My mother says, 'Mike is older. We'll talk to him later.'

The question arises in part from the desire to deflect attention from my own neediness and fear. But it is more than that. I *am* worried about Mike, in the way a child worries about a pet left behind when the family goes on holiday. The way a child thinks, *We should write kitty a letter so she won't be lonely*, as though kitty, despite her inscrutable and alien nature, has needs just like our own. And the question is a sign that I am panicking. That I am trying to insist on our continued togetherness. I want everyone accounted for, gathered round, as though we have just passed through some dangerous terrain and it's time for a reassuring head count. But my timing is off. The fact is, terra incognita is all before us. We have only just begun to lose each other.

My father comes into the room and my mother looks at him and says, sadly and with the slightest trace of accusation, 'She asked if we still love each other.' Of my father's response, I have no recollection.

The next thing I know, I'm standing at the sliding glass door in the kitchen, looking out at the mist – that not-quite-drizzle that is the Oregon winter. I'm like something from a thousand films I've seen since – a solitary figure gazing at a grey world. I am older, suddenly, than I want to be. The sense of time-lapse is reflected in the memory-image itself, for every time I call up the snapshot, I find

myself taller than I could possibly have been at the time. The cos-
tuming, however, is historically accurate. I am wearing a beloved
staple of my eleven-year-old wardrobe: a polyester brown blouse
with coloured flowers all over it. As I stand there, I am coming to a
momentous conclusion. The conclusion I am coming to is that this
business, this divorce business, is adult business. I don't know who
to blame or who to be angry with, and so, I decide, I will refrain
from feeling anything at all until I am old enough to understand
what the right thing to feel is, at which point I will commence feeling it. I am aspiring, in the best Aristotelian sense, to be angry with
the right person, to the right degree and for the right purpose.

After some time gazing out the window – twenty seconds or ten
minutes – I decide, like a good soldier, to get on with my day. I have
plans, after all. As on so many Saturdays, I will cross the scrubby
field beside our house and make the quick dash across Kerr Park-
way to Tanglewood Drive, to the house of my little boyfriend (he *is*
little, his littleness accentuated by his billowing head of black curls
and the extremely puffy down jacket he wears) in order to play two-
square in his driveway.

My mother questions the wisdom of this. 'Are you sure you feel
like going out to play?'

'Yes,' I say, 'I'm sure.' What else is one to do?

When I get to Ben's house, I tell him the news. It's like a movie
then, too. We are child actors, adrift in a world that is beyond our
comprehension, wanting to be a comfort to one another but with
no vocabulary, either verbal or physical, for doing so. Ben screws up
one side of his mouth and tilts his head. Both of these gestures are
habitual, and will one day belong to his own quirky repertoire of
flirtation, but for now they are simply an expression of self-
consciousness and sympathy. Ben is genuinely sensitive, and he
adores me. But he is eleven. What can he do? So we stand there
in the damp driveway, Ben holding the red rubber ball loosely
against his stomach – for though he has no idea what to say, he
knows enough not to play two-square through the story of my
parents' divorce.

Ben will move that summer to Seattle and it will be thirty years before I hear anything of him. He will email me, out of the blue, saying that he'd come across our class picture while he was cleaning out his attic. By then he will have two children, younger than we were that day, and he will be in the middle of his own divorce.

For the moment, we cannot imagine ourselves any older than we are right now. Finally, he lets the ball drop and knocks it gently into my square. The game resumes. Muted, rhythmic, familiar. And we are a comfort to each other, together, as though encircled by something we cannot see, with the ball bouncing between us, under the not-quite-drizzle of a winter's day.

In the beginning, my mother tries to talk sense into my father, to remind him of where he belongs. She believes the decision to divorce is a kind of temporary insanity brought on by the difficulties of the previous two years. Her own mother saw the toll they took when she wrote, *I feel sorry for him when the band stops playing.* Now she sends a two-page treatise she has written titled 'What is a Divorce?'

> *Just some 'low' name which disconnects you from your duties (love) and a sneaky legal way to dump your faults and blame it on your partner . . .*

In 1976, such sentiments can still be uttered without irony – especially if one is a septuagenarian. My father's own mother is devastated. She tells Fanny that she cut a picture of Jack out of *Sports Illustrated*, with his shaggy seventies hair and paintbrush moustache, and sent it to him along with a much older one she had fished from the attic, which showed her son clean-cut. She enclosed a message: *What are you hiding from? Take off the mask.*

My mother's views on marriage are much the same as those of her mother and mother-in-law. She and my father have lived more than half a lifetime together, often in happiness. She has two children still to raise and one grown son she is trying to shepherd back to sanity. But there's no reasoning with him. And so, in June, we leave the ugly green house, and my mother takes Tim and Mike and me to live in a house on the other side of town.

150

She doesn't grovel, make scenes or become noticeably depressed. She regards that sort of carry-on as undignified. Life makes its demands and you rise to them, with generosity and a sense of humour. A thousand years ago (as she would say herself), as a reporter for Immaculata's school paper, she had transcribed the words of John Powers, head of the famous Powers' Modeling Agency:

Always be the natural girl and everyone will love you. If you wish to be truly charming, spend yourself for others, forget yourself, and the glow of charm will brighten your face.

Now, after the changes wrought by feminism and the sexual revolution, such advice smacks of condescension and chauvinism. Yet, in a way, it still describes her. Self-obsession is alien, as is regret. Such are the secrets of her equilibrium. Six months after my father has moved out, she will write to her mother:

Please don't be bitter and think that I've had an unhappy marriage. We had a lot more good years and laughs than most people have. If I had the choice to make all over again, even knowing what I know now, I'd still do the same thing . . .

★

Somewhat surprisingly, perhaps even a touch masochistically, we spend that Fourth of July evening – my mother, Tim, Mike and I – at our beloved old house, the guests of its current owners.

You may remember it's high and off the back hill is a great view of the fireworks on the lake. The house looks good, and they let Molly go through (we all could have but didn't) to see her old room, etc.

I know, even from a distance of thirty-five years, what it is I am looking for as I prowl about the house. I am eleven, old enough to intuit that physical locations are like handrails we use to grope our way into the past, but still young enough to confuse the spatial with the temporal. What I am looking for is the past, embodied, *our* past, that beautiful sunny dream we had. It lives on here without us, I am sure, like a pet we couldn't bring along and so entrusted to the next owners. And I am coming back to visit us, as we were in all our glorious and blissful ignorance, prior to our expulsion from paradise.

By that summer, something elemental and fine has left our lives. It is faith, the unconscious belief that the future will unfold as splendidly as has the past, that it will always be a case of better and surer, that the people we love can be relied on to behave in a predictable and reassuring manner.

To see myself at such an age mourning the loss of paradise – groping about, even, for a point of re-entry – does not surprise me. What surprises me is that the others hadn't come along, that my mother allowed me to go spelunking, all alone, down the long hallway to my old bedroom, on such a big doomed errand.

Fourteen

My motive that July evening in 1976 was instinctive and hazy, but in the decades that followed, as I found myself regularly visiting houses we'd once lived in, the agenda grew more explicit. It involved a conscious calculation of effects, an orchestrated déjà vu. I wanted to cast my present level of awareness back, like a net, over the past and enjoy it all afresh, properly conscious of its preciousness. It is not unusual in my family, this going back to old houses. We are always looking for ourselves, peering at the structures that have contained us, as though they are those puzzles in which objects are hidden. We roll past in cars, slow as kerb-crawlers, or we walk right up to our old doorsteps. We knock and smile and say, 'Hi! We used to live here.'

But we only ever do that with the houses of our suburban years, on streets we could easily picture ourselves living on today. We never come back to places like Mount Airy, to the apartments of my parents' early marriage, to the neighbourhoods gone grim with wear.

In early spring 2006 I began a trip that would take me from New York to Florida, connecting the dots of the first decades of Mike's life. His first home was the grandly named Stenton Manor at the corner of Belfield and Sharpnack in Mount Airy – *Garden apt, 2nd from the right, ground floor*, my mother had written by way of directions. The friend who was driving me around Philadelphia was Wendy, whom I'd first met in Ocean City during the summer of 1984. Wendy has lived in Philadelphia all her life, and not always in the most exclusive neighbourhoods, but she grew edgy as we approached Stenton Manor. A clutch of young black men hanging on the corner – all attitude and sidelong glances, their pants riding low – took note of our arrival: two white girls who must be lost. The dreariness of the neighbourhood was heightened by the weather. The sky was a flat pale grey, the air ominously still, the trees bare.

My plan was that once I'd found the right apartment, I would knock and I would say, *Hi! My parents lived here in 1950*, and the occupant (hand slapped to forehead) would say, *Whoa! You gotta be kiddin' me!* He or she would invite us in, would tell us about life in Stenton Manor in 2006, and together we would marvel at how the years fly by.

The problem with my mother's description was that there was more than one building in Stenton Manor, so determining which was '2nd from the right' was not as straightforward as I'd expected. Based on the memory of a photo of my mother standing in front of one of the buildings (she is twenty-five years old and looking uncharacteristically dowdy, in a long skirt and shapeless sweater), I decided to knock on the door I guessed might have been theirs. A heavy-set woman appeared at the plate-glass window. She had pants on but from the waist up she wore only a bra – voluminous and stark white against her black skin and housing, even in this age of breast implants, the largest breasts I had ever seen. I thought to myself, *Those are real*.

I told her that we were looking for the apartment where my parents used to live. She stared at us as if to say, *And I'm supposed to care?* Then said, rather redundantly, 'Well, I'm not dressed right now.'

I looked left, then right. I said to Wendy, 'I don't think this is it.' We apologized and turned away.

I recalled something my mother had said about their apartment being on the corner. And I remembered that in the photograph I had seen, in which my mother is standing next to the Stenton Manor sign, there is a sapling in front of her. This block was U-shaped, and didn't have a tree in front of it, but there was a tree in front of the next L-shaped building, now thick-trunked and very tall.

There were two apartments on the ground floor of the L-shaped building. The one on the right had a doormat that read, *Welcome to My Muslim Home*. No one answered our knock. We tried the door to our left. A woman peered out from between the slats of a plastic venetian blind and white iron vertical bars. There was a smaller set of eyes to her right. The woman was holding a cordless phone; she was in the middle of a conversation. I explained what I was looking for, and I thought she was trying to be helpful, though all I could see

were her eyes, and it was difficult to guess her expression behind the crosshatch. I felt instinctively that this was my parents' old apartment. But I also knew that the woman was not going to invite us in to talk about how time flies and how much the neighbourhood had changed. We thanked her and headed back to the car.

Though Stenton Manor was Mike's first home, when he was just out of hospital in May 1950 my mother took him to her parents' place on Wayne Avenue in Upper Darby. Once a tree-lined, middle-class section of Philadelphia, the area subsequently went the way of Mount Airy. Driving there, my friend and I asked directions three separate times – once of a man behind the counter at a gas station who might have been Iranian ('I am not saying black or white, but neighbourhood is bad – after nine o'clock, don't go there'), then of a taxi driver who tried, unsuccessfully, in Urdu or something, to get directions for us on his mobile, and finally of a Latino man on the street who said, 'I no speak English.'

'*Estoy buscando Avenida Wayne*,' I said, not because I thought he might know where Wayne Avenue was in Spanish any more than he did in English, but because I wanted to make him feel welcome in my country.

He answered in Spanish. I heard the word Ecuador, and then something about his not knowing the neighbourhood.

'*Entiendo*,' I said, though I wasn't sure I did.

He told me my Spanish was good, which it was not. We were all smiles now.

'*Mucho gusto!*' he called happily as I rolled up my window.

'*Mucho gusto!*' I cried.

After much circling, we found the house on Wayne Avenue, which I recognized immediately from photographs. There was a single light in the downstairs window and for a moment I could see them framed there, my grandparents, cardboard cut-outs frozen in the midst of some domestic activity, as though they had waited through the decades for me to happen by. Something was odd about the small front yard: it was as though a hurricane had torn through this single property and taken all trees and plant life with it, leaving nothing but the odd stick poking up out of the ground and a few lucky blades of grass. Even the several ceramic plant pots were empty. A slimy, grey-green film was growing down the walls from under the rafters. Inside could have been anything from a meth lab to a pair of work-worn parents helping the kids with their homework. But like every old house of ours I've ever seen, it was remarkable for looking exactly as it does in photographs taken decades ago, as if to say, *Yes, it was all just as you have been led to believe.*

The day of Mike's arrival here is preserved on a tiny passport-sized photo in which my mother sits up in bed cradling her firstborn. On the back, Fanny has written:

Anita & Mike just home from Hospital
7118 Wayne ave

Fanny would paper-clip the photo to a postcard she received from Mike in December 1975. Out of what impulse did she pair this image of absolute innocence with a reminder of his twenty-fifth summer, the summer he gave them scabies, and Father Flynn administered the Sacrament of the Sick? The picture and the card remained together for three decades, the paper clip wearing a pair of rusty parallel lines into the photo and the front of the card, which shows a reproduction of a woodblock print entitled *That Oceanic Feeling of Love.*

DEAR FANNY AND NONY,

*JUST THE NAME OF THIS CARD WHICH A FRIEND MADE
AT SCHOOL REMINDED ME THAT I SHOULD WRITE TO
YOU AND THANK YOU GREATLY FOR THE LOVELY SUMMER
WHICH I SPENT WITH YOU AND THE LOVELY CHRISTMAS.
TOOK SOME OF MY SUMMER MONEY OUT OF THE BANK
THE OTHER DAY AND LOST IT SO I HOPE IT TURNS UP IN
THE NEXT DAY OR SO. CAN'T GO WITHOUT MONEY.
CAN'T STAY WITH IT EITHER BUT YOU'VE GOT TO
HAVE IT. OR ELSE YOU'RE OUT OF IT. PLEASE BE GOOD.
ALL MY LOVE, MIKE*

The friend who'd made the woodblock print postcard was one of those I met that spring, as I travelled from New York to Florida. I met them at bus terminals and train stations and pre-appointed street corners. They mouthed my name uncertainly across train tracks. They lived, a lot of them, in the fairy-tale towns of the eastern seaboard, in the muffled stillness peculiar to affluent neighbourhoods. One had a cellphone on which he showed me a video shot, at 120 miles an hour, from the front seat of his race car. Another said to me, as we drove away from the station where he'd picked me up, the silence accentuated by a thick blanket of spring snow, 'In there, they live up that road.' He was referring to the Clintons, whom he occasionally bumped into at the grocery store.

Thirty-five years before, they'd played catch on the quad at Duke and talked about civil rights. Now they had offices in preserved buildings or glass towers, or they worked from home, managing portfolios or filing copy from desks that overlooked expansive yards and well-stocked driveways. A few were unconventional – creative, artistic, intellectual. One lived on a latter-day commune, and after we spoke in his studio I was invited to break bread with what felt like a small group of hold-outs from a bygone age.

What they told me depended not only on the kind of people they were and the roles they had played in Mike's life, but at times on what they thought I needed to hear. They believed, not entirely in error, that my mission was to reassure myself that Mike, too, had known happiness. That he was someone I could be proud of. Sometimes they felt consoled by what they told me and other times discomfited – when they reached, as they inevitably did, the point in the story at which Mike vanished from their lives, or simply became incomprehensible.

Once or twice I was embarrassed, when the stories had a sexual component, though I was also happy for him on occasion. Late spring of his junior year, after he'd broken up with Susan, there was a long weekend when Mike had stayed on campus and found himself incredibly amorous. Ross, who was telling me the story as we sat on his living-room sofa, said that Mike had just walked by the nurses' dorm and picked up a chick. Ross was impressed and envious. But he wasn't surprised. 'He was an open guy with good vibes,' he said, 'and I thought that on some primal level his spirit was very strong.'

Another day I sat in a meeting room and a man named David placed on the polished oval table a scrapbook from 1968–9, freshman basketball at Duke. I had never met David before, but I liked him. He was a big man with a soft Southern drawl, and he had an unambiguous wholesomeness about him that made me feel safe. He leaned his large frame back in the leather chair and looked me in the eye and told me how much he had respected Mike that year they played together. David was on a basketball scholarship and Mike wasn't; and yet, David said, Mike came out every day and gave 110 per cent, knowing he wouldn't get game time, just because he loved it.

He turned the pages of his scrapbook and together we peered at the tiny print of the box scores. The high point of Mike's season was the Freshman Preliminary at North Greenville Junior College: he was five for ten from the field and grabbed three rebounds. Otherwise, his presence in the box scores was scant. Sometimes his name didn't appear at all. Sometimes it appeared with a string of zeros after it: he had gotten in the game but wasn't able to rack up a single stat. In one box, the first letter of his name was missing and he was identified as Ike McCloskey. More than all those zeros, more than David with his nice life and his kindness, it was the missing 'M' that got to me.

One day, as I said goodbye to Mike's old friend Kevin and walked down Market Street in Philadelphia, I thought, *Wouldn't it be nice to invite Kevin down for a day to our family get-together in Ocean City this summer?* It had been more than thirty years, but everyone remembered Kevin, at least by name. He remembered all of us. Kevin is successful, intelligent, compassionate. The image of him (less his wife and children, I noticed) in the midst of my family filled me with an immense, disproportionate warmth. I realized almost immediately what I was doing. I wanted us all to be able to pretend for a day that Kevin was Mike, that this was who Mike had become, and I felt ashamed of the impulse, and of its obviousness.

In North Carolina, I stayed with my brother Steve. During the days, when he worked, I drove through Winston-Salem, to the places that had been a part of our lives. It was raining and misty and the oaks dripped overhead and I felt like I was in the middle of a fable. Since we left North Carolina in 1972, I hadn't spent more than a few hours there, but I could feel, in some barely conscious way, that it belonged to my life.

During my rounds of Winston-Salem, I wandered through the country club where my father had golfed and my parents had dined and danced, and where we kids had spent our summers swimming. In the more than thirty years since I had seen the swimming pools, I had thought about them countless times, likely because the designations by which we had referred to them – Baby, Middle Sized and Big People's – had been imprinted on my mind as a crude map of my progress through life. What I had given no thought to at all was the peculiar faded pinkness of the footpath that snaked between them. And yet as soon as I saw that colour something in me stirred. More than any landmark I had so far seen, it was at that moment of looking down that I knew – not from any photograph (for this oddly coloured path was captured in no photograph), not from any story passed down through the years or any letter (it was inconsequential) – that I had been here before.

One night Steve took me to a Mexican restaurant and there, for the first time in our lives, we had an actual conversation about our

brother. Whatever we'd said to each other before had taken the form of elliptical asides – no different, really, from the kind of exchanges I'd had about Mike with my parents. It was a quasi-silence that in thirty years I had never thought to question. It wasn't that the subject of Mike was verboten, or that anyone was in denial. Mike is not so much the elephant in the room as a mined area we approach with caution. Any real discussion of him is painful enough that it needs sufficient justification – a link to some practical action or a decision that needs to be taken. Otherwise it is just going over sad ground to no purpose.

When we lost him, Steve suffered more than any of us kids, though not because the two of them had enjoyed any natural affinity. They were always opposites. Steve was gregarious, extroverted and rebellious, while Mike was a model son, self-contained and so reserved that when the family moved down south, Steve felt obliged to compensate by being extra friendly, lest people take them for northern snobs. Physically, they were opposites, too. Mike was lean, at times even gaunt, with a suggestion of the ethereal. Steve was blocky, earthbound.

But Steve suffered because they grew up side by side, just two years between them. Autumn Saturdays on Ferguson Avenue in

Broomall in the mid sixties, playing touch football with the neighbourhood kids, the air knife-sharp and the leaves in tufts against the kerbside. Or basketball at the hoop behind the garage, their father rebounding and the two boys rotating in half circles, a quick-fire drill to improve their jump shots. Or going one-on-one against each other while their father refereed. They were pitcher and catcher in Little League, and they were altar boys together – scrub-faced and smart in their black cassocks and white surplices. They shared a room in the Ferguson Avenue house, and Steve, lying in the bottom bunk, lights out and the obligatory prayers said, would hear soft cheering sounds coming from above: *Heah, heah, heah.* It was Mike, playing the role of adoring crowd at his own fantasy basketball game.

Steve first saw the change in him in 1973, when Mike was drifting around North Carolina and Steve was at college in Virginia. Reports filtered up that Mike had been seen behaving oddly. Steve put it down to tripping and didn't worry, until he met him at a party during spring break. Mike was laughing at things he shouldn't be laughing at, giggling to himself, speaking in non sequiturs. At first, Steve wondered if he was doing it for attention, putting it on the way people did then. But, no, there was more to it than that. Steve just didn't know what it was. Embarrassed by his own brother, he'd shied away from him, and felt ashamed of himself then, too.

Steve had given me, when I arrived, his copy of *A Beautiful Mind*, Sylvia Nasar's biography of John Nash, the Nobel Prize-winning mathematician and economist who suffered from schizophrenia. (Steve has seen the movie several times and occasionally – he is a good mimic – does Russell Crowe doing John Nash, though it is always the quieter, not-quite-broken Nash rather than the florid psychotic.) He also gave me CDs of the Grateful Dead and Country Joe & the Fish, bands that had once been favourites of Mike's, and I listened to them as I drove, these wistful druggy riffs on the whole sad, tired business of living. Travelling along I-40 East in the cool spring sun, heading towards Durham – the road Mike would've hitched between home and the university, the road he would've taken with my parents on those first trips to Duke – I wept to the strains of Country Joe's 'Here I Go Again' in a way that both embarrassed and consoled me.

At Duke, I found Mike's old dorm – House P on Kilgo Quad. It was March, so the trees on the quad were still mostly bare, though it was warm enough that the students had set up tables outside, each devoted to a worthy cause. The guy manning the 'End Slavery in Niger' table wore a Hurricane Katrina sweatshirt that said, *Make Levees, Not War*. Across from House P, a white sheet with a red ribbon painted on it hung from a second-floor window: GET TESTED. Pasted on the door of Room 109 – *his room* – were two cheerful blue cardboard nameplates that read *Jorge* and *Muhammad*, evidence that Duke's demographic was now more varied than in Mike's day. What hadn't changed was the safety net of money and privilege. Whatever natural disasters and communicable diseases and distant violations of human rights were a part of the collective consciousness, these were the children of affluence and good fortune, and they would be protected from almost anything.

Steve had contacted our old next-door neighbour in Winston-Salem, still living in the same house, so that she could arrange for me to visit the house where we had lived. I had been back there once before, years ago, on a cross-country road trip, but only outside. It was 1989, a sunny late spring day, the buzz of bees amplified and distinct. The house, the street, the whole neighbourhood were preternaturally still, dreamlike – all so contrary to my memories, which have a kinetic quality to them, as though we were forever tumbling, breathless, from one source of fun to the next. Whatever dust we'd kicked up had long since settled. The place was neat and trim and silent. The owners were not at home. I skulked around the side yard, towards the dank, shadowy no-man's-land underneath the raised deck my father and brothers had built, until the next-door neighbour called to me from her own deck, 'Can I help you?'

I looked up at her and said, 'I used to live here.'

We recognized each other immediately. Alice's husband Jim – the paediatrician who had come to our rescue in the middle of so many nights – appeared beside her and they said Southern things like *Golly*

and *I'll be damned* and then we drank iced tea on their shady deck among the bird chirps and the buzzing bees and talked about I don't remember what. All I remember is the stillness. The sense of it being *after*. As though some massive churning thing had passed and left us bobbing in its wake.

By 2006, when I went back, Jim was dead. He'd had Alzheimer's. Alice was still very much alive, astonishingly alive. Still with her trilling quick-fire Southern accent and her kooky irreverence. Before I went over to our old house, she and I sat chatting in her living room and she looked at me the way people do – fascinated and slightly unnerved – when you arrive out of the distant past, a time traveller sitting blithely on the sofa.

Our old house was still owned by the people who had bought it from my parents: a laid-back, amiable couple who were sitting in the living room reading the day's papers when I knocked. Before they released me to my solitary explorations, we made small talk in the foyer.

'The living room looks so nice,' I said. 'It's different than we had it. There used to be gold carpet, didn't there?'

'The room was gold and black,' the woman said.

'The whole house was gold and black!' her husband said. We laughed. He scratched his head, bewildered, and said, 'Yeah . . . we were like, what's *that* about?'

On behalf of my mother, I felt mildly offended. What *that* was about was reported in the *Raleigh News and Observer* on 28 January 1968:

> Mrs Jack McCloskey decorated her living room in gold and black, the Wake Forest colors. Spanish pieces reflect her Puerto Rican background . . . Large driftwood floor lamps and hanging wrought-iron tables add a dramatic atmosphere to the gold and black color scheme.

Though the gold-and-black colour scheme was perhaps a bit over-done, it reflected her loyalty to the forces in her life.

More small talk – *We had the sofa there . . . Oh, we've got ours here* – and then the man waved his hand in a gesture of release. 'Take your time,' he said. 'Don't worry.'

I felt a greedy impatience, a Christmas-morning kind of excitement. I had a strange desire to tear through the house with my arms spread like the airplanes we used to play at being, making sputtering motor sounds with my lips. Instead I proceeded at a polite pace and tried not to appear to be looking too closely at anything.

Their aesthetic was one of thoughtfully acquired and meticulously arranged clutter. Bits of retro-Americana on the walls. A bumper sticker from the 1960 presidential election. A Singer sewing machine that was actually in use. There were huge old black travellers' trunks plastered with faded stickers: Paris, Palermo, Hungary, Algiers. There were paint sets, train sets, unidentifiable electronic gadgetry. A reproduction of the *Abbey Road* album cover. The style was casual postmodern, with its layers of eras, its toys for grown-ups. It was as though their lives were a constantly unfolding school project.

Our decor, in contrast, had not been playful, ironic or unfolding; it contained no references to popular culture or politics. There was something about our house, the way we had 'done it up', which still smacked of the fifties. It was functional and uncluttered without being consciously minimalist. Our interiors lacked the sense of decor-as-self-expression that developed in later eras. We had our flourishes – the velvet curtains hemmed with black tassels, the octagonal side table suspended from the ceiling by faux antique silver chain-link, the high-backed living-room chairs upholstered in black 'fur'. But none of this mix 'n' match was done with ironic intent. We didn't have that kind of distance on ourselves.

As I poked around the ground floor of the house, details I didn't even know I'd stored materialized before me like dream fragments flashing through a day. (The kitchen cupboards were still the same. And the cupboard handles, like spades in a deck of cards; how fancy they had once seemed to me!) What was really drawing me, though, was downstairs, the old family room. As I stood at the top of the stairwell, I felt a strong sense of the uncanny – something welling up the stairs to meet me, like a vaporous substance that was the essence of us. I felt I would reach the bottom of the stairs and turn the corner into the family room and there we would be – shades that rose and shrank before my unbelieving eyes, or perhaps perfectly substantial, turning to greet me with the joviality and naturalness of cocktail-party guests welcoming a late arrival.

With a slight vertiginousness not dark enough to call foreboding – on the contrary, I couldn't wait to meet us – I descended the stairs and entered the dark-panelled space where we had lived our lives. There was nobody there, of course, but the air was heavy with a residue I had never sensed in any other place. Despite and amidst the copious detritus of other lives, we were there, all of us, frozen in a time and a space in which our collective presence had been concentrated and consistent enough to sustain. This, then, was where we had left ourselves.

Fifteen

What had looked like a miracle in the spring of 1976, Mike's determination to study to become a medical technician, turned out not to be so. Although in August he managed to pass his chemistry course, in September he had what my mother described as 'a spell': another psychotic episode which was bad enough to land him back in Dammasch, the mental hospital. The spell could have included one of a dozen disturbing episodes that have, in the years since, come unmoored from any certain narrative.

Most likely, that September it was the incident at the Catholic church on the main street in our small downtown, the church we'd attended since moving to Oregon. There are several versions of this story, sometimes told by the same person – my mother – on different occasions. In one of the versions, Mike is inside taking off his clothes (not during Mass, thankfully) and the police come and he is carted off to Dammasch. In another, there is a large mailbox in front of the church – one of those that house numerous smaller boxes – and he is perched on it, naked, doing things to himself, things generally considered anatomically impossible. In a third version, the church doesn't figure and the mailbox is located several blocks away, on Sixth Street, along the school-bus route. The school bus passes and all the kids see him. In Tim's version, the police come to the house to talk to our mother; as they are talking, Mike comes strolling, naked, down the street. Tim recalls incredibly vivid sunshine, and being in awe of his big brother's panache.

Mike will have his own account of that day. He will say to an old friend he meets soon after that the incident did take place on the mailbox outside the church, though he will add his own flourishes, which include my mother running screaming from the church, crying, 'I don't know him! Take him away!' (Not only would my mother never have said those things, she is simply not the running, screaming type.) Why did his mother have to put him in the hospital that day? he will ask. Why couldn't she have just taken him home, or sent him to live with his grandparents? For a time, he will keep returning to this scene, obsessing over it.

Whatever happened, it was serious enough to put paid to the belief that Mike was capable of undertaking a demanding two-year academic course. Instead, some time after his admission to Dammasch, he became a 'working patient' at the hospital, where he remained for the next several months.

> He won't be doing medical tech stuff – he's not ready for that yet, but more like an orderly – delivering laundry to wards etc. It's about 15 miles from here & they have employee facilities, so he'll stay there the nights he works (5 in a row, I think) & then come home for 2.

Never again was there mention of his becoming a medical technician. A sad silence sat around such topics. Mike was trapped in a demoralizing cycle, each false fresh start bringing with it a diminution of confidence. Gradually, the expectations of him were growing humbler, from the high hopes of the late sixties to the day our mother wrote, after a 'record' week-long spell working at a local cafeteria some years later ended in his being fired, *I would rather have a happy bum than a tense worker.*

And yet, throughout the mid seventies, my mother's letters were still peppered with lines like:

> He is a changeable little rascal, but better now than he's been for years.
> He's happy, alert, reading, and better than he's been in three years.
> Mike is better each day, and I am hopeful that he may be his old self sometime.

I know why my mother kept hoping. It wasn't that her unfailing optimism blinded her. It wasn't even because she was his mother. It was to do with the nature of the illness – the way, in those first few years, acute psychosis would alternate with periods of lucidity and calm, during which the symptoms would dramatically diminish, and we would all be lulled into believing that the worst was over.

167

Mike is getting more realistic every day. It's a painful process – coming back, but I honestly think he is coming back . . .

★

In the summer of 1977, Mike left the hospital, withdrew his money from the bank and, without telling anyone, took a bus to North Carolina. His first letter home gives the impression that this latest escape is somehow different from his other sudden flights. It is possible to imagine, reading it, that the breakdowns, the hospitalizations, the drugs that made his body spasm, the pessimistic doctors and the wavering faith of his own family had together acquired a critical mass that propelled him into a state of resolve.

Dear Mom and Everyone,

Everything here is fine. I'm taking my meds even though they are very expensive and I feel good. I'm living in a private home and I have my own room with a private bath . . . I shaved my beard off for a job interview and I'm keeping my face shaven. I wish I had a picture of myself to send you. No job yet but I'm working through vocational rehabilitation here and they may be able to find me something . . . Haven't quit the cigarettes yet but I've cut down some and I feel good. I hope that I didn't scare you by the way I left but I just couldn't take being in the hospital any longer. Please Mom try to understand. Haven't talked to Steve but if you send me his address I'll write him and Robin too as I just bought some writing paper and envelopes and a pen . . . I have a bicycle from Jeanette so I can get around . . . I'll put off buying a car until I have a job. Please don't worry about me I can take care of myself. I haven't had any spells lately and I think it's because I'm out of the hospital environment.

All my love,
Mike

Jeanette, the woman my mother referred to at the time as Mike's 'east coast surrogate mother', had been at Duke with him, though they had only met properly after graduation, when Mike was passing through Durham. Mike had been shooting baskets in a friend's driveway, bragging that he'd been on the Duke team and could still sink them. And he could. He sank ten in a row, which surprised her. By then, he didn't look the athletic type.

When they met again in the summer of 1977, he told Jeanette he had left the mental hospital and nobody knew where he was. Jeanette convinced him to phone home a few days later. By then, my mother, so wearied by it all, had written to Fanny, *I just have to face the fact that Mike will always be the prodigal son & may never settle down . . . he is one of God's special people, and I am through worrying and struggling.* Contrary to her worst fears, six weeks after having left Oregon, he appeared to be doing fine.

Dear Everyone,

Greetings from the sunny south. I hope everything is going well with y'all. I'm doing well. I have a job now working on the grounds crew of Durham County General Hospital. I walk about a mile to the bus stop every morning at 7.30 and then again back to the house at 5.30. The job is hard and I only make $2.81 an hour but it's not too boring as we move around to different hospitals . . . I wish I could be in Ocean City with you all but that's impossible now that I'm working. My supervisor is strict but pretty nice. Today he took me to Goodwill to get some work clothes . . . I've been taking my meds and I feel pretty good. I went over to Jeanette's the other night for dinner, she cooked a nice rice and vegetable dish and I washed the dishes . . . You should see me without my beard. It's a whole new me. Just took a shower. I really get dirty at work, but I'm happy. Please write or call as I love and miss you all very much.

Love,
Mike

What he didn't tell my mother was that his supervisor had taken him to the emergency room and that he had spent a few days in the hospital. When Jeanette asked him about it, he told her his diagnosis was CUT, chronic undifferentiated type (a subtype of schizophrenia that includes symptoms common to paranoid, catatonic and hebephrenic subtypes). By the time he wrote the letter, he was getting on with his life again. But the episode probably had something to do with the fact that by September, he was no longer working on the grounds crew and was once again unemployed. Although he still sounded lucid and determined, the reference to his 'nerves' in a letter home in late September suggested a setback. The buoyancy of midsummer was quietly leaching away.

Dear Mom and Everyone,

How's everything? Things here are really looking up. I walked all over west Durham today all the way out to Interstate 85 looking for a job. I applied at five places, all restaurants, and one told me to come back tomorrow, Hardee's. I'm hoping to get a part-time job so it won't be so bad on my nerves. Some asked me if I could cook and I told them a little bit. I need a haircut, so before I go for any interviews I'll get a trim. Please don't worry about me I'll be taking care of business. How are Timmy and Molly? Is Timmy playing football? Is Molly studying? I hope they're doing well? How's your boyfriend doing, Mom? I'd love to meet him and I'm sure I will next summer. I missed sending Dad a birthday card so I'll write him a letter soon. Got a letter from Robin recently and she sounds really good. I'm sure she has written you and given you all the news . . . Well not much else to say except that I feel real well and I miss you all very much. Take care and write soon.

Love,
Mike

After that, there were no more letters from Durham. When Jeanette saw him just weeks later, he was standing on her front doorstep, the pockets of his woollen jacket filled with cigarette butts, the smell coming off him so strong it turned her stomach.

By the time Kathy met Mike, not long after, he was unrecognizable. Kathy – his first high-school sweetheart, who had picked him up for school in her little Ford station wagon – had lost track of him around 1972, after he graduated from Duke. In 1977, she was managing a café in downtown Durham. The city was full of homeless people then. Many were former mental patients, liberated from the asylums by the federal government in an attempt to shift patient care from hospitals to community-based mental-health services. Kathy's place was homeless-friendly. She was used to the bedraggled and the confused. A lot of them she knew by name.

One day in late autumn, a young man appeared who was, even by the standards of the homeless, filthy. His hair was matted and he smelled. He was incoherent, babbling to himself and laughing. He sat down at one of the tables and Kathy went over and tried to talk to him.

'How ya doin? What's your name?'

He didn't answer – he was away somewhere, he was really gone, this poor guy – but he did look at her. So she kept standing there, trying to make conversation. She wasn't getting anywhere but she kept eye contact, looking into his eyes because there was something about them. His eyelashes. They were so long, so beautifully long.

And then she realized that this filthy, foul-smelling person sitting in her café, unable to speak his own name, was the same person she had kissed on a hayride eleven years earlier.

'Mike,' she said, 'is that you?'

He didn't recognize her.

She gave him a sandwich and he sat there all afternoon, staring or chattering away to himself. Finally, at some point late in the day, he looked at her and said slowly, 'I remember you . . . yeah, I remember you.'

She phoned her husband. She said, 'The guy is clearly crazy but he used to be my boyfriend.' She brought Mike home with her that evening and she and her husband got him showered and fed. They washed his clothes. He stayed with them for a couple of weeks. She even gave him some shifts at the café washing dishes. (She already had one guy with schizophrenia working in the kitchen – he drank beer straight from the tap.) At home in the evenings, Mike watched TV. Sometimes, they talked. He told Kathy that he had escaped from a mental hospital. He said he was 'on the run'. One night they were sitting in front of the television and he looked over at her. It was like he was emerging from a fog, she thought, or had broken through the surface of something. For a moment, she saw someone she recognized. It was brief, this reappearance, but before he returned to staring at the screen, before he sank back down again into whatever world he inhabited, he said to her, sadly and with utter clarity, 'Most of the time I'm pretty lost.'

That winter, he drifted, homeless or living in boarding houses, my mother wiring him money when he phoned to tell her where he was. Slowly, he made his way north, though not to his grandparents' – my mother had forbidden that. When he got to Philadelphia, he phoned Kevin, his old best friend from his first years at Duke. They'd had no contact since graduation. Kevin, by then embarked on a career in law, went to the Greyhound terminal on 10th and Filbert to pick Mike up. He was shocked by what he saw. He took Mike to his house in a nearby suburb. That evening, they went to a restaurant where there was a poetry reading. Kevin thought the poet was bizarre, but Mike started interacting with him, really relating to him on some level – or thinking he was relating to him, Kevin couldn't be sure. It was obvious to Kevin that Mike was in bad shape, though he wasn't coherent enough to talk about what had been going on with him. He chattered and giggled, and Kevin couldn't make sense of any of it.

So, Kevin did what everyone did. He called my mother. What he would remember, three decades after the conversation, was my mother saying of her son, 'He is the first thing I think of when I wake in the morning and the last thing I think of before I go to sleep at night.'

During the period when these things were happening, I kept Mike in the blind spot I'd constructed and got on with the business of adolescence. I didn't ask and the members of my family generally didn't tell. Although my mother always tried to make Mike welcome in our home, she also tried to shield me from information or stories that were sad or frightening. But things trickled down. Phrases or place names acquired resonance despite an absence of context. I was about thirteen when I first heard the words Orange Sunshine. It was Tim who introduced them into my vocabulary.

My knowledge of things adult was often arrived at via Tim, after he had interpreted, sieved and repackaged the information for my consumption. In this case, I didn't know if he had overheard our parents discussing it, or if it was one of those precious nuggets of information to which his two years' seniority tended to entitle him. Nor was I sure how much he knew. He had a habit of hinting that he was in possession of information which he was required, on account of my age, to withhold from me.

His manner of enlightening me on the topic of Orange Sunshine was typically elliptical. He wanted me to know that there was more to the story than he was at liberty to reveal and that having to harbour this knowledge alone pained him. It probably did pain him. Back then, rightly or wrongly, we both connected LSD with our brother's present state of mind, with the fact that, instead of building a career or applying himself to a postgraduate degree or even experimenting with subsistence farming in the wilds of somewhere, he was sitting in the living room with his woolly cap pulled low, waggling his leg and giggling at nothing.

By 1977, my parents knew that Mike had done lots of drugs, but more specifics were revealed, according to Tim, during a walk Mike took along the beach in LA with a friend of my father's. Mike was drifting around California for part of that year, and my father was living in LA, having landed a job the summer after the divorce as an assistant coach with the LA Lakers. (The suspicion I had harboured – that it was *we* who'd been dragging *him* down – was only confirmed by the fact of his migration to the land of sunshine and movie stars, some of whom sat courtside at the games.) My father had informed this friend of his, who apparently knew something about such things, that his son had a 'drug problem'. That was the way he couched it, not as a psychological problem but as a *drug problem*, as though Mike had been sucked into a chemical vortex from which he could not escape – hooked on the hallucinogens which, in reality, he had long since stopped ingesting. He arranged for his friend to meet with Mike. The two of them walked the beach, and afterwards, the friend informed my father that Mike had done some 'pretty heavy stuff', including smoking ground-up magic mushrooms and dropping a whole lot of Orange Sunshine.

When this news travelled from the rarefied world of beachside condos to our rain-soaked, shag-carpeted existence in Oregon and down the chain of command, what stuck in my head was the incongruity between the words and what they stood for. Orange Sunshine sounded not like a mind-altering substance that could launch a person into insanity but like something we might've drunk with our morning cereal.

Over the years and decades that followed, an association took root in my mind between Orange Sunshine and the little I knew of Mike's travels in Florida in the mid seventies, especially his stay in Gainesville. What exactly happened in Gainesville during those weeks when my mother prayed we'd hear from him never became clear in any detail, and the association I'd made between the drug and the location was likely erroneous; Mike was by then intermittently psychotic, and was no longer dropping acid.

The reason for the link was probably as simple as the link between Florida and oranges and sunshine, and what I had long imagined was the sheer brilliance in which those days were bathed. I thought of Mike, and whoever he was with, as the last true hippies, vegetarians and Deadheads, still dropouts when most of their peers had rejoined the mainstream. A hallucinogen called Orange Sunshine fitted neatly into the picture I'd constructed.

It was a gross, if innocent, romanticizing of that period. Because what I learned from my mother thirty years later was that in Gainesville, Mike squatted in a big burned-out house with a bunch of other strung-out people. He told my mother that some of them 'took advantage' of him. Maybe they did, maybe they didn't. His accounts were not always reliable. But whatever happened there, Gainesville did not represent the halcyon days of his hippydom. Rather, it was just one more place where he fell apart.

Sixteen

My mother had inhabited her role as my father's helpmate as though she'd been born to it. But the way she took to her new life seemed to suggest that she'd been waiting three decades to live it.

During the year we lived in the green-carpeted house – the year my parents' marriage fell apart, a year from which not a single photo survives – my mother was already changing: helping to pay the bills with her part-time job, growing increasingly independent and yet, more than ever, the one who held things together. Aside from that snapshot memory from the early seventies – she and my father walking arm in arm down the concrete corridor of the Coliseum after another trouncing – I hardly recalled her in her supporting role. I can look at the *Raleigh News and Observer* of 1968, in which she gushes about how lucky she is to share with her husband 'so much of the agony and glory of the game', and I have to believe that she meant it. But my own vivid memories of her date from a subsequent incarnation, one defined by an unsentimental strength and a matter-of-fact acceptance of present circumstances:

It ain't what ya do, but the way that ya do it . . .

What survived the transition from wifely cheerleader to reluctant divorcée was her sense of fun and curiosity. Though the split was heartbreaking for her, she welcomed the opportunities that single life afforded. Through her job at the local newspaper, she continued to meet colourful and inspiring people, people whose company my father would not have been interested in. She met a woman her age who had backpacked through Europe with her children, she met artists and psychologists, a blind lawyer, a South African couple, a gay man. She met others recently divorced – divorce, if no longer a scandal, was still a shock then, and its casualties banded together for succour. She spent evenings with other parents of mentally ill children. She even ran for the Oregon State Legislature – something she'd never have done while married – under the slogan 'We Need Anita'. She won the Democratic primary but lost in the general election, her chances perhaps undermined by the fact that her campaign manager and lifelong pal Jean had a habit of referring unofficially to theirs as the 'Champagne Campaign'.

Before the divorce, before my mother took Tim and me to live in the house downtown on Fourth Street, life's difficulties had been things that we would collectively absorb, survive and emerge from in recognizable form. Now, with just my mother at the helm, anything seemed possible, in a way that was by turns unsettling and exciting. Both feelings hinted at a truth about life – that it was not, as I had previously supposed, governed by a set of principles I would gradually discover and apply (like the principles of grammar, ordering what would otherwise be random), but that sometimes there was true randomness, and all you could do was your best in the face of it.

Our lives during those years were makeshift and often fun. My father had always been the disciplinarian, and in his absence the atmosphere around the house became more tolerant and freewheeling. Though my mother was discreet and, as far as we were aware, chaste, she was forever going on dates. Most of the men seemed misshapen and anaemic compared to the blocky solidity and unequivocal vigour of my father, though there were a couple of exceptions. She interviewed, then briefly dated, Walt Morey, the author of the famous children's book *Gentle Ben*, who lived on a sixty-acre filbert ranch and whom I wanted her to marry. The man who wanted to marry her drove a Rolls-Royce and gave her gifts of gold. He lived in Ocean City and flew to Oregon to visit us. He was large and exuberant and our house seemed even humbler with him in it. I thought I wouldn't mind if she married him. I liked the idea of being suddenly, filthily rich, more for the sense of safety I thought it would bestow than out of any rampant greed. But my mother wasn't swayed. And the day he refused to stop and help a driver who was stranded in the rain with a puncture, she knew he wasn't the one.

No doubt, after twenty-eight years of sharing a life with my father, she was lonely. But she dramatized nothing, including her own losses, and regarded whatever happened as a challenge, a lesson, 'life's little adventure' (though surely she was fudging when she wrote of my father in a letter two years after the divorce, *He just seems like someone I knew a long time ago . . .*). She exhibited not exactly a stiff upper lip but a thoughtful equanimity and a high-spirited resolve, qualities reflected in her musical repertoire, which included 'Que sera, sera', 'My Sweet Lord' and fragments of the more harmlessly funky seventies hits. Of one of her favourites, she could remember only a single line – 'Evr'budy was kung fu fi-i-tin!' – which she always followed with the requisite *hungh!* kung fu grunt.

Our house was open and our friends were always welcome. My mother often invited acquaintances – the guy who'd come to clean the gutters whose wife had died of cancer, a single mother raising a child with cystic fibrosis, the young man behind the counter at our local grocery store who was working his way through community college – for Sunday dinners with our family. On the small concrete porch, which backed on to an alleyway (a horizon so constricted compared to the sweeping view she'd had at our hillside house), she mingled these everyday heroes with the wackier well-heeled friends from her former life, women who wore designer pant suits and lived on the lake shore and loved a party of whatever stripe.

As John was away at college, and Steve still lived on the other side of the country, Tim – at fourteen – became the man of the house, his secret life of recreational drug use matched only by his devotion to my mother and his rage for order. We had only one shower in the house and Tim devised, on his ever-present clipboard, a schedule to which the three of us were expected to adhere each morning as we prepared for school and work: *Mom 7.05–7.18, Molly 7.19–7.32 . . .*

My mother tried to make up for what Tim and I had lost by creating for the three of us an atmosphere of pleasure and adventure. Each Christmas, she staged a treasure hunt, writing clues in rhyming couplets and hiding them throughout the house. She cooked our favourite dinners and sneaked us into the movies and took us for weekends in the mountains or days out at the coast. Once, quite soon after the divorce, she brought us to San Francisco for a few days. Photos show us all looking slightly dazed (Tim and I deep into the dislocating landscape of puberty but still sporting the last vestiges of baby fat), our outfits an odd mishmash of themes and patterns, as though a blind person had dressed us, our hairstyles shapeless and unfortunate. My mother's frizzy helmet was especially regrettable; with her electric hair and her purple-tinted glasses, she looked ever so slightly mad. She called us the Three Musketeers and said we were raising each other now.

During those first couple of years in the house on Fourth Street, Mike lived sometimes with us, sometimes in apartments nearby, experiments in independent living that tended to end with my mother cleaning rotting food out of his refrigerator and sweeping cigarette butts up off the floor. Some days he would walk the few blocks to our house to spend an afternoon or to have dinner with us, and I would glimpse him through the living-room window – again and again, his same slumped gait framed beyond the shrubs and the white fence – and my heart would sink at the sight of him.

Once, as the four of us drove home from a pizza dinner on Tim's birthday, Mike became agitated and started flipping the door handle. When we pulled up to our house, he jumped out and began running in circles around the small front yard, Munka yapping at his heels. He was bent slightly at the waist and he was lifting his legs high in the air and making whooping sounds. It was as though something had taken possession of him, quite suddenly, and whatever was happening was more, my mother knew, than she could handle. By that night, Mike was back in Dammasch, and my mother set to commence another round of Sunday visits. She would put Munka in the car and they would go for walks on the hospital grounds with Mike. Sometimes, Mike wasn't fit for visitors, and she could only look at him through a window. Once he was crouched in the lock-up with just a shirt on. There were faeces on the floor, and he had his arms wrapped around his knees, and though his face was hidden from her she thought he was crying. When she came back home to us on those Sunday evenings, Tim and I would be watching television

in the living room and my mother would hug us in turn very tightly, like we were the one good thing in her life and its anchor.

During the years in the house on Fourth Street, when Mike was not in the hospital, my mother attempted on several occasions to pair him up with other lost souls, twenty-somethings in various forms of limbo. Maybe a woman she had met while doing a story for the newspaper on vocational rehabilitation, or a guy who mowed lawns in the neighbourhood and was, in some way you couldn't put your finger on, not quite right. There was a woman named Mary who joined us a few times for dinner, and once on a rare family picnic. Mike knew her from the hospital, or maybe from some community-care programme, but he didn't speak to her much when she was with us, and my mother always ended up trying to play the encouraging interlocutor between them, as though Mary and Mike were two shy five-year-olds at a birthday party. Though Mary was unattractive and clumsy, Mike's disregard for her seemed nothing personal. He didn't interact with anyone.

At some point, Mike had become incapable of forming new

friendships. By 1978, all the bonds he had so far forged in his life had frayed to the point of non-existence; after that, none of his college friends, apart from Susan – his old girlfriend from Duke – attempted to stay in contact. Even his family began to fall away. Of his siblings, it was probably Tim who tried hardest to make time for him, compelled by the same intrinsic decency and familial devotion that had motivated him, even as a rambunctious and hormonal teenager, to write carbon-copied letters every single Sunday for a decade to his two sets of grandparents.

Only my mother has been a constant, the one sustaining relationship in his life. Theirs has always seemed to me a kind of love story, forged in the years after Mike's diagnosis and after my father had gone. It wasn't that my mother hadn't cared for Mike before; of course she had. But when the illness took hold and all the obvious things to love had vanished – not only the pleasure of his company, but all hope of future pleasures – a different kind of bond was forged. My father had tried to help – he had raced to the Rocky Mountains when Mike had gone missing, jumped on a plane to North Carolina to bail him out of jail, wanted to send Susan to Portland, all expenses paid, to try to guide Mike back to sanity through Transcendental Meditation – but the more intimate, less obviously grand gestures were left to my mother. When Mike arrived at the green-carpeted house with boils and body lice, it was she who put on her bathing suit and scrubbed him in the shower. It was she who went for walks with him after dinner and on Sunday afternoons when not one of us was eager for his company. It was she who praised his small accomplishments: now he helped tidy the house, now he can find his way alone on the bus, now he showers without being told.

Unable or unwilling to shop for himself, Mike wore what my mother picked out. She meant well. She bought him a blue pants suit for special occasions – slacks and a short jacket made of polyester and patterned in faux-patchwork to resemble a hippy's denims. There are photos of him wearing this, images steeped in pathos, both because of my mother's good intentions, which missed the mark by a mile, and because my brother, who had been so cool in his twenties – the drugs, the beard, the dangling cigarette – had allowed himself to wear this get-up.

The last letters Mike wrote that were addressed to anyone other than my mother were produced in a brief flurry during the summer of 1978, while he was living at the Salvation Army in Long Beach, California – his final period of drifting before he came back to Oregon for good. From Long Beach, he wrote to our father, our grandparents, our brother Steve, his high-school girlfriend Lara, our family dog Munka and me – short muddled notes on small squares of paper headed 'OTTO LACAYO for senate'. (The notes were never sent and somehow my mother ended up in possession of them.) He addresses us all with warmth and benevolence.

DEAR MOLLY AND MUNKA,

YOU ARE ALL VERY SWEET TO BE WELL AND HAPPY SO BE GOOD TO MOM AND GET GOOD GRADES IN SCHOOL. SURELY THE SUMMER WILL NOT LAST LONG. SO ASK A GIRL AROUND TO TRY TO GET YOU A LITTLE TIME TO YOURSELF AND GO BACK TO THE WAYS YOU KNOW BEST AS I WILL BE COMING UP TO SEE YOU SOON AND I KNOW THAT IT IS VERY IMPORTANT TO BE SMILING. THAT'S ALL FROM HERE.

LOVE MIKE.

Apart from a few tortured lines that surely unsettled my mother – *Around 9 o'clock at night the rain poured down from the sky and Lucifer polished his gun* – those he wrote to her during that period strike a note of hallucinatory good cheer. Metaphorical, inadvertently poetic, shot through with truth, the Long Beach letters to her are his most beautiful. Their details tap into the collective symbols of our lives. Their streams of consciousness have the logic of dreams. They are suffused with an affection which must have moved her all the more for the distorted quality of its expression. For some reason, they were almost all written in caps.

MOM,

*WHO CARES WHO WINS OR LOSES IN THE FIGHT OF LIFE
BUT I KNOW THAT I LOVE YOU AND YOUR OLD WAYS.
ANYTIME YOU FEEL LIKE CRYING JUST CALL ME AND WE'LL
GET TOGETHER IN A LITTLE CHIT-CHAT. FOR THE WAYS OF
TIME ARE VERY WELL UNDERSTOOD BY THE ONES YOU
LOVE AND IT CAN BE VERY SOOTHING TO BECOME A CHILD
AGAIN. AS WE SEE THE CONSTANT CIRCLES AROUND THE
SUN WE KNOW THAT THERE IS A REASON FOR OUR SUF-
FERING IN LIFE. ONLY GOD CAN GET A GLASS FOR YOU. AND
ONLY MIKE LOVES YOU. SURELY YOU CAN GIVE IT A TRY FOR
ME AND LET ME KNOW ABOUT TIMMY AND MOLLY. ANY
TIME WE ARE AT AN IMPASSE IN NEGOTIATIONS FOR OUR
SILLY LITTLE OUTBURSTS OF TEMPER REMEMBER THAT IT
IS JUST A WAY OF THE WORLD, COULD IT BE ANYTHING
ELSE. OR IS THAT JUST THE WAY WE FEEL. GOD KNOWS IT
COULD BE NOTHING ELSE. JOIN ME IN A FRIENDLY SALUTE
TO THE OLD TIMES AND BECOME A PAL OR A MONKEY OR
ANYTHING. AND BE YOURSELF BECAUSE AS I AM LEARNING
LIFE IS NOT JUST A HALLOWEEN PARTY. GO TO THE STORE
AND SMILE. I MISS YOU AND CARE FOR YOUR WELL BEING
AND IT WILL BE A JOY TO FEEL THE OLD TENNIS RACQUET
IN YOUR HAND. ANY WAY THE MONEY YOU SENT WAS
GREATLY APPRECIATED AND I WILL BE SURE TO CATCH UP
ON MY WRITING. CIGARS ARE ALL AROUND THE ROOM
FOR US HERE SO DON'T WORRY. KINDNESS IS A VIRTUE
AND COFFEE IS A STIMULANT. BE HONEST WITH ME IN
YOUR NEXT LETTER. I LOVE YOU.*

MIKE

The letter is a classic example of the 'formal thought disorder' that is a symptom of schizophrenia. Yet for all its seeming randomness, there is a strange, quiet authority to this letter, something age-old. In his attempts to reassure and to provide succour, he seems to be the elder here, or to feel himself the elder. The letter is steeped in nostalgia, as well as an awareness of the pitfalls of nostalgia. He sounds as though he would like to shepherd his mother through something, to help her over some loss. He was aware that she was on her own, and aware that our father had remarried the year before. He knew that none of it had been easy for our mother. He ends another letter from that period, *P.S. THE WHOLE WORLD LOVES YOU. EVEN DAD.*

There is from that same period a letter to Mike from Fanny, which also ended up in my mother's possession. Though my grandmother had by then some understanding that Mike's problem was not mere fecklessness – *Tony said Mike is sick and cannot think like other people* – she was nevertheless a woman of her time who couldn't help believing that an inability to bounce back from adversity could be put down to self-indulgence. Life, in the end, was about pulling up your socks and getting on with it. Not realizing just how out of touch with reality Mike was by then, and apparently under the impression that he was working at the Salvation Army rather than availing of its charity, she sent him one last motivational letter.

Dear Michael:

We hear you have another opportunity to use your lovely personality and show you can keep yourself to make good in this confusing world. It is all up to you. We all love you so very much but none of us can keep you and be responsible for you at your age. Tony and I are 78 *and* 80 *years old. You are very fortunate we are all not depending on you as the oldest of the generation after ours and your parents. You should have more pride and confidence in yourself. How many fellows your age, looks and education would act as you have done.*

This letter is just to tell you so many love you but you have to find your own way. Your mother is working at her age (52) and the others, even Tim working to make money and a future for themselves.

It is all up to you dear Mike and we know you can do it. We are both getting so old this could be your last letter from us.

Remember you are on your own.

Our love and prayers,

Fanny and Tony

By the end of 1978, Mike was back in Oregon. From that point on, he would never leave the state, and he would never be off medication for more than a couple of weeks at a time – experiments that invariably ended in psychotic episodes. By the early eighties, he was living in a group home a couple of miles outside of town – the grandly named Riverview Manor – with others not well enough to live independently, not unwell enough to be hospitalized. He shot baskets in the driveway and came to us for Sunday dinners and frequented an ice-creamery and coffee shop downtown, close to my mother's office, where the girls behind the counter knew him by name and treated him with generosity and kindness.

In 1984, my mother left Oregon and moved back east to her parents' Ocean City house, into the upstairs apartment, with its claw-foot bathtub and its sloping turquoise kitchen walls and its warren of memories. It was something her mother had been encouraging her to do since the divorce.

Whenever you are happy then we are the same. When you are sad so are we. The years pass so quickly and everyone takes to the road. At least here you should feel at home having spent all your summers here . . .
This is all a message of Love. Do not worry. Come home.

When my mother finally made the move, it was for her parents' sake rather than her own. They were growing too senile to be safely alone in the house. Separated from Mike now by 3,000 miles, my mother wrote to her son faithfully each week for the next twenty-five years. Though he was not quite as consistent – *My letters are becoming more frequent not because of any altruism but because I realize you really do like to hear from me* – she was the only one from this point on to whom he ever wrote.

By the time of my mother's move, Mike was a changed person, and his letters reflect this – the emphatic all-caps long since replaced by an often-shaky scrawl (a consequence of his medication) and his subject matter decidedly banal. All metaphysics have been banished. The world is small and his concerns are few. But if these subsequent letters are tentative and somewhat flat in comparison to the florid performances of the late seventies, they are striking in their own way.

Dear Mom,

Thank you for sending me the letter with the check in it. I'm doing well and I enjoy myself when I get the coffee and cigarettes I need. Every day I do my chores and I'm not afraid to take on the responsibilities that living at Lake House requires. We went to the beach last Friday and I was feeling sentimental about the ocean and rock formations and it was a sunny winter day. We packed a lunch and we stopped at the Tillamook cheese factory for coffee. I'm sure Howard is doing well and I thank him for the restaurants and the shopping. No big new news but I'm doing better every day and I'm sure you'll be proud of me in the very near future. Write soon.

Love,
Mike

The letters are the only record of Mike's emotional life – the only indication, really, that an emotional life exists, for he neither shows his emotions, nor speaks of them. His voice is monotone, his stare flat and blank. For decades, he has treated my mother, the person dearest to him on earth, with no particular warmth, and seemed largely indifferent to her presence. His attitude towards her – towards all of us, towards the world in general – is, or appears to be, one of boredom, irony and a tolerance verging on disdain. And yet his letters to her contain expressions of affection that are consistent, simple and genuine.

I miss you like crazy.
I miss you and think about you every day.
I miss everyone and love you.
Dear Anita . . . Another short letter to remind you that I'm thinking about you.

Over the years, the syntax reverts to its former peculiarities and a slight formality creeps in. His writing assumes at times an oddly archaic, almost courtly, quality.

God bless you and this will reach you on a good day.

In December 1995, on a slip of paper smaller than an index card, he writes simply:

From far away you came and I knew the Christmas time couldn't have been any better.

Love,
Mike

His letter-writing self never reports feeling bad or depressed, never expresses a wish that things were otherwise. He is even, at times, philosophical: *I didn't think anything was new but it's all relative. If it seems new and exciting in life then that's what it will be.* In this refusal to consign complaints to paper, he is like his mother. His most consistently repeated wish is that she not worry about him.

Please don't worry, I'll be fine.
Don't worry too much about me I'm a big boy and can take care of myself.
Don't worry be happy. My mind is just as keen as it ever was.
I'm getting better every day.

★

The discrepancy in a person with schizophrenia between the subjective experience of emotion and its outward expression was noted as far back as the 1920s by, among others, the Swiss psychiatrist Eugen Bleuler. (It was Bleuler who coined the term *schizophrenia* in 1908.) That people with the illness experience a range of emotions in the absence of observable cues, particularly facial cues, has been confirmed in the ensuing decades. But while those of us without the illness may be able to conceive of this disconnect, we cannot fill in someone else's blanks. Not being able to laugh, or to smile, or to furrow one's brow in empathy – and at the precisely appropriate moments – makes relationships almost impossible.

Mike, like all of us, is layered. In his case, though, the difference between what is hidden and what is shown – between felt emotion and affective expression – may represent a rupture rather than a continuum, so that he could not, even if he wanted to, move between the two realms. Before I read the letters, I had assumed that he felt little. I had read about anhedonia – the inability to experience pleasure, thought to be a common feature of schizophrenia – and I had believed that the deficit of expression corresponded to the lack of an inner life. I had taken him, literally, at face value.

In a similar way, I had mistaken my mother's lack of melodrama over the years as evidence that she had made her peace with what happened to her son, that it no longer shook her. She had always kept up her good cheer in his company, unlike the rest of us, who tended to become stiff and self-conscious in his presence. In an application of twisted logic, I had regarded the fact that she could be so consistently herself with him over the decades of his illness not as a testament to her strength of feeling but as proof of the distance she had achieved. It was only in 2006 that I saw how wrong I was.

I was visiting her at her house in Florida, where she now lives happily with Howard, her second husband, who she married in 1987. (She and my father had known Howard and his wife back in the early sixties, when they were neighbours on Ferguson Avenue in Broomall, playing bridge and going to basketball games together. After Howard's wife died in 1985, he and my mother began dating.) She goes swimming every day, and she and Howard attend cocktail or dinner parties most nights. When I was there, she and I spent a few afternoons lying on the twin beds in the spare room and talking about Mike. I would ask her questions and she would do her best to answer, though there were times she would sigh and say quietly, 'Oh, I don't remember . . .'

Once she added, 'Or maybe I've made myself forget.'

Just as our minds often refuse to retain even the rough outlines of what happened, so too do they adopt events from the minds of others and treat them as their own. On that awful weekend in 1973 when Mike was first diagnosed, did I see him standing in the kitchen and barking like a dog? I have a very clear image of this in my mind.

His hair, his beard, his T-shirt, are all exactly as they were in a photograph taken around that time, in that kitchen, when he was sitting down to dinner. I can hear the bark. It's entirely possible I witnessed it. But I also have a fairly clear picture of him sitting naked on the mailbox on Sixth Street as the school bus passed – his lean bare limbs jutting this way and that like a grasshopper's – and for various reasons I am almost certain this is not something I witnessed. Both of these images were likely created not by the events themselves but by the people who described them to me – in the case of the school bus, by my mother, who is herself uncertain as to whether it actually happened that way. It's as though we just waltz into each other's heads and draw pictures there. And then the pictures become indelible, their outlines clearer than those of many of the actual moments of our lives.

When I asked my mother, four or five times over the course of as many years, what she remembered of visiting Mike at Dammasch, again and again she came up with a single image. Mike crouched in the lock-up wearing only a T-shirt. His face hidden. Crying, maybe. Faeces on the floor. It's as though this single memory has agreed to act as representative for all the others. And why not. It's enough, isn't it?

One day during my week with her in Florida, my mother received two photographs of Mike, attached to an email sent to her by his social worker. Mike had finally cut his long hair, and my mother wanted to see the new look. She was unable, though, to open the attachments and asked me to do it for her. Once I had, I called to her, offhandedly, to come and see. She swished into the room, almost gaily – 'Show me!' – as though it were my latest holiday snaps on the screen. She sat next to me at the desk and I clicked from one photo to the next. Her expression went slack, and we both fell silent, abashed by our own momentary imprudence. Then she turned her face away and stood up. She looked, I thought, like someone in a movie who has just identified a body in a morgue.

'Tcht,' she said sadly. 'He looks like an old man.'

In truth, he looked terrible. Though he hadn't been homeless for years, he showed those same telltale signs of physical neglect. In one of the photos he is hamming for the camera, opening his mouth as though saying *aaahhhh* at the dentist's. There is a brown-yellow nicotine stain running up the centre of his tongue, and several of his teeth are missing. In the other, he sits quietly, and what the eye is drawn to is his own eyes. Unnaturally small due to the drooping lids and the bloated face, they have a glazed, sad cast to them. His mouth hangs open slightly. The effect – despite his looking, indeed, like an old man – is one of innocence and incomprehension.

Why had the photos so upset her? It's not as if she didn't know what he looked like – she saw him twice a year or so, every time she travelled to Oregon. Presumably it was because in person his residual intelligence, his sarcasm, his laughter, belie his appearance. What she brings with her each time she meets him is knowledge, history, memory, so that in a gesture or a tone she detects, without even trying, allusions – not to a former self but to a whole self. To a more complete truth about him than the digital image, with its excision of a single moment's reality, could even hint at. When they meet, it is not only their present selves in dialogue, but all the roles they've played opposite each other, a lifetime of incarnations.

Their written correspondence – or his side of it – ended unceremoniously on 5 August 2002.

Dear Anita and Howard,

Just thought I'd drop you a note to let you know that I think about you and how I'm doing. Every day has been really nice this summer and I'm relaxed and feeling well. It gets a little noisy downtown and the whoever they are a real pain but I live through it. I don't know when you will be coming west again but I'll be looking forward to seeing you. I go to the same place for coffee in the evening and I really enjoy it. Timmy took me out to lunch for my birthday and he is working on his project for remodeling houses. I don't think I'll be coming back east soon so I hope you're feeling well.

All my love,
Mike

Seventeen

In February 2008, I began a four-month sublet of an apartment on the rue de Seine in Paris. I had just come back from eighteen months in Nairobi, where I'd been working for a UN office, and I was happy to be back in Europe, to feel proper cold, to no longer worry about carjackings or the sound of shooting at night. But I was alone in Paris, and each day I spent hours on my own, reading and writing about schizophrenia and acid trips and the forms that fear and insanity could take. Looking at drawings made by people undergoing LSD birth-regression therapy – of faces stretched Bosch-like in terror, of mothers with three heads and Cubist, anatomical distortions. Trying to understand how all of this related to someone to whom I was intimately connected but hardly knew. Though I tended not to think much about it all once I quit working for the day, it was there, in my unconscious, a crowding and sometimes malevolent presence.

The sense of isolation I was beginning to feel only increased when I left the apartment. My grasp of French was limited, and it is easy to feel alienated in Paris. In the wrong frame of mind, one can feel unequal to the magnificence of the city – not only the grand cathedrals but the haute couture and the meticulously arranged rows of pastel macaroons. The narcissism of Parisians, the attention to each exquisite detail, can fuel a suspicion that there is nothing and no one underneath. Packed into their tiny tables sipping thimblefuls of espresso, they can look like slightly menacing lemmings. I had a few friends in the city, but I hadn't known them long, and that was no substitute for belonging – for that feeling of being contextualized, one's own history woven into the mesh of a place. Instead I felt perched atop a writhing heap of complex stories, none of which had anything to do with me.

After a few weeks in that apartment, I found myself waking each morning to a kind of fear with which I was not unfamiliar. Brittle, invasive, extremely wordy. I had been through it before, chronic anxiety and its grim climax, the panic attack. During the years when I had experienced intermittent free-floating anxiety, I had cast about for an understanding of it. I'd read Kierkegaard and Schopenhauer and Pema Chödrön's *The Places That Scare You*. I'd read *What to Say When You Talk to Yourself* and *The Panic and Anxiety Workbook*. I had applied the techniques of cognitive behaviour modification. I had quit drinking. I had taken up meditation. Gradually, the fear had left me. And yet, here it was, back again, waiting for me each morning.

I ordered Rollo May's *The Meaning of Anxiety*, and read with interest May's description of experiments in which animals are kept in states of unrelieved vigilance – that is, unable to answer two basic questions about their safety and their environment: *What is it?* and *What happens next?* In this constant state of tension, the animal soon becomes frantic, its behaviour disordered. May likens this 'experimental neurosis' to what happens when humans begin to break down under the weight of severe and constant anxiety.

Over the course of the working day, my own paranoia and anxiety would lift of their own accord. Around three or four, I would go out, usually to meet someone. By evening I was invariably fine, delighted to be in Paris (even looking in the windows of estate agents at apartments for sale), feeling safe and snug in my little nest, my neighbourhood and my neighbours benign-seeming, my luck unquestionable, the fears of the morning as unreal as last night's dreams. I smiled indulgently at my poor beleaguered self of so many hours before and assumed that I would wake the next morning in a continuation of my present mood, which of course I never did.

One of the people I saw regularly in Paris was a young psychiatrist named Azad, whom I had found on a conversation exchange website. We met twice a week, he to practise his English and I my French. Azad was a mix of French and Armenian. He had decided to become a psychiatrist largely because he had seen his only sister succumb to schizophrenia – an unhappy coincidence that we discovered on our first meeting and that immediately bound us. He was kind and sensitive and a true Renaissance man – a polyglot, a polymath, an aesthete, an intellectual – and he did his best to educate me in a dozen ways, pointing out minute architectural features hidden in the nooks of laneways, alerting me to moments in French history that had occurred on the street corners on which we found ourselves standing. On café napkins, he sketched timelines of the successive Republics of France and snakepits of dashes and arrows tracing the barbarian invasions of Europe.

He was like an angel who'd been appointed to guide me through Paris, gentle Beatrice to my confounded Dante, and I could never quite understand what he was getting out of our meetings. His English was already near perfect, and I was often a slightly glum or tentative companion. It wasn't romance he was looking for – Azad was gay, a fact that freed our friendship from any awkward or ambiguous agendas. (My other conversation partner was a Congolese financial analyst named Hippolyte, who was flirtatious and charming and not to be trusted, and whose teasing banter and tendency to glance too often at my breasts provided an amusing contrast to Azad's courtly but sexually disinterested attentiveness.) Whatever the topic on which we began – gargoyles or Visigoths or the glories of Titian – we invariably ended up conversing in English about psychosis and other forms of mental illness, a busman's holiday for both of us, but a subject we seemed unable to stay away from.

When I mentioned the daily pattern of my moods to him, Azad said gently, 'Well, you know, this may be a sign of depression . . . because of the way the cortisol levels change throughout the day . . .' I remembered reading something about cortisol, about how depressed people tend to feel more depressed in the morning. But hearing him say it sent my relatively good 5 p.m. mood plummeting, and my anxiety level spiked. I stiffened and looked at my hot chocolate – which, due to the shaking in my hands, I did not now trust myself to lift – and thought exactly what I had always thought when I'd found myself, in the past, in similar states: *Just don't let him see that you're falling apart.*

The anxiety was unpleasant enough in its own right, but it was more frightening still for what I knew it might herald. In the past it had preceded depression, and the two states had then combined to produce a new form of awfulness.

In the late autumn of 2000, a confluence of unhappy external circumstances and my catastrophic interpretation of them had put me in an unfamiliar and slippery state of mind. I was standing at an ATM on Grafton Street in Dublin one day as taxi after taxi rounded the corner, each driver blowing his horn. At first, I thought it was a taxi strike. But then I noticed that there were children riding in the taxis, and that they all had Down's syndrome. The children looked tragic and beautiful, and I felt moved to tears. In fact, many things had become catalysts for tears: kittens, small kindnesses, an ad for the Special Olympics. There was a young and hefty Tanzanian guy who worked at my local Tesco, and a tiny elderly woman named Marie would follow him around, peering through her thick eyeglasses. She would stand in the fruit aisle, munching away on grapes she had no intention of paying for and saying, 'Jaaaysus, didja ever see wedder like it in yer life, didja?' And the big Tanzanian would chat softly to her, always gracious, and this too made me want to weep.

Experiencing the world as a sentimental drama full of heartbreaking details was not a totally uninteresting sensation, but the quality of the sadness soon began to change. I felt steeped in a darker form of grief that both emanated from me and rose to meet me. I marvelled at the fact that we all kept going in the face of so much sadness. I felt deeply connected to people, which I tried to view as a bonus; but the empathy was so indiscriminate it was crippling, and it was tinged with the narcissism of depression. I felt sure that others could see me more clearly than I could see myself, that there was whispered agreement on the fact that I was falling apart, that this irrevocable dissolution was somehow preordained, and that the only one who hadn't seen it coming was me. I sat through a disastrous job interview certain that my fraudulence was evident. Believing that I shouldn't compound that fraudulence by trying to hide it, I reasoned that I should come clean and admit to all my failings. Fortunately, the grim effort required just to sit there was enough to render such an explication impossible.

After a sleepless week, the awfulness came to a head one Friday night, during which the gloom that enveloped me assumed more frightening shades. My housemate Gabrielle cancelled her plans for the evening and encouraged me to phone St James's Hospital, to find out if I could see someone. As it was a Friday night, the woman I spoke to said that instead of my coming in, someone could come to my house and 'give me something'. Then she asked if I was alone, and whether I thought I was in danger of harming myself. I said no, and no. The second no was a lie, but I told it because although those thoughts were certainly going through my head, I knew that deep down, I did not want to harm myself. I had never before entertained thoughts of suicide. That night, though, my mind kept returning to the idea – or, more accurately, the idea kept returning to my mind, zinging past like tracer fire. I had the disconcerting sense that it was not me who was having my thoughts, but my thoughts that were having me. As frightening as the idea of harming myself was, the fact of being asked such a question was possibly more frightening. Suddenly, I was someone one had to check with on such issues.

The woman asked again if I wanted someone to come to the house. I did not. There was a long-standing link in my mind between psychiatric professionals making house calls and people being taken to mental institutions. If confronted with such professionals, I was not at all sure I would be able to behave like someone who didn't need to be hospitalized. The woman and I agreed that I would see how I felt in the morning, and if things were no better I would come to the hospital then.

The next morning, I was no better. Gabrielle drove me through the city to St James's. It was one of those days that are bright without being sunny, when the light is a metallic, headachy white. The world looked blank and flat and uninviting, and all the people we passed had an unreal quality to them, like figures in an architect's mock-up. At the hospital, the doctor gave me a baby dosage of Valium and said I should visit my GP on Monday to discuss with him what medication, if any, I should go on.

Monday morning, with my head in my hand, my elbow on my doctor's desk, I cried, my tears actually dribbling on to the desktop before he reached for the tissues. I had always found my doctor attractive and, as the large bloopy drops issued from my eyes, I saw the two of us as from a distance, my crumpled, pathetic self and his composed, blond loveliness, and I knew that if ever I'd had a chance with him, I didn't any more. He gave me the number of a therapist he knew, a prescription for Seroxat and another one for sleeping pills.

The following evening, I fainted. I was standing in my bedroom, talking to Gabrielle about nothing much, when suddenly I felt a panic creeping, rising, swelling, threatening to overwhelm me. The most obvious and helpful thing would've been simply to sit down. Instead, I thought, *Say nothing. Don't let on. Soon she'll finish talking and you can excuse yourself and close the door . . .* The next thing I knew, I was lying on the floor. Gabrielle was crouched over me, saying, 'Are you okay? Are you okay?'

I had never fainted in my life. I had never seen anyone else faint except in the movies; I'm not sure I even believed in fainting as a phenomenon. But the anxiety was such that I had collapsed with the effort of trying to conceal it. Eventually I got up and sat down on the bed, and where the panic had been there was a physical stillness, an emptiness. But there was also something new to fear: now my body, as well as my mind, was betraying me.

The next day, I phoned my doctor and asked him for something to quell the anxiety until the Seroxat kicked in. I tried to sound like someone who would never abuse prescription drugs, but at the same time like someone troubled enough to need something, *now*. He gave me a prescription for Xanax, which I rushed to fill. It made me woozy and tired. Like someone in a cartoon who gets bopped on the head and sees stars before toppling over, I had a few moments of sudden-onset sleepiness before falling into a deep slumber for the rest of the day. I didn't take Xanax again.

Because I had never felt like this before and didn't know what to do, handing myself over to an antidepressant seemed as good an idea as any. But I was also extremely uncomfortable with the idea that I needed it. And, after the previous week's insomnia, I was now finding it difficult to do much of anything but sleep. I didn't know whether my exhaustion was to do with the antidepressant, the sleeping pills, the crash the depression had precipitated or a combination of the three. But spending hours in bed during daylight made me feel guilty and scared.

One afternoon, Gabrielle came upstairs to sit with me. Even though it was November, she said, 'Can we open a window?'

'Does it smell bad?' I said, without lifting my head off the pillow.

'It just smells like a sick room.'

She didn't mean a room of mental illness, but when she said it, I thought of the smell of Mike's bedrooms in our succession of houses, the smell of his clothes, layers of them, even in summer. He hated taking showers in those days, and he hated leaving his bed. Presumably, the controlled environment of his bedroom was preferable to the random and unceasing stimuli that raged beyond his bedroom door. But it was likely depression, too – depression often follows a psychotic period – and the fact that any activity at all was exhausting. When he did emerge, it was with his head hanging and his eyes averted, looking as though he were trying not to be seen.

> . . . the preoccupation with being seeable may be condensed with the idea of the mental self being penetrable, and vulnerable, as when the individual feels that one can look right through him into his 'mind' or 'soul' . . . in psychotic conditions the gaze or scrutiny of the other can be experienced as an actual penetration into the core of the 'inner' self.

R. D. Laing is referring, in the above passage, to feelings experienced by the schizoid individual, but the sense of permeability can apply to the depressive state as well. The feeling of being under a spotlight is not, however, mere paranoia. When you are mentally unwell, people *do* watch you much more closely. They are like animals sniffing the air for signs of trouble, monitoring your mental vital signs for indications of deterioration or improvement. They try to read behind what you're saying, or behind the silence. They ask if you're in danger of harming yourself, and when you say no, they doubt you, not only searching for the cover-up but deciding whether you could even recognize your capacity for self-destruction.

There are two things I took from growing up around my brother, both of which I was reminded of that winter. One was an awareness of the loneliness of mental illness. There was a woman I used to see a couple of times a week in Dublin, always either on Nassau Street or on College Green, across from the front gates of Trinity. Her skin was grey and her hair was shoulder-length and also grey, though she was probably only about forty. She was always on her own and I never saw her speak to anyone. A few times I slowed down and walked behind her, watching her. I was pretty sure she had schizophrenia. She had the same slumped gait that Mike did, the same dead look in her eyes. She was quite obviously medicated and looked profoundly depressed. What always struck me was how alone she was, how sealed off she seemed, as she made her slow, steady way through the streams of human traffic. And then weeks went by and I didn't see her. I never saw her again.

The other thing I took from witnessing Mike's illness was an active fear of going mad. Growing up, I saw nothing that protected me from what had happened to him – this thing that had caught us all so unawares, this force that, whatever we did, whatever he did, just kept bearing down on him. Insanity seemed to me then as though it were a thing that might swoop any time, like a flu in winter, if I failed to exercise proper vigilance. I developed over the years a tendency to catastrophize unpleasant states of mind, to suspect that any significant sense of unease signalled the onset of total and permanent psychosis. By the autumn of 2000, I had long since dispensed with any concept of a continuum where mental health was concerned, and so was terrified that this was *it*.

In one of Mike's letters home, during the period in the late seventies in which he expressed himself in a disjointed and metaphorical prose, he wrote that he was *just a bit aback from the picnic*. It seemed an apt, if deceptively offhand, assessment of his current state. From the first time I read that line, I imagined that the picnic he had in mind was life – life lived cheerfully and at its best, under sunny skies and in a festive and communal spirit.

One night during that unhappy winter of 2000, as I sat slumped on the sofa, I saw myself, in a moment of terrible clarity, through the eyes of those friends who'd been observing me with such concern. I realized that they regarded me as being on the other side of some divide. I realized that they no longer expected me to behave like the person they had known. My life, suddenly, seemed like a false floor, far easier to crash through than I had ever imagined. In a panic, I wondered how long I had before people permanently recategorized me and gave up on me for good. But just as I feared the speed with which this might happen (relegating me for all time to a life in which I would achieve nothing, love no one and never feel any joy), equally I saw how easily I might acclimatize to my new persona. In this moment of clarity, I had glimpsed that bizarre paradox: the safety in helplessness, the seductiveness of giving up the struggle, even when the struggle was against misery and a kind of non-being.

It was the cold comfort of bad faith that beckoned, what Sartre termed *mauvaise foi*. Kierkegaard had already written of this kind of self-negation, in which the individual attempts to shut out the demands of freedom. What I had glimpsed was the relief of denying my freedom – of handing over responsibility for myself to other people. No longer would I have to make decisions or choices, or to exercise agency. I had understood that I could commit one great failure, after which I would never again have to fail at anything.

But whatever relief I intuited in such an abdication was immediately shunted aside by the fear of what lay beyond. What terrified me about this strange place that beckoned, what rendered its apparent seductions most suspect, was that in it, there was only me. I shuddered. I thought, *I can't live here alone*, and what I meant by here was my own head. My mind would become a sad and scary room that nobody would want to visit and that I would never be able to leave, and the overwhelming loneliness of that made me want to get better, fast.

Eight years later, in Paris, I felt myself slipping again. I tried to think like the Buddha: these are just thoughts, arising and vanishing.

Instead I thought like Nietzsche: only the weak need other people. I tried to lose myself in distractions and sometimes it worked and I would realize with a spasm of relief, perhaps while reading the newspaper (which, oddly, with its catalogue of horrors, always tends to lessen my anxiety), that the tormenting inquisition had ceased. Of course, once I realized that it had gone, it came right back.

I began to think I needed to get out of Paris. I was experiencing the distressing, and not entirely unfamiliar, reversal of ownership in which my thoughts seemed to be having me rather than my having them. I was considering a weekend visit to a friend in Geneva, but then she emailed and said she'd just taken a three-month contract in Tajikistan.

Don't worry, I wrote, *I'll come to Tajikistan!*

Yes, that was it! I would fly to Tajikistan! I'd had enough of bonbons and daintiness and unrelieved beauty. I wanted to be in a place where the men were earthy and had fingers like sausages. I googled, I checked flights, I read UN reports. There was a major power shortage in Tajikistan and the country was in the midst of the worst cold wave in forty years, and I could guess what a freezing Tajikistan with no electricity might be like. There I was, in Paris, the City of Light, in a centrally heated apartment in the 6th arrondissement, and Tajikistan seemed the one place on earth I needed to be.

Clearly, I was panicking. At the intensifying sense of psychological isolation and the exponential speed with which I seemed to be spiralling down, knowing that there was a line I was capable of crossing after which I would be undeniably, inarguably depressed. I was casting about for some way, any way, to break the mood.

Tajikistan!

Hell, of course, is not other people. Other people are merely irritating. Hell is the unrelieved self. What I needed was not Tajikistan in February but someone I could trust. Miraculously, in the midst of my fact-finding on Tajikistan, an old friend wrote to say she was coming to Paris in three days. I could not have chosen a better visitor, for though I knew Maria well enough to confide in her how I'd been feeling, I also knew that she shared none of my depressive, paranoid, neurotic tendencies, and so would not peer worriedly at me (as Azad had) but would instead insist that we enjoy being in Paris, something that I, in my abusive state of mind, had become incapable of.

Pascal, in *Pensées*, held that the great majority of human diversions were attempts by people to avoid thoughts of themselves, for were we to pause for self-contemplation, misery and anxiety would rush to meet us. Indeed. But all things have their time. One awful day in the awful autumn of 2000, I lay in bed reading Voltaire's *Candide*, at the close of which the eponymous hero – after all his travails and the assaults on optimism, after all the philosophizing and the theorizing and the witnessing of the rottenness at the heart of man – declares, '. . . we must go and work in the garden.' It struck me with the force of revelation. There are times, I realized, when self-scrutiny is called for, and there are times when one is ill-equipped to wrestle with metaphysics or the darkness, when it is wisest, simply, to do the next right thing. Show up. Put one foot in front of the other. Attend to the simple tasks. Re-establish your capacity to do the small things. With their rhythm and familiarity, they are a bedrock. They won't let you down.

The moment Maria arrived, she began to take me out of myself. We went to Montmartre and the Pompidou, we ate onion soup and overpriced macaroons. We laughed, we talked, she recognized me. I felt safe. By the time she left, the worst of the mood was broken. The anxiety was a thing on which I could cast a cold eye, and I regarded myself with renewed compassion. The lure of Tajikistan receded and I sat in my apartment and sighed and smiled because when the dread lifts, there is no calm like it. The thousand fears that have pressed so frantically fall away. The need for vigilance evaporates. Everything is fine, exactly as it is, and the world shines in a fresh manifestation of miracle.

A couple of weeks later, sitting in a café in the Louvre with Azad and feeling tip-top, I explained to him my aversion to psychotherapy, an aversion based on the fear (a fear I can regard with bemusement in such tip-top moments) that if anyone were to probe deeply enough, he or she would realize that I was crazy. The mask would slip, and the whole house of cards would come tumbling down. In a way, I had Azad himself in mind when I said this. For while I could keep up the front with my other casual Paris acquaintances, with Azad there was no pretending. As we talked that day in the café, I realized that his wisdom and gentleness and insight had presented me with an almost irresistible invitation to fall apart. He leaned across the table and looked me in the eye, seriously but lightly, and said in an untroubled, confidential whisper, 'We are all crazy.'

Eighteen

My father walked crab-wise. From the waist up, he listed to one side as though assailed by a strong wind. He was eighty-two and had scoliosis. As he sidled across the gleaming mid-court of the Palace in Auburn Hills, Michigan, he looked like someone who had just got out of bed and was hamming up his aches and pains. His second wife and five of his six children sat in a semicircle behind him.

It was 2008. I had come to Detroit for the weekend from Paris to help celebrate the high point of my father's career. In 1979, after a few drifty years during which it looked like his NBA career might fizzle out (he was fifty-three by then, there weren't a lot more chances left), my father took one of the least coveted jobs in the league, as general manager of the Detroit Pistons. For decades the Pistons had been one of the worst teams in the NBA. The year he took over, they won sixteen of eighty-two games. Within a few years, my father had, through a series of clever and controversial trades and draft picks, turned the team into contenders and rescued himself from the brink of professional oblivion.

By the time he left the club in 1992, the Pistons had made five trips to the Eastern Conference finals and three to the NBA finals, and had won the NBA championship in 1989 and 1990. The second of those titles was won against the Trailblazers in the Coliseum in Portland. Until that series, Detroit hadn't won a single game in Portland since 1974 – the year my father was fired as coach of the Trailblazers – and so to win the title there, the scene of so much frustration for my father a decade and a half earlier (the final game clinched at the buzzer, on a shot with 0.7 seconds left on the clock), must have tasted especially sweet. After the Pistons won their first championship, my father said to me, 'How many people can say they're the best in the world at something? You can't measure that if you're a surgeon. But we can say that right now we're the best in the world at what we do.' He wasn't bragging, just stating a fact. Actually, he seemed humbled by his good fortune.

During my father's tenure in Detroit, the team acquired the sobriquet Bad Boys because they played, depending on your point of view, either tough and aggressive or just plain dirty. In the book *The Franchise: Building a Winner with the World Champion Detroit Pistons, Basketball's Bad Boys*, Cameron Stauth called it Coalminer Style, in reference to my father's roots. Now, the architect of the Bad Boys was being honoured. At half-time of a Pistons game, a banner with my father's name on it would be raised to the rafters. For us – his children – there was an added resonance to the occasion. This was the first time since the divorce, thirty-one years before, that the five of us had come together to see him. For the thirteen years he had lived in Detroit, and over the few subsequent years he'd lived and worked in Minnesota, I had never once visited him in his home. How had that happened? Was it my decision? Was I ever invited? I can't remember. By 1989, I had moved to Ireland, meaning that my father's habit of visiting us when he happened to be in town on business – scouting, usually – didn't apply. Five or six years passed during which I didn't see him at all. Aside from Mike, who my father says kept him for years on a list of people he didn't want to see, I saw less of him than any of my siblings did. I would read about him in the paper and find myself slightly surprised to be reminded that there was someone out there in the world with whom I shared so much of my DNA.

Throughout the weekend, I kept noticing my father's hands. As a child, I'd been intensely aware of them: square and thick, callused, the plentiful hairs like wire. That these hairs should sprout in the spaces between his knuckles had struck me as fabulously animalesque. I have memories that specifically concern his hands. He had a habit of drumming his fingers on the table-top in time with a tune (he'd played the piano all his life), producing a deep thrum that with my skinny girlish digits I couldn't replicate. And the way he held a tumbler of vodka and tonic and, with the index finger of the same hand, stirred the drink, imprinted itself on my mind as masculine and authoritative, signalling an easy command of the physical universe.

The hands were still square and strong, unchanged, really, from what I remembered, their familiarity deep and uncanny and also disconcerting, for they called attention to how much he was otherwise changed. Though it had only been two years since I'd last seen him (we'd played tennis; his frustration with my erratic forehand hadn't lessened), he was otherwise dramatically diminished.

He spent the weekend flanked by three or four massive black men, all former players of his who looked like they might at any minute burst out of their designer suits. He appeared almost childlike among them. (One of the four was Vinnie Johnson, who had sunk the winning jump shot against Portland in 1990.) But it wasn't my father's seeming smallness, or even the recent drastic increase in the curvature of his spine, that was most striking. It was the eyes. They had long had a slightly sad cast to them, a look suggestive of unexpressed emotion; now they were rheumy and bloodshot, giving him a lost and abstracted, even frightened, look. It was the look of incipient senility, and it lent him an air of vulnerability that was totally incongruous with the person he had been. This was the guy who'd told me, 'I always say that my business is the business of winning.' This was the guy who'd said, 'A winner is a loser who just didn't quit.' Now he was a man who looked, at every moment, as though he were trying not to cry.

On the night of the banner-raising, there were speeches at half-court. My father's own contribution was brief. He singled out a few of his contemporaries for praise – his scouts Stan Novak and Will Robinson, the Pistons' owner Bill Davidson, and Chuck Daly, who my father had hired to coach the team. Of the four, one – Stan – was already dead. Stan and my father had known each other for over sixty years; they'd been at Ie Shima together in 1945. Of the other three, Will would die four weeks later. Bill would die in March the following year. Two months after that, Chuck would die of pancreatic cancer.

After he spoke, my father was led over to a photo collage commemorating his achievements. The collage was unveiled by two ample-breasted blonde cheerleaders wearing shiny white pants and halter necks. He was instructed to pull a curtain rope to reveal the banner, his name against a white background, trimmed in the team colours. The banner rose to the rafters as rousing triumphalist music blared. Every time I watch the YouTube clip – his crab-wise walk that looks excruciating, his doe-in-the-headlights expression, the faltering voice – it is that music that finally brings tears to my eyes.

The previous night, we had all attended an informal dinner for my father, along with Chuck and some of the players from the Bad Boys era. Everyone who wanted to say something about my father was invited to do so. Following a panicked flurry of nods and whispers, we decided that Tim would speak on our behalf. It was not an easy task, and Tim was a risky choice. He has always been the most unselfconsciously good-hearted among us. But his interior monologue tends to be exteriorized, and so he is the one most likely to blurt out precisely the wrong thing. He pulled it off, though. He told a story of when he was ten and went to basketball camp and was greeted by a now-famous coach with a growling, 'You'll never be as tough as your old man.' A generic enough tale pitched to the crowd at hand (a crowd for whom toughness was the ultimate attribute) and tinged, ostensibly, with admiration. For those of us who knew better, it was also an unwittingly sad anecdote, for it was a reminder of how deeply in my father's shadow all his sons had felt.

Towards the end of that evening, the five of us kids ended up sitting around one of the tables with my father. He signalled that we were all to join hands. Six of us in a circle holding hands, as though we were having a seance. He squeezed the hand on either side of him and his eyes filled with tears. We knew he was going to say something deeply sentimental. He is the opposite of my mother, who, though a warm and caring person, is astonishingly devoid of sentimentality, whom I have never once seen shed a tear through all of our miseries, or through her own. My father, on the other hand, can tear up at the slightest hint of emotion, particularly when he says, 'I love you.' Or, his more emphatic, signature phrase, 'God, I love you.'

The eyes of his five children darted from side to side, in our swapped glances a mix of apprehension, sentiment, slight embarrassment at this weird public display, and the temptation to giggle.

But we summoned the necessary gravitas and waited for whatever was to come.

Finally, my father said, 'This one's for Mike.'

If there is anything that binds us to our father, it is basketball. There is a strange photo taken in our rec room in North Carolina when I was about three. I am perched on the coffee table – an upturned tree stump my father had converted into furniture. My father, my sister Robin, John and Timmy are sitting in a row on the sofa, facing me. My father is holding a basketball, offering it to me as though it were a sacramental object. I am eyeing him with what looks like dubious reluctance, showing no sign of taking the ball. (It looks, in fact, like it would be too heavy for me to hold.) My three siblings stare expectantly at me. A huge amount appears to be riding on my acceptance or refusal of the ball.

He saw me play once in college. When he met me outside the locker room after the game, I burst into tears, ostensibly on account of my poor performance but really in the throes of a much more fundamental anxiety: the fear of love's conditionality. His old friend

Stan Novak, the Pistons' scout, was with him, and I can still see the look on Stan's face: tender and wide-eyed. Stan was a softie. My father's expression, a forgiving and somewhat abashed smile, suggested that he thought my tears disproportionate to the situation. We both knew that my performance on the court was essentially irrelevant; by then it was clear that I was not going to crash through some glass ceiling and become the first woman to dunk the ball, or even develop into a college player of minor significance. I suppose I should have felt relieved, but instead I felt adrift. If we weren't linked by this, then by what?

That weekend in Detroit we had a minibus for the family and the friends of my father's who'd come for the weekend from out of town. As we drove between the hotel and our various activities, I felt sad and oddly envious. It seemed to me that my father and I were essentially where we had been when I was eleven – neither closer nor further apart – and yet so much had happened to him since. It was as though at some unconscious level I had assumed that, because he hadn't added to *our* story since 1976, he hadn't added to the story of himself. But his life had had a whole second act. By 2008, he had been married to his second wife for nearly thirty years. His best friends were people I had never met or even heard of. They spoke of him intimately, drawing on a store of recollections that none of his children could match.

I had last seen my father in 2006 when I'd visited him in Georgia to talk to him about Mike. We sat in the office in his house, surrounded by photographs, trophies and memorabilia, including an autographed photo of Babe Ruth, a home-run ball Steve had hit in a Little League game when he was twelve, and a framed crayon drawing I'd made at the age of four, depicting the heads of several ladies who had just been to the hairdresser's – a drawing my father had hung over various desks and dressers since the day of its creation. He had told me that he was glad I was writing about Mike and that he wanted to help. Like my mother, he seemed to feel that it was a form of tribute. But when the time came for us to talk, he was guarded and slightly ill at ease. It was understandable. This was the first time we'd ever set out to have a conversation about Mike.

My father had seen him about a year before, when he was out in Oregon. 'He gave me a big bear hug before I left,' he said, and I thought of the way Mike had held on to me when I left him in the lobby of Shari's the week of Tim's wedding. He said that Mike had talked about his days playing ball at McGuinness and about the Catholic League championship. In fact, much of what my father told me about Mike that day was linked, in some way, to basketball. During Mike's first year at Duke, when he was playing on the freshman team, my father only got to two of his games, because Wake Forest usually played on the same nights. My father's impression – not shared by everyone – was that although Mike had been happy to play that first year, he wasn't disappointed when it was over.

'He knew he wasn't good enough for power schools,' he said. Then he smiled sadly and shook his head. 'But he sure could shoot the ball.'

When Mike was finishing high school, my father had hoped that he would choose a smaller college where he could play regularly. He still wondered whether it might have anchored him and kept him away from the drugs he always implicated in Mike's demise.

My father didn't think that, apart from the usual arrogance of college students, Mike changed for the worse during his years at Duke. It had never entered his mind that there were mental problems. Nor did he believe that there were indications of any problems growing up. He saw a boy who studied hard, got good grades, had friends. 'Mike might've been a little serious,' he said, 'but he was a normal kid.'

I asked him about a story I knew only dimly, about his having bailed Mike out of jail in the mid seventies. Mike was drifting on the east coast then, living in boarding houses or sleeping rough. One day my father got a call from the Durham police department saying that Mike had been arrested on the Duke campus.

'What was he arrested for?' I asked, afraid to hear the answer.

'Vagrancy,' my father said. 'He was shooting baskets in the gym.'

My father flew from Oregon to North Carolina, making his way to an old dilapidated jail where he found Mike in an enclosure made of high chain-link, more like a cage than a cell. With him in the cage were about a dozen big black guys. Nearby, there was another cage full of women. Two of the women were fighting over one guy, and all the guys could see this and were picking sides and cheering. The place was chaos. Mike – skinny, scared, disoriented white boy – looked at his father and said, 'Dad, get me out of here.'

My father shook his head and chuckled at the memory, not because he took the jail scene lightly but because it wouldn't be in him to offer an explication of the pain it caused him. Instead, the sadness is embedded in the humour, implicit and bearable. The story, if told properly – with affection and elan – provides adequate cover. And my father loves a good story. When he tells one that involves himself, particularly one in which he has done something silly, he manages to render his incompetence charming, implying that proficiency in such a situation would be somehow *womanly*. And he has done some silly things. Like setting his own pants alight (it was 1973, they were polyester) while attempting to get the fire in the den going by adding lighter fluid to it. He didn't know there was a difference between a reluctant barbecue and a log fire. He is rigid in his way, and fanatically disciplined, but he can laugh at himself. And it was with a similarly bemused exasperation that he recalled some of the scrapes Mike had got himself into.

There was another incident he described which I must have witnessed myself, though I have no memory of it. It took place at a Trailblazers' game in Portland in the mid seventies. My father recalled that he was just taking his seat on the bench following a time-out when he spotted a guy coming into the arena, wearing a long green army coat with big brass buttons. He had unkempt hair and a scruffy beard. The whistle blew. My father turned his attention back to the game, not even registering who it was he had seen until he felt a tap on his shoulder and heard a familiar voice behind him saying, 'We gotta get you out of here. We have to go.'

He turned around and found himself staring into the mad eyes of his own son.

'I can't leave now,' my father said. 'Go sit with Mom in the stands.'

'No,' Mike said, 'you have to get out of here.'

My father hadn't seen Mike in some time, but he was hardly in a position to have this conversation; he had enough on his plate – in the middle of a game, in the middle of a losing season, holding on to his job by a thread.

Later that night, he took Mike for a walk on the golf course and Mike got down on his knees and wrapped his arms around my father's legs. It was the sort of thing nobody does in real life, a flamboyant enactment of filial piety straight out of Shakespeare or a film about the Cosa Nostra. He pleaded with him, 'If you don't get out of coaching, you're going to have a heart attack.'

My father blamed it on the drugs. It was a neat and simplifying explanation, one that allowed for the conclusive denunciation of all that he had found troubling about the last several years. The self-indulgent hedonism of the young. Their blithe disregard of the sacrifices of past generations. The way they ridiculed the country he loved while living off the fat of its prosperity. He looked at his son, down on his knees in the wet grass, the old army coat, the wild eyes, and saw the madness of the last decade embodied.

Nineteen

In the summer of 1987, when she was on her way to a job in Alaska, Susan, Mike's old girlfriend from Duke, stopped to see him in Oregon. She hadn't seen him since 1974, when he'd showed up at her house in Fort Meyers, Florida, where she was teaching Transcendental Meditation, but she was the only one from college who'd tried to keep in touch with him. Every year she sent him a Christmas card he never answered. She still had a book of Chinese love poems he'd given her for her birthday in 1970, inscribed in the front, *To remind you always of when we were young and hopelessly in love.*

She arrived at the group home outside of Portland, dressed conservatively in a long flannel skirt and a blouse, driving a rental car. Mike was in the driveway, shooting baskets and smoking. She waved cheerfully as she approached.

He greeted her affectionately, though with slight disdain: 'You look so . . . *American.*'

They spent the day together, doing touristy things, going to the Japanese Gardens and the Pittock Mansion. Apart from his yelling at her in the checkout line of the Safeway for what he considered an indiscreet comment about their personal life eighteen years earlier, and the fact that he kept picking up cigarette butts off the ground, he seemed 'fairly normal' to her. The impression she came away with was of someone who was still a hippy, still striking an anti-establishment pose, but now in an aimless way. Knowing him as she once had, she didn't find the attitude out of character. There had always been something in him, she thought, that needed to feel unique, 'a star'. His disdain for conventional society had been strong. Seeing him now, she believed there was something 'almost conscious' in the persona he was projecting.

The phrase 'almost conscious' sticks in my mind, for it introduces the question of choice. There is no one in my family who thinks that if only Mike had tried hard enough, he could have been the things he'd once dreamed of being: a lawyer, a psychologist, a medical technician. But on occasion we have wondered whether he might, over the years, have done . . . *something*.

In her book *A Beautiful Mind*, Sylvia Nasar describes how the mathematician John Nash, who won the Nobel Prize in economics for work he had done as a postgraduate student, succumbed to schizophrenia in his early thirties. For about twenty-five years he was frequently in the grip of paranoid delusions, psychotic, unemployable and occasionally hospitalized; and during much of this period he refused to take antipsychotic medications. Then, in his fifties, Nash experienced a remission. He described the process of his emergence as one that involved 'both a growing awareness of the sterility of his delusional state and a growing capacity for rejecting delusional thought'.

It is estimated that between 10 and 20 per cent of people with schizophrenia experience some degree of improvement late in life, a burning out of acute symptoms and the development of some degree of insight into delusions. For Nash, remission was not a clear case of before and after. Though the 'noise level' quietened significantly, Nash reported that he was still plagued by paranoid thoughts and voices, and he likened the maintenance of rationality to the constant vigilance and willpower required for dieting. He was never able to resume teaching or research at anything like the level at which he was working before he became ill. According to Nasar, Nash believes, 'rightly or wrongly, that he willed his own recovery'. It is a belief that likely contributes to a sometimes callous attitude towards one of his own sons, who was diagnosed with schizophrenia in his teens. 'I don't think of my son . . . as entirely a sufferer,' Nash has said. 'In part, he is simply *choosing* to escape from "the world".'

For argument's sake, let us say that Mike has made some choices about his life. That in the grey area (if one exists) between the impossibility of going back to who he was before his first breakdown and the decades of doing, essentially, nothing, there was a life he might have constructed for himself. Supposing he had wanted to work. What kind of job could he have managed? Something fairly simple, maybe stuffing envelopes. He would have been working alongside people whose intellectual capacities he deems far inferior to his own, the kind of people he labels 'retarded'. Given his personality, his pride, would he have found such work a boost to his self-esteem? Or would it have served only to make painfully explicit certain facts he seems to acknowledge only implicitly?

Given that same pride, it is possible to imagine why he might have greeted his old girlfriend as he did, and why she read into his attitude the hint of something 'almost conscious': it was as though he wanted her to know that what he was refusing was not the half-life of menial labour that was available to him but a place in *her* world – her bourgeois, salaried, rental-car world. For in spite of the myriad humiliations and all the assaults on his freedom, there remains, I have to assume, a desire to save face. If he tells me, as he once did, that he cannot leave Oregon because he is working for Clackamas County Mental Health and many people are depending on him, my best guess (though it is only a guess) is that this is not a simple delusion – that he does not literally believe that what he is saying is true. He is, instead, insisting that I collude in a lie that somehow preserves a necessary vision of himself.

But if I choose to emphasize the signs that Mike has a basic grip on reality and an ability to make meaningful choices, and if I extrapolate from these signs a vision of him as a person capable of work and a greater degree of independence, am I simply underestimating the subtler ravages of schizophrenia? The hallmark of the illness, after all, is not psychosis but the daily tedium of functional impairment. Another hallmark is a lack of insight about oneself and about the illness – a lack that can persist throughout a lifetime.

In an effort to arrive at a picture of the 'average' schizophrenic brain – and to create an aggregate image of the disease process – neuroscientists at UCLA, in conjunction with laboratories around the world, have taken hundreds of brain scans over a period of years of children and adults with schizophrenia. They collated these images in order to map some of the damage associated with the illness, as well as to try to see patterns of difference between healthy brains and the brains of people with schizophrenia. The damage they recorded manifests as grey-matter loss, or brain-cell death (the younger the age of onset, the more significant the loss), beginning in the parietal cortex and pushing forwards into the frontal lobe. The parietal cortex is the part of the brain that makes sense of what we hear, see, taste or touch, and impairment here is associated with hearing voices – the auditory hallucinations characteristic of schizophrenia. The frontal lobe helps us to analyse information and make decisions, and thus to organize our lives. Loss of volume here may result in nerve damage which could impair connections needed for verbal memory, attention, reasoning and meaningful speech.

And what about Mike's medications? Though his own cocktail has been remixed several times over the years, the effects have often been a hammer blow to the brain and body. Two of the four drugs that he is on – loxapine and lithium – have between them the potential to produce lethargy, slurred speech, insomnia, agitation, cataracts and the worsening of existing glaucoma, decreased concentration and attention span, impaired memory, and involuntary movements of the mouth, lips, legs or arms. Depending on the intensity and prevalence of the side-effects, we may imagine they are preferable to the torments of psychosis. But they are an enormous hindrance when he rises to face the world each day.

Elyn Saks was a young woman of exceptional intellectual promise. She was studying at Oxford as a Marshall Scholar in the 1970s when she had her first full-blown psychotic breakdown and hospitalization. Her diagnosis, as she writes in her book *The Center Cannot Hold*, was 'chronic paranoid schizophrenic with acute exacerbation'. Her prognosis: 'grave'. Saks's treatment, as well as relying on antipsychotic medication, has also included decades of psychoanalysis – a therapy very rarely used for people with schizophrenia. She credits her analysts, who regarded her psychotic thoughts as 'unconsciously motivated and meaningful', with helping her to live with (as opposed to recover from) her illness. Her own – highly unusual – view of her psychosis is that it is, at least in part, an attempt by the unconscious mind to protect the conscious mind from painful thoughts and feelings.

Saks has managed, in spite of several severely psychotic periods in the decades since her diagnosis, to become a professor of both law and psychiatry. She was a recipient of one of the MacArthur Foundation's so-called genius grants. She knows that she is exceptional; indeed, she notes that only one in five people with schizophrenia comes to live independently and hold down a job (let alone a job like hers). So rare are her circumstances that one of her colleagues, in urging her to publish the book under a nom de plume, asked if she really wanted to become known as 'the schizophrenic with a job'.

Saks's analysts, on the other hand, urged her not to define herself in terms of something which even highly trained professionals don't fully understand. Nevertheless, she felt the full weight of psychiatric labels for years. One clinical judgement which designated her as suffering from 'schizoaffective disorder, depressive type' felt, she writes, like death; upon receiving the news, 'as if to fully inhabit the diagnosis, I quickly started to unravel.'

To the catalogue of obstacles and horrors, then, that Mike would have had to contend with in order to build even a slightly different life for himself (the illness, the breakdowns, the exhausting effort of will required to sort the real from the unreal), we must add the challenge of trying to see himself as more than a 'paranoid schizophrenic'. This is extraordinarily difficult, and not just because of societal views of schizophrenia. The illness has its own seductions.

Lori Schiller speaks explicitly of these in her memoir *The Quiet Room*. Like Saks, Schiller came from an affluent family of high achievers. She developed schizophrenia in her teens, and suffered several nightmarish years of intermittent severe psychosis. Just as she was looking at permanent confinement in a state hospital – doomed to the 'wretched half life of a chronic mental patient' – she was put on clozapine, the antipsychotic drug that appeared in the late eighties and proved exceptionally effective for some patients whose response to existing antipsychotics had been poor. Though it did not return her to a pre-illness level of functioning, it is hardly an overstatement to say that clozapine gave her back her life. But the bond she had forged with her illness was not easily broken. 'After years of begging [the voices] to go . . . when they finally did leave,

I found to my surprise that I missed them . . . I felt like there was a neon vacancy sign flashing.' In the absence of the voices, Schiller felt she had nothing to think about. She missed the voices enough that, for a time, she brought them back. 'By focusing my attention on them I was able to coax them out. I welcomed them like lost friends. They were horrible, cruel and profane, but at least they were familiar.'

For Mike, the known world of mental illness, however isolated, however terrifying, must gradually have come to seem like home. Every time he attempted to re-enter life, the world had shifted, everyone he knew had moved on that bit more. At a certain point, perhaps, trying again became more painful than giving up entirely.

Please pray for me Fanny at church in the morning as I think we can make it. Just think if we all had jobs and were moving around in the city what the news would be like at dinner time . . .

In *The Meaning of Anxiety*, Rollo May writes, 'An inadequate organism may seek to shrink its world to that in which its essential capacities are adequate, thus avoiding the catastrophic situation.' Yet we are all the inadequate organisms of May's description, no one among us possessing unlimited capacities. As May points out, we each have a threshold beyond which additional stress renders a situation catastrophic. Knowing this as we instinctively do, we construct our lives within limits. In order to avoid catastrophe, we are always shrinking our worlds, in ways that are generally neither conscious nor neurotic.

I can recall only two occasions when Mike asked me about my life. The first time was in May 2007. Tim and his wife had just had their first baby, and I had come to Oregon from Nairobi for a week to visit. Mike didn't know yet about the baby; he never questions why we turn up out of the blue – sometimes several of us at once – from our various corners of the country or the world. Sitting across the table from me that day – my mother, Howard and I were having lunch with him at Shari's – he seemed a little shaky and ill at ease.

My mother was talking about something I'd written, and Mike's eyes were flicking up and down between the table and me. And then he said:

'How did you start writing? Do you sell many books? How do people make money in Africa? How did Kenya get its name? Is it a Swahili word? I thought it was something Americans came up with because it was easy to pronounce.'

His attitude was an awkward mix of tentativeness and challenge. He gave the impression of being afraid to risk being interested in what happened beyond the borders of his world. Then, as suddenly as he'd begun to question me, he stopped. He sank back into his own thoughts and didn't emerge again that day.

One of the signs of a healthy mind is the capacity to enter imaginatively and accurately into the thoughts, feelings, hopes and fears of another – and to allow the other access to one's own inner life. This idea is related to what is more broadly known as the 'theory of mind' – the ability to attribute mental states to oneself and others, to recognize that others have thoughts, desires and intentions that are different from one's own, and to understand that these mental states can be the cause of another person's behaviour. Impaired theory of mind has been linked with certain cognitive and neurodevelopmental disorders, including autism and schizophrenia. The functional impairments suffered by people with schizophrenia – deficits of attention and memory; finding it difficult or impossible to identify emotions in others on the basis of facial expressions; their own deficits of expression – make relating to other people highly problematic.

From a psychoanalytic point of view, there is also the idea that the mutual bleed of inner lives that occurs in a genuine exchange threatens to the core someone whose 'self' feels insubstantial, or insufficiently defined. The living reality of other people may feel threatening and implosive. Laing referred to this sense of penetrability when he spoke of the 'plate-glass' feelings of the psychotic.

Mike is not psychotic. He sits quietly at Shari's and eats his burger. But he deflects attention. He refuses to answer any but the most superficial of questions – if I ask how he is, he says, every time, 'I'm ıne' – and, for the most part, he doesn't ask them. When I meet him, it is often as though we shared no past at all, so flat is his emotional register, or at least the expression of it.

Once I asked him what he remembered of me when I was small. In all the binders of photographs my mother has amassed over the years, there is only a single photo of Mike and me alone together. I am three and perched atop his shoulders in our backyard, on an autumn day devoted to the raking of leaves. (Because the photo was so rare and precious to me, I chose a very special place to keep it, so special that now I cannot find it.) And there is a letter from my mother to Fanny from 1971. The last three lines of the first page read: *Don't worry about molly & the basketball games – they are all Sat morning or afternoon. It is a good distraction to get her through the first weepy week of school. She is fine now, & does perfect work. Mike thinks she*

The second page of the letter has been lost.

When I asked him what he remembered about me, he said, 'I remember you playing "American Pie" over and over again on that little orange turntable in your bedroom.' He'd just come in from having a cigarette and he told me that that was what he'd been thinking about when he was outside smoking.

'You were?' I was touched, and amazed, to think that I lived in his mind like that.

Then he said, 'You didn't say much when you were small. Do you remember why you were like that?'

I thought for a moment. I shook my head. 'You were introverted, too,' I said, thinking of what people had told me.

'I wasn't really introverted,' he said, his tone blasé. 'I just don't like to waste time.'

The day he blurted out his questions, about me and about Kenya, I imagined I could feel the porousness of him. I felt raw myself as a result, and slightly anxious being with him, as though I were witnessing someone in the act of taking a physical risk.

I had taken him to Kenya with me, just as I had taken him to Kosovo. The letters were all in my apartment in Nairobi. A stack of photographs was on my desk. One morning I wrote about him before going into work, and when I got to the office I felt queasy and exposed in the midst of all that bustle and water-cooler bonhomie. I felt a sudden, sharp loneliness. So I learned to leave him to the weekends. But after a few months he got completely crowded out, by the demands of my job and the mental space it occupied.

The office I worked for coordinated humanitarian assistance for Somalia, and I travelled to that country a handful of times. Each time, the same two thoughts returned to me. The first was to do with Mike, the way he used to hitch around America as though it were nothing. I thought of how his friend Rob, with whom he'd driven across the country in 1972, had said Mike would just pick a canyon and follow it to wherever it led. And then I thought about how small his world was now, his absolute insistence on its limits. I had watched his world contract until it came to include only the house where he was living and whichever neighbourhood café or diner he could feel comfortable in. What struck me each time I saw him was that he was exactly as I had left him. I could go to the moon, I thought, and when I came back he would still be there, riding the #33 bus to Shari's, sitting outside the door of his house, smoking, no more affected by my appearance than if I'd come from next door.

The second thought had to do with my own past. My world, circa 1996. The two pubs on the peninsula that had become the lodestones of my existence. I remembered how on some days a degree of mettle was required to step outside my door at all. I was too paranoid to go to the village shop, too nervous to sit in a café and drink a cup of coffee, afraid to answer my phone. Now, here I was, calmly sipping tea and eating goat in one of the most dangerous countries on earth, as armed teenagers ambled a desultory patrol about the restaurant's perimeter. Was this progress? Or compensation?

The other time Mike asked about my life was one day in December 2007 when he said out of the blue, 'Do you have anxiety?'

We had just finished lunch. I looked out the window. Did I have anxiety? Indeed I did. I needed to think no further back than the drive to Mike's place that morning, and how, as always when on freeways, I had imagined horrific pile-ups, conflagrations and carnage.

'I have general anxiety, like everyone, I guess. And then I have particular anxieties,' I said. 'Like financial.'

'Or like love,' he said.

'What about love?'

'Do you have people you love in Dublin?'

I was taken aback, by the question and by the bluntness with which he asked it. I thought about my life in Dublin, which always seemed strangely underpopulated when I saw it from a distance.

'Yeah,' I said. 'I do.'

He said nothing and looked at me as though he knew more about me than I'd ever given him credit for. I wanted to know what he had to say about love, but that was the end of that. He went outside for a cigarette and when he came back to the table, he said he had to go. It was nearly one, time for him to be in Shari's smoking section – an area separated from the main restaurant by a pair of saloon doors. He belonged to a 'coffee group' that convened there. He called them the Nazis. This was not as crazy as it sounds. He was using the term Nazi in the way many people use it – to mean a fundamentalist of some sort. The men were Second World War vets who complained that America was going to the dogs because the young people were all sissies.

'I stand up for the younger generation,' Mike told me.

He also told me that the men spoke German and that the police had hired him to listen to the things they said. This was as crazy as it sounds.

He saw me to the door of the restaurant before turning to go back inside, something gallant in the gesture and in his attitude. We hugged goodbye, perfunctorily. (The protracted and heartfelt embrace of two years earlier had never been repeated.) Though I'd told him I'd be leaving Oregon the next day, his 'See you later' was delivered with the same drowsy nonchalance as if we were going to meet again that evening.

I decided to use the bathroom before I left, and retraced my steps into the restaurant. On my way out again, I peeked over the swing doors into the smoking room. If he was with the Nazis, I would catch his eye and wave goodbye. It would give him a boost, I thought, to show them that he wasn't alone in the world. But he wasn't sitting with the Nazis. He was sitting on his own at a table in the centre of the room, smoking and staring out the window. At an adjacent table there were three grizzled older men hunched over cups of coffee, all looking vaguely put-upon. They had a clubbish air about them that made me sure they were the vets. Mike didn't see me and I ducked quickly out the door before he did. Later, when I mentioned it to my mother, she said that sometime, she wasn't sure when, the Nazis had told Mike they didn't want him to sit at their table any more.

In the summer of 2009, Mike decided that he no longer wanted to speak to anyone in the family. It had started with my mother, about a year before. She had pressured him to get a test for diabetes – which Mike's doctor was strongly recommending because of his weight and other factors, and which Mike was refusing, presumably due to his horror of needles. My mother, worried about him and not knowing what else to do, applied economic sanctions – withholding the bit of extra cash she sent him every month, which he put into his cigarette and coffee fund. She relented after two cheques, but the damage was done. He stopped taking her calls. Nor would he see her when she was in Oregon at Christmas. She felt she'd made a terrible mistake. That summer, the day before I arrived in Portland, she had driven out to his house, and had managed to have a brief exchange with him in the kitchen. He was civil, but repeated that he didn't want to speak to her any more.

My mother was eighty-three by then. They had been through a lot together. But just like that, he had cut her off.

I was staying at my brother John's house for a few days in July and had phoned Mike to see if I could meet him the following day. Someone else at the house had answered and I could hear Mike in the background, refusing to come to the phone. He had never refused to speak to me.

On the one hand, I felt I should respect his wishes and leave him alone. On the other hand, to acquiesce so easily seemed a misapplication of principle – respecting his wishes *because* he was mentally ill (would I have given up so easily on another family member?). It would also, if I were honest, be an acquiescence arising partly out of selfishness. Wouldn't I be relieved of a burden? Wouldn't I have more fun spending my days in Portland swimming or having lunch with friends downtown rather than trucking across myriad freeways for an hour's dispirited exchange with him?

When I arrived at his place the following morning around 11.30, I expected he'd still be in bed, and I let myself in the living-room door. My attention was drawn to the guy asleep on the sofa, and so I didn't immediately notice Mike and was startled when I realized he was sitting at the table to the left, a glass of water and a pack of cigarettes before him. He was expressionless and gave no indication that he was surprised to see me there, as though, like some Bergmanesque figure of Death, he'd been waiting in a timeless realm for my inevitable arrival.

We exchanged hellos and I asked if I could sit down. 'I called yesterday,' I said. 'But you didn't feel like talking to me?'

'No,' he said. And with no ceremony and no inflection, he added, 'I don't want to talk to anyone in the family.'

'Do you want me to leave?' I asked.

'No,' he said flatly, 'it's okay.'

I asked what he'd been up to and he told me they'd all gone on an outing to the beach the other day. The Miss Oregon pageant contestants had been in Seaside, all dressed up. He didn't have to say what he thought of this. I knew that he would view such events, and the women who participate in them, with derision. That night, he said, everyone in the house was going to IHOP for dinner.

'Will that be fun?' I asked. 'Or you don't really want to go?' I was wondering if his not wanting to see us was part of a larger antisocial drift. The house social worker had told my mother than Mike had stopped going to Shari's. Mike had said he was 'taking a break'. We all wondered if some unpleasant incident had occurred, resulting in his no longer being welcome – that was often how his association with a favourite place came to an end. But the previous day my mother and I had called into Shari's to enquire, and a waitress who knew Mike assured us that nothing had happened.

'No, IHOP is all right,' he said. And then he asked me to take him to McDonald's for lunch.

I hesitated. I didn't have a car of my own. My friend Stuart had driven me here and was parked outside. Stuart and I had agreed that if Mike sent me away, he and I would go straight to lunch. If Mike was willing to see me, then Stuart would wait for me. I hadn't foreseen that Mike might want to go somewhere with me, and I wasn't sure I could ask Stuart to drive us around.

Stuart and I had known each other for twenty years, since I was just out of college and working as a lackey at the newspaper where he was already an established name, but our friendship consisted of lunch every other year and a few emails in between. It was possible, I thought, that he would find the encounter interesting, being a journalist and a writer and thus a student of human nature. And, though Stuart had never met Mike, he had once played a bit part in his story.

In 1998, Mike had made one final bid for autonomy. He'd stopped taking his medication and disappeared from the house where he was then living. Our brother John, who didn't actually know Stuart but knew that I knew him, enlisted his help. Stuart didn't write about Mike's disappearance himself (it wasn't exactly news) but he did have something to do with getting a small missing-person item into the paper, which ran with a photo of Mike. Mike had been gone about a week when he was recognized by the police. They picked him up downtown – immediately upon leaving his house, Mike had joined the ranks of the scavenging homeless – and phoned John, who brought him to his place for a couple of days, then got him settled again at the group home.

Later, Mike wrote to my mother, *I've been getting a lot of rest but I've been active in the neighborhood and I hope I don't get in any trouble like I did last summer . . .*

The tone of contrition is heart-rending. He was too vulnerable to survive out there, and he knew it.

'I don't have a car to go to McDonald's,' I said. Stuart had already gone far out of his way to pick me up from John's house and bring me here. I couldn't ask him to wait outside while Mike and I sat in McDonald's. Nor could I ask him to join us. Mike simply doesn't tolerate the company of strangers. And if Stuart just dropped us there, how would we get back? I had no idea where McDonald's was. 'A friend drove me here,' I said. 'But I can take you tomorrow. Do you want to go tomorrow?'

'No, I don't want to go tomorrow. I just want to go today because I missed the BLTs here.'

'Are you sure? I could definitely take you tomorrow.'

'No,' he repeated, 'I don't want to go tomorrow.'

'It looks like you've lost weight,' I said, changing the subject. He had. It was remarkable. He'd done nothing but gain weight for twenty years.

'Yeah,' he said, 'I was getting really fat. I feel better since I lost weight.' He told me he'd just decided to start eating less. The real reason was almost certainly his teeth. They were rotting, and were causing him a lot of pain, particularly when he ate, but he had refused for several years to visit a dentist.

'That's good,' I said. I paused for a moment before returning to the other topic. 'Did something happen to make you not want to talk to us?'

'No,' he said. 'I just don't feel like talking to anyone.'

'So you're not mad at us?'

'It has nothing to do with you,' he said. 'It's just me. I just don't want to see anyone.'

There was a trace of impatience in his voice, but otherwise his tone was marked by an unusual calm, a clarity of intent, as though this was a decision he had deliberated over and with which he was at peace. And, indeed, he seemed to bear me no ill will, even for being there against his wishes, though neither did he seem particularly interested in my company. I was simply an emissary from a world he had declared himself ready to leave behind.

I glanced out the plate-glass window and swallowed. 'For ever?' I asked. 'Or just for a while?'

And then, as though it were nothing at all, he looked straight at me and said blandly, 'For ever.'

I had no idea what to do. The moment was at once pivotal – family members didn't just write one another out of their lives every day of the week – and strangely lacking in drama. Was this really the message I would carry back to my mother? *For ever.*

'Okay,' I said. 'Well, I don't want to bother you.'

'Okay,' he said. Then, bizarrely, he reached a hand across the table to shake mine, as though we'd just agreed an amicable end to some long professional association. I had never shaken his hand in my life. But I did then.

'Can I have a hug?' I said.

'Sure.' He stood up, like someone standing up after a board meeting. We hugged, briefly. I moved my hand over his back and felt beneath my fingertips, beneath the rough texture of his polo shirt, a slightly raised bump below his right shoulder: a mole. I thought to myself, *Remember this.* A memento, like the little sea-urchin fossil he gave me when I was nine. Like when he said, *I remember you playing 'American Pie' on your orange turntable* and it was as though in telling me, he had handed me an actual keepsake.

We disengaged and he picked up his cigarettes, said, 'See ya,' and turned and walked towards the stairs, his pyjama bottoms baggy, his shoulders hunched, his posture and the odd stiffness in his long fingers reminiscent of my mother. I turned, too, and stepped out into the sun, wondering if such things really ever happened this easily.

Stuart's car wasn't there. Probably he'd gone for gas or just to check out the neighbourhood. I reached in my pocket for my phone and realized that the phone I had on me was one I'd borrowed for the week, which had none of my numbers programmed into it. The phone with Stuart's number in it was in Stuart's car. I stood in Mike's driveway and looked around. I was ready for someone to yell, 'Cut! What happened to the goddamn car?'

After a few minutes, Stuart arrived back. I got in beside him and we chuckled about the mix-up as we drove away, and it was only as we pulled on to 99 that I started to cry.

★

People with schizophrenia are like people without the illness, in that their subjective level of satisfaction tends to be linked to how well they are doing relative to those around them. But in the case of someone with schizophrenia, an increased level of functioning brings with it an awareness of just how far behind one is. Hence, one may be doing better – experiencing greater lucidity, for example – and feel worse as a direct result. This helps to explain why the danger of suicide for people with schizophrenia is highest not during a psychotic episode but afterwards, when a degree of clarity returns and the individual realizes just how ill he or she is.

I don't know why Mike suddenly decided he didn't want to see us, but I can imagine how seeing us had, over the years, made him feel worse rather than better. (I think of my father, how painful it can be to fail before him. I think of Tim, the most forgiving of us all but also, with his strapping physique and his enthusiasm, the one most bursting with vitality.) We had even talked about it among ourselves – whether our visits were a burden to Mike – and we had long ago developed the habit of withholding happy news about our lives because we assumed it would make him feel unhappier about his own. So a desire to withdraw would not be difficult to understand. But why now?

It seemed to me that he was more lucid – his strange, businesslike calm, a focus that was untypical – and I wondered if some incremental improvement had given him the sense of autonomy required to make the decision. I thought about remission, as I occasionally was prone to. What if he emerged? I have often imagined that he might be like a long-time prisoner of war tossed back into the world, raw and bewildered in the face of it all. Could he say what it had been like? Could he bear to see clearly how much time he had lost? Would he accuse us of having given up on him?

After much discussion and hand-wringing, my mother and I decided we would try again. So the following day, she and Howard and I were back on the road to Mike's house. Howard has accompanied my mother on every visit to Mike for more than twenty years, but given the delicacy of the situation, he decided to wait in the car when we arrived. Howard is a saint. My mother sometimes says this to him, 'You are a saint.' Howard, in turn, likes to preface news about my mother by saying, with emphasis on the *your*, 'Your mother . . .', which he then follows with a recounting of her most recent and fabulous feat, or act of kindness, or wacky antic.

We found Mike upstairs, sitting at the kitchen table. He was doing nothing, listening to the radio: 106.7, 'classic rock' – Elton John, America, the Eagles, Joni Mitchell. Again I had the feeling that he'd been waiting for us. But then I thought, *No, that's just the way it seems when someone has nothing to do and nowhere to go.*

My mother sat down at the table. I leaned against the counter, reluctant to join them, given that we weren't even supposed to be here. But Mike offered us coffee and seemed no more opposed to our presence than he normally was. There was something slightly absurd in the way we kept reappearing, despite his declaration, and the way he kept receiving us, in spite of vowing not to. It was as though yesterday's conversation had never taken place. His hand-shake, my tears, my directive to myself – *Remember this* – it all looked a bit melodramatic now.

I took a seat. The conversation passed much as it always did, though it was actually more relaxed than those lunches at Shari's tended to be. We talked about the music playing on the radio and which of the old bands he liked. When I said I was going back to Ireland the next day, he recalled watching *Darby O'Gill and the Little People* when he was nine.

Before we left, he took us outside and showed us the garden. The plots were overflowing with zucchini, beef tomatoes, eggplants. 'Wow,' I kept saying, lifting the leaves and peering at the vegetables beneath – vegetables so large they seemed mildly obscene. That summer, I was for the first time growing edibles in my own tiny urban garden, and I tended my patch with obsessive care. I lived in a land of untrustworthy weather, and I waited, anxiously, for a sum-mer of rain to wash my brave little shoots away. I sensed that the more impressed I grew, the prouder Mike became, though I knew that since the tomato debacle of 2005 – when he'd insisted on water-ing his plants on the deck above where his housemates were sitting – he didn't join in the gardening any more.

'It's no big deal,' he said to me. 'You just throw the seeds in the dirt and they grow.'

Howard, seeing from the car that all was going well, had joined us. The four of us loitered in the garden, like suburban neighbours swapping the news, until it seemed time to go. We hugged good-bye, Mike hitched up his jeans and turned back towards the house, and we three trooped off in the direction of the car. It had all gone far better than expected – Mike had said nothing about not wanting to see us – and as we pulled away, my mother was beside herself with happiness. All evening and into the following day, she was beside herself with happiness.

The next time she called him, he wouldn't come to the phone. When my father was in Oregon towards the end of that summer, Mike refused to see him. In September, Tim went out to Mike's house. Tim and his wife had had their second daughter in May. Some months after their first was born and they had told Mike about her, Mike had made his one and only visit to their house. He wouldn't hold the baby, he was too nervous, but he looked at her and wanted to be near her. Now, Tim thought the new baby might draw him out.

'Hey,' he said, 'you're an uncle again. We'd love you to come out to the house.'

Mike said no.

'Are you sure?'

'I'm really busy,' Mike said. 'I think I'm going to be busy for a long time.'

Afterword

No one in my family knew anything about schizophrenia when it entered our world. My parents were groping in the dark. They blamed LSD. Depleted zinc. A bad diet. Excessive introspection. Hippy culture. Or they blamed themselves, or each other. Sometimes, when it seemed he should have been able to pull himself together, they blamed Mike. Their ignorance was by no means unusual, nor would it be today. For although schizophrenia affects approximately 1 per cent of the general population over the age of eighteen (which means that nearly everybody knows of someone who has been affected by it, either directly or through a family member or friend), and although advances in neuroanatomy and brain imaging have enabled us to see certain differences in the brains of people with schizophrenia, the illness is widely and deeply misunderstood by the general public, and is still deeply mysterious even to those who devote their lives to its study. Causes seem to be myriad and overlapping. Diagnosis is an inexact science. It is still not clear whether there is a single illness called 'schizophrenia' and not, instead, many different forms of the disorder, each with its own particular causative factors.

Though it unfolds over decades, the origins of schizophrenia are thought to be present at birth or even before. It is believed that people who develop the illness have inherited a predisposition that likely involves the interaction of many, perhaps hundreds, of gene variations, some having very small effects. Genes, however, are not the whole explanation. (If they were, the concordance rate for schizophrenia for identical twins – who share all of their genes – would be 100 per cent, instead of the 40 to 50 per cent that it is.) Rather, the illness arises from an interplay between genetic and environmental factors.

Studies have shown that obstetric trauma, high fever as an infant, head injury, heavy drug use, and growing up in an urbanized environment, all have the potential to increase the risk of schizophrenia in people with a genetic predisposition. Other environmental factors are prenatal. It is possible, for instance, that maternal influenza during the second trimester – the period when neurons are setting up connections with other neurons – may be a factor in some cases. If these connections are disrupted, information passed between neurons will be processed in a less than optimal manner, leading to problems in the areas of attention, memory, perception, executive functioning (planning, problem solving, alternating between tasks), and some aspects of language and social cognition (the ability to perceive emotion in others, to infer what others are thinking, to understand the roles and rules governing social interactions). Such neurocognitive deficits lead, in turn, to functional impairment – problems in everyday living.

But if abnormalities are present before birth, why do they take years to manifest? The peak onset period for schizophrenia – if onset is defined as the appearance of clinical symptoms – is between the ages of twenty and twenty-five years for men and between twenty-five and thirty years for women. The reason for the lag may be that the underlying disruptions involve brain regions that are not fully developed or required for cognitive operations until the second or third decade of life. Interactions between neurotransmitters and hormones may also play a part.

Advances in brain imaging have not been matched by advances in treatment, which has not – despite the billions of dollars spent on research – progressed significantly since the first antipsychotic drug, chlorpromazine, came on the market in 1953. Chlorpromazine – which Mike would know as Thorazine – was developed in the laboratory of the pharmaceutical company Rhône-Poulenc in Paris. It replaced wet packs, prefrontal lobotomies and insulin coma therapy to become the primary treatment for psychosis. What chlorpromazine could do that nothing else before it could was to calm the frantic psychotic, dissolving delirium and hallucinations without rendering the patient unconscious. Unfortunately, as soon became clear, while chlorpromazine could effectively treat acute psychoses, it had only a suspensory action in most chronic psychoses.

Antipsychotics, possibly by blocking the effects of abnormal dopamine release, are effective in controlling hallucinations and delusions, but the 'negative' symptoms of schizophrenia have been remarkably resistant to medication. And it is these that primarily constitute the chronic illness. Back in the 1970s, my parents made a common mistake when they assumed that once Mike's hallucinations and delusions were brought under control by medication, the illness was in retreat and Mike should be able to recommence normal life, exhibiting previous levels of ambition, industriousness and focus. My father did not understand why, when he went to the trouble of getting Mike a job, Mike couldn't be bothered to show up.

Mike's life, and his illness, may have taken roughly the same course whatever the context of their unfolding. But knowledge is always a good thing, or almost always, and so there is value in asking, If we'd known more than we did, if we'd seen it coming earlier, would it have mattered? What if my parents had heard of the 'prodromal stage', that period when the illness begins to flicker and hint, before it erupts in a first psychotic break?

Early detection can, perhaps, make a difference. It has been noted that the quantum of stress required to produce a psychotic break in someone with early-stage schizophrenia seems to decrease as time goes on. One theory as to why this should be is that psychotic episodes are brain-toxic: the more of them a person has, the greater the likelihood he or she will have more (loosely akin to how a sprain or break will predispose a weakened joint or bone to further injury). Or the explanation may be less mechanistic. Psychotic episodes tend to result in gross interruptions of an individual's life. Self-confidence is shattered, again and again. So the fewer of these a person undergoes, the better. And though medication doesn't cure the illness (there are many debilitating symptoms it hardly touches), it can, in almost all cases, prevent the recurrence of full-blown psychosis.

In the decades to come, certain advances are possible. Treatments may be developed that address underlying neurobiological vulnerabilities and provide protection against environmental risks. Medications to treat the symptoms of schizophrenia that have remained most resistant – the cognitive impairments and the so-called negative symptoms – might also be developed. If treatments improve, greater general awareness and earlier intervention will become all the more important – because, to put it bluntly, there will be more to play for.

What if we *had* seen the signs a little earlier? What if we'd recognized them for what they were? Would it have mattered? Maybe. Maybe not. Mike was a drifter, a seeker, someone who loved to be out on the road. After his diagnosis in the seventies, when stability and rootedness were likely what he needed most, he chose instead to cut loose, again and again. That was him. Insisting on his freedom, and as much in the dark as any of us.

Acknowledgements

It would have been impossible to write the story of my brother's life without the help of so many of his old friends who generously shared with me their memories, correspondence and photographs. Family members were also generous with their time and their recollections, and I am especially grateful to my mother, who responded openly and patiently to my endless queries and calls for assistance. Family members and friends read drafts and made helpful comments and corrections, as did Adrian Frazier at NUI Galway and Camilla Hornby at Curtis Brown. Thanks to Brendan Barrington for his superb editorial guidance; to Michael Gill, Professor of Psychiatry, Trinity Centre for Health Sciences, St James's Hospital; to Wendy McEwen, for all her help in Philadelphia; and to Ciaran Benson for his help in Dublin. I am grateful to the Arts Council of Ireland for their continued support.

A number of books were extremely useful to me in the writing of this book. They include: *The Fifties* by David Halberstam; *The Quiet Room* by Lori Schiller and Amanda Bennett; *The Center Cannot Hold: My Journey Through Madness* by Elyn R. Saks; *A Beautiful Mind* by Sylvia Nasar; *Ten Years That Changed the Face of Mental Illness* by Jean Thuillier; *The Divided Self* by R. D. Laing; *The Meaning of Anxiety* by Rollo May; *Acid Dreams: The Complete Social History of LSD: The CIA, The Sixties, and Beyond* by Martin A. Lee and Bruce Shlain; *Realms of the Human Unconscious: Observations from LSD Research* by Stanislav Grof; and *Schizophrenia, Culture, and Subjectivity: The Edge of Experience*, edited by Janis Hunter Jenkins and Robert John Barrett.

The *Ladies Home Journal* cover photograph of September 1953 is reprinted courtesy of Pratt Institute Libraries, the Virginia Thoren Collection.